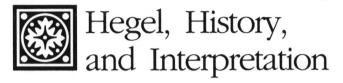

Hegel, History, and Interpretation

SUNY Series in Hegelian Studies
William Desmond, editor

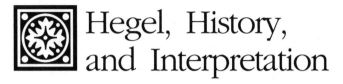

Hegel, History, and Interpretation

edited by
Shaun Gallagher

State University of New York Press

Cover concept courtesy of Michael Tunney, S.J.
Dept. of Fine Arts, Canisius College

Published by
State University of New York Press, Albany

For information, address State University of New York Press
State University Plaza, Albany, NY 12246

Production by Dana Foote
Marketing by Nancy Farrell

Library of Congress Cataloging-in-Publication Data

Hegel, history, and interpretation / edited by Shaun Gallagher.
    p.   cm. — (SUNY series in Hegelian studies)
    Includes bibliographical references and index.
    ISBN 0-7914-3381-1 (hardcover : alk. paper).— ISBN 0-7914-3382-X
(pbk. : alk. paper)
    1. Hegel, Georg Wilhelm Friedrich, 1770–1831.   2. Hermeneutics.
I. Gallagher, Shaun, 1948–   .   II. Series.
B2949.H35H44   1997
    193—dc21   97-12083
                                                            CIP

We dedicate this volume to

George L. Kline

*teacher and colleague, in recognition of his singular
and invaluable scholarly contributions to Hegel studies,
and in grateful acknowledgment for the generous help
and encouragement he has provided to so many
scholars in a great variety of fields.*

*Hence the vague look on the face of the Muse of Time.
It is because so many eyes have stared at her with
uncertainty. Also because she has seen so much energy
and commotion, whose true end only she knows.*
　　　　　　　　　　　—Joseph Brodsky, "Profile of Clio"

Contents

Introduction

The essays collected in this volume take their bearing from texts and themes provided by Hegel. Some of the essays celebrate Hegel, others take issue with his philosophy; so it has been, and continues to be, since the time of Hegel. Yet, within the terms of this mixed reception, Hegel is consistently recognized as having a major influence on nineteenth and twentieth-century Western thought. Thus, Maurice Merleau-Ponty, even as he distances himself from Hegel, suggests that "all of the great philosophical ideas of the past century . . . had their beginnings in Hegel."[1] Michel Foucault, too, although he maintains that "our entire epoch struggles to disengage itself from Hegel," admits that Hegel remains always "close to us."[2] Jürgen Habermas, even as he challenges the critical spirit of Hegel's mature works, joins the consensus in his own way, claiming no less than that "Hegel inaugurated the discourse of modernity."[3]

The mixed influence of Hegel can be clearly observed with respect to those issues that define the contemporary field of hermeneutics— the validity of historical interpretation, the question of philosophical foundations, the crisis of reason, the understanding of others, and the possibility of a critical social theory. Hegel continues to have a voice in the ongoing philosophical conversations that shape these issues; his

---

1. Maurice Merleau-Ponty, *Sense and Non-sense*, trans. Hubert Dreyfus and Patricia Allen Dreyfus (Evanston: Northwestern University Press), p. 63.

2. Michel Foucault, *The Archaeology of Knowledge*, tran. A. M. Sheridan Smith (New York: Pantheon Books, 1972), p. 235

3. Jürgen Habermas, *The Philosophical Discourse of Modernity* , trans. Frederick G. Lawrence (Cambridge, MA: MIT Press, 1987), p. 51.

texts continue to be a living force which elicits both sympathetic and agonistic responses.

Traditionally the modern discipline of hermeneutics, defined as the theory and practice of interpretation, has been associated, justifiably, with Hegel's colleague at the University of Berlin, Friedrich Schleiermacher. Schleiermacher, unlike Hegel, developed an explicit theory of textual hermeneutics. In the twentieth century, however, philosophers like Heidegger, Gadamer, and Rorty have developed hermeneutics beyond its traditional conception as method for textual interpretation. Hermeneutics has become a more general philosophical approach. In this broader context Gadamer suggests that Hegel may play a more important role than Schleiermacher, and that "if we are to follow Hegel rather than Schleiermacher, the history of hermeneutics must place its emphases quite differently."[4] For Gadamer, hermeneutics not only takes the Heideggerian turn away from the tradition of Schleiermacher and Dilthey, but also becomes more widely conceived by retrieving certain Hegelian elements. Outside of the work of Gadamer, however, the connections between Hegel and hermeneutics have been left relatively unexplored. The majority of essays collected in this volume develop these connections outside of the constraints imposed by Gadamer's own hermeneutical theory. The authors explore themes that form the common ground between Hegelian philosophy and hermeneutics conceived in the expanded sense of philosophical hermeneutics.

The term *common ground,* however, may be misleading in two respects. The ground is often contested rather than shared. Moreover, one of the issues that is hotly contested is whether anything like an epistemological ground or metaphysical foundation is possible. In terms of the much used metaphor, the 'conversation' of philosophy more resembles a debate among parties that do not always communicate. Not everyone agrees with Gadamer, that Hegel has a positive role to play in the field of hermeneutics. Other contemporary theorists such as Derrida, Foucault, and Habermas challenge the Hegelian legacy in a number of different ways. These voices too are echoed in the essays that follow.

Hegel and Hermeneutics

Hegel's *Phenomenology of Spirit,* as an interpretation of the history of human consciousness, involves, according H. S. Harris, a hermeneutical

---

4. Hans-Georg Gadamer, *Truth and Method,* 2nd rev. ed., revised translation by Joel Weinsheimer and Donald G. Marshall (New York: Crossroad Press, 1989), p. 173.

recollection. This recollection follows a path through the *Phenomenology* to arrive at the self-comprehensive nature of absolute knowing. Harris, in the opening essay, defending a Hegelian interpretation of the rationality of history, argues that absolute knowing is comprehensive and universal because it acquires a standpoint from which absolutely everything—every historical occurrence—can be viewed as meaningful. This concept, however, does not exclude differing or developing interpretations of history. Absolute knowing is not something that can be measured in epistemological standards of certainty, that is, by standards that are defined from the 'standpoint of consciousness.' Rather, it is the standpoint in which the human community interprets itself. Thus, according to Harris, absolute knowing is not the endpoint of knowledge, the closure of interpretation, but genuinely the beginning, the opening of self-understanding. It involves a different conception of truth. Not truth as *adequatio* or correspondence, certitude, or absolute objectivity, but truth as self-comprehension. This is a concept of truth that involves the finitude of a discursive process.

In this respect Hegel differs from Kant, in the same way that hermeneutics differs from epistemology. Although this point will be contested in later essays by Robert Dostal and Walter Lammi, Harris suggests that Hegel, in contrast to Kant, deals with actual historical experience and not just possible experience. Harris insists that the realm of Spirit for Hegel is the realm of historical actuality and that it displaces Kant's notion of an intelligible realm beyond the bounds of possible experience. Spirit, in effect, is a hermeneutical concept, and we enter into the realm of Spirit through conversation and study, practices through which pure thought is actualized in experience.

Quite in contrast to Harris's reading, Robert Dostal finds in Hegel "a rationalism which is relatively innocent of experience." On Dostal's interpretation, both Kant and Hegel unsuccessfully set out to bring metaphysics to fulfillment. Kant, however, differs from Hegel in that he did not regard the metaphysical enterprise as a quest for foundations. For Dostal, Kant is not primarily an epistemologist, but a critical metaphysician. To bring metaphysics to fulfillment meant two things for Kant: first, to bring to an end dogmatic or foundationalist systems that take their starting point from abstract concepts like Being and non-Being (as in Hegel's *Logic*); and second, to develop a critical metaphysics that takes experience as its *arche*. Kant's non-foundationalist appeal to experience is too quickly overlooked by contemporary thinkers, like Rorty, who, in putting an end to philosophy hastily abandon the Kantian transcendental project and its further development in contemporary phenomenology.

Dostal champions a more metaphysical conception of Husserlian phenomenology, that is, a more Heideggerian conception of phenomenology. For the early Heidegger, to seek the conditions of experience is also to seek Being. This approach still begins with experience and, according to Dostal, is thus distinguished from a Hegelian subjective idealism. Heidegger, of course, construes Hegel to be a representative of modern subjective epistemology, especially to the extent that Hegel speaks of absolute knowing. So Heidegger would view the phenomenologies of Hegel and Husserl as parts of a modern metaphysics of subjective idealism. The later Heidegger even comes to view the early hermeneutical-phenomenological Heidegger as too metaphysical in the wrong sense. Dostal, however, is in favor of retrieving hermeneutical phenomenology as a way of developing a non-foundationalist speculative thought. But is it possible to retrieve such a project without also retrieving Hegel? Is it right to claim that Hegel's rationalism was innocent of experience? These are questions posed by Walter Lammi in his essay on hermeneutical experience.

Lammi examines Gadamer's fusion of Hegel and Heidegger, and asks on what criteria one can retrieve Hegel. The answer to this question requires an investigation of the concept of hermeneutical experience—a concept shared by all three thinkers. For all of them, experience is not a cognitive accomplishment so much as something that we undergo or suffer, something in which we are unavoidably involved. Moreover, it involves us in a transformative movement, a playfulness in which we are put at risk. For Heidegger, however, the "end of philosophy" involves the abandonment of the Hegelian notion that experience can come to an absolute completion. Despite Heidegger's rejection of what he takes to be Hegel's subjective idealism and foundationalism, despite his critique of the absolute, the dialectic, and the metaphysics of presence, Gadamer shows that Heidegger shares with Hegel the realization of the historicity of experience and the transcendence of subjectivity involved in it. Hermeneutical phenomenology, no less than Hegelian phenomenology, retains a sense of transcendence, either a movement toward the future or from out of the past, that opposes any easy conception of epistemological subjectivity.

The issue, for Lammi, is whether it is legitimate for Gadamer to choose Hegelian historicity but reject the Hegelian absolute. Are Gadamer's interpretations of Hegel within a Heideggerian framework, and of Heidegger within a Hegelian framework, cases of hermeneutical violence? Is it legitimate to turn Hegel's concept of objective, historical Spirit "against his Absolute?" The answer, for Gadamer, lies in *experience*. Experience, the issue at stake in his interpretations, turns out to be the very criterion required to justify the interpretations. This hermeneutical circle depends a great deal on the language that is available to express experience. Experience, however, is not distinct from language, since language as it comes to us is linguistic experience. The language used by Hegel and Heidegger to express experience transcends the intent of the authors, but does not transcend experience itself. The very nature of experience, which, as Heidegger points out, allows Hegel to conceive of the dialectic in the first place, and the very nature of language, which, Gadamer points out, involves a dialogical openness to the unsaid, speak against the closure involved in the notion of an Absolute. Thus Lammi shows that Gadamer's concern is less a retrieval of either Hegelian or hermeneutical phenomenology than a transformation of them worked by letting experience speak for itself.

The kind of hermeneutical transformation that Gadamer engages in is, for John Caputo, too Hegelian, too domesticated. Caputo claims that Gadamer's reading of experience does not face up to the radical facticity of experience. The essence of experience, which for Caputo, following Heidegger and Derrida, is an abyss rather than a firm ground, is covered over by Hegelian metaphysics. Thus, he argues, the strategies of deconstruction need to be employed to push hermeneutics toward the edge. This does not mean that we give up on finding truth. But truth is not to be found in a hermeneutical reproduction of tradition—a set of forces that tend to level down our understandings. Rather we find ourselves in truth by confronting our own unavoidable facticity which undermines any aspirations we have to absolute knowledge. Over and above our wanting and willing, truth is given; it is a form of givenness. *Es gibt.* Although Gadamer demonstrates how the factical finitude of understanding both limits and enables understanding, according to Caputo, he fails to recognize what Heidegger calls the *Es gibt,* and he substitutes in its place a virtual Hegelian absolute framed in terms of the process of tradition that operates according to laws of mediation and appropriation.

A more radical hermeneutics, modeled on Derridian deconstruction, faces up to the facticity of the *Es gibt.* There are no presuppositionless beginnings; rather we are "always already" thrown into the difficulty of understanding something without understanding its origins or its complex implications, and we never get clear of this hermeneutical situation. We can never occupy the position claimed by Hegel, outside the hermeneutical frame, able to explain everything once and for all in neat dialectical stages. This realization, however, does not leave us in a state of nihilistic skepticism, with some firm conviction about the impossibility of truth. Rather, it calls us to a different conception of truth; a textualized truth that can only be worked out within the framework of uncertainty and suspicion.

Yet this is not the obvious interpretation of deconstruction. Numerous commentators from a variety of positions have suggested that deconstruction leads us into a free play of signifiers without the possibility of reference to a real world. Deconstruction moves away from the heights of Hegelian speculation only to fall into the abyss excavated by Nietzsche. This is an argument explored by William Desmond in his essay, "Rethinking the Origin: Nietzsche and Hegel." Desmond, starting from an insight provided by George Kline, attempts to chart a course differentiated from both Kantian and Nietzschean attitudes toward metaphysics, as well as from both Heideggerian and Derridian deconstructions. Metaphysics is not only unavoidable but the rightful destiny of human understanding. This is not a simple matter of endorsing philosophy over art, or Hegel over Nietzsche; it involves a complex interpretation of both. It is impossible to divorce art from metaphysics, and despite the postmodern and deconstructivist readings of Nietzsche, we do not find this divorce in Nietzsche's texts. His texts are more equivocal than this interpretation would allow; equivocal enough to allow both the Heideggerian interpretation, that Nietzsche is the last metaphysician, and the Derridian one, that Nietzsche deconstructed metaphysics. Nietzsche was playing with absolute spirit, as Hegel defined it. Art, religion, and philosophy are not only Nietzsche's topics, defined in the *topos* of the will to power, but, as Desmond makes clear, they are places where he seeks out origins.

Of course, the intention is not to conflate Hegel and Nietzsche, and Desmond explicates the differences between them. The point to be made is that Nietzsche, no less than Hegel, even if in a different way than Hegel, was everywhere seeking origins. Even in those of Nietzsche's texts celebrated by postmodern deconstructive readings, an interpreter can find, on the other side of the equivocation, metaphysical reassurance: the "generosity of being," the *Es gibt*. Yet, as it is construed by radical hermeneutics or as it is worked out in terms of Nietzsche's will to power or his concept of *amor fati*, even as it displaces modern subjectivity, the *Es gibt* is nothing other than an erotic origination in which an authentic self can come into its own. The task, according to Desmond, is not to think of it as another remnant of metaphysics to be further deconstructed, but to rethink it as a positive possibility of human understanding. For Desmond, and seemingly in contrast to Caputo, this means that the notion of the *Es gibt*, rather than a deconstructive force, should be understood as a positive, agapeic, metaphysical possibility. The thought of the giving of being that reduces the transcendence of the *Es gibt* to an erotic origin or repetition—and this includes the thought of Hegel and Nietzsche, as well as deconstructive and radical hermeneutics—fails to recognize the agapeic possibility.

History and Critical Reason

"Whatever happens," Hegel writes, "every individual is a child of his time."[5] The truth of this assertion motivates individuals and cultures to pose the same question: how to interpret what no longer is, how to interpret an absence. Historical interpretation, however, has a significance that goes beyond a concern for the past; it extends through our present circumstances to the future in which we ourselves will be past. Our own sure demise motivates our interest in both antiquity and the fixing of the future. Historians are motivated by the same interest, and that makes all history personal. But history is also personal in a second sense: the historical existence and demise of every individual are always personal and particular events, and in this regard, never of universal scope. Every historical occurrence has a singular nature, and this has ethical implications for the practical distinctions between victim, survivor, and onlooker, as well as the theoretical distinction between fact and interpretation.

All of this puts into question Hegel's idea that history is completely rational. Although this idea fits well with the role of the interpreter, it is impossible for the victim. As Joseph Brodsky recently put it, "to accept history as a rational process governed by graspable laws is impossible, because it is often too murderous."[6] Still, interpretation always has the last word; the rationality of history is always more persuasive than history conceived as an irrational force. In certain instances, however, the cool distancing of objective, rational, historical interpretation falls short of persuasiveness and is overcome by the force of historical events.

Hegel, as Heidegger once indicated, was a philosopher who experienced the force of history.[7] Acknowledging the constant ending and starting of historical movement and its importance for Hegel, George Lucas in his essay on recollection and forgetting, develops a neo-Hegelian ontology and sets out to explore the implications it has for an ethics of historical interpretation. In contrast to the kind of resurrection or immortality that remembrance brings, forgetfullness obliterates

---

5. Hegel, *The Philosophy of Right*, trans. T. M. Knox (Oxford: Oxford University Press, 1967), §11.

6. Joseph Brodsky, "Profile of Clio," *The New Republic*, (February 1, 1993), p. 61. I want to note with some regret and sadness that Brodsky's essay was to have been included in the present collection. Various complicating factors, including his untimely death, however, prevented his essay from appearing here.

7. Martin Heidegger, "The Anaximander Fragment," in *Early Greek Thinking*, trans. David Farrell Krell and Frank A. Capuzzi (New York: Harper and Row, 1975), 14; also see Walter Lammi's essay in this volume.

victims. Yet even historical interpretation can be murderous. Recollection remains possible, however, only because the past remains to haunt the present, an absence that persists as an evidence that is always a potential testament to hermeneutical murder, to the terrorism of imposed silence.

Pursuing an ontological distinction made by George Kline, Lucas argues that the being of past events cannot be reduced to their interpretation. They have an ontological status that transcends remembering or forgetting. Lucas examines the forgetting of the past—both the natural and inevitable kind of forgetting, and the forced forgetting involved in revisionist and Orwellian history. Following Hegel's suggestion that forgetting forces us into the continual movement of history, Lucas demonstrates by several well-chosen and pointed examples that forgetting does not imply the erasure of history. The past still has an effect on the present even in the forgetting of it.

If the past does not reside in memory, where, external to intentional consciousness, does it reside? Here Lucas builds upon the past views of Hegel and Whitehead, as well as the current views of contemporary hermeneuticists and scientists. The past resides in the present. On cosmic levels, and in the complexities of living genes, the past continues to have an effect, positively or negatively, in present experience. On a cultural level, even the forgotten past, in a negative fashion, that is, precisely insofar as it has been forgotten, constitutes the "material ground" of the present. Like the negative moment of Hegel's dialectic, like Whitehead's negative prehensions, like Gadamer's concept of *Wirkungsgeschichte*, Lucas conceives of forgotten pasts as having determinate effects in the present.

If the real effects of history have an implicit and often hidden impact on current social practices, are we able to explicate and change them through critical philosophical reflection? Tom Rockmore, in his examination of issues that concern Hegel and the social-political function of critical hermeneutics, addresses the often-raised question of whether philosophy has a social function. To answer it he works out an interpretation of Hegel's attempt, within the context of his critique of Kant, to define the difficult relation between theory and practice.

Many commentators, most famously Habermas, argue that in contrast to the early Hegel who was a liberal intellectual activist, the later Hegel adopted the conservatism of the 'official' philosopher. On this reading, the later Hegel's contention, that philosophy cannot instruct the state on "what it ought to be; it can only show how the state, the ethical universe, is to be understood," is construed as an abandonment of political practice in favor of a detached hermeneutics.[8] Rockmore takes issue with this interpretation by showing that Hegel solves the problem of theory and practice in a way that makes theory always hermeneutically contextualized within social circumstances.

Hegel defines his position by taking up one side of a Kantian antinomy that opposes the traditional view of "theory as independent of, but indispensable for practice," to the more innovative view that theory is subordinate to practice. Hegel pursues the latter, innovative thesis and contends that theory is both subordinate to, and yet influential for practice. Theory is subordinate to practice in the sense, made famous by Hegel, that theory is an attempt to explain retrospectively the social practice that has already occurred. Hegel then must show that retrospective hermeneutics can have a prospective effect. A prospective effect is possible only if the theory correctly interprets its object and remains intrinsically related to the social context. For Hegel, however, both theory and practice share the same spirit. Theory is not independent of practice; interpretation is not separate from its object. Theory, as a form of culture, is part of its own historical and social context and for that reason remains essentially linked to practice. Theory is not free from the finitude of experience, or the "stresses and strains of existence."

Thus, for Hegel, reason necessarily has a social function because reason unavoidably has a social effect. On this view, the theoretical enterprise of showing how social and political arrangements are to be understood cannot help but have practical effect. Rockmore suggests that this realization has importance today especially in the wake of certain scandalous experiences involving recent philosophers in the infamous political contexts of the twentieth century, an importance that extends in its relevance to the current turn toward pragmatism.

My own essay, like Rockmore's, is an attempt to give Hegel a voice in the contemporary discussion about the nature of critical social theory. My intention is to place Hegel in a debate between Habermas and Foucault; between a utopian conception of critical theory and a non-utopian critical hermeneutics; between a search for the universal and remote, and a regard for the particular and local. Habermas views himself as the heir of a tradition of critical theory that starts with Kant and develops through the early Hegel and Marx. I argue that there is an alternative conception of critical theory to be found starting in Hegel, especially the later Hegel who is dismissed by Habermas. This alternative conception is developed in Foucault's genealogical analyses of historical discourse and practice.

---

8. *Philosophy of Right*, §11. Also see Jürgen Habermas, *Theory and Practice*, trans. John Viertel (Boston: Beacon, 1973), 178–179.

Habermas seeks to work out his critical theory in terms of a universal solution based on an ideal communication procedure in which, as Foucault puts it, "the games of truth could circulate freely, without obstacles, without constraint, and without coercive effects. . . ."[9] Foucault suspects that this is a utopian dream. The question, then, is whether it is possible to develop a critical theory that faces up to the force of the past and the circumstances of present power structures. I contend that a more hermeneutical model of critical theory would allow for the possible transformation of past traditions and present conditions and yet recognize that this possibility is inescapably constrained and limited by the effects of past and present resistances.

Like Desmond and Lucas, I am influenced here by an important theme developed by Kline. Kline's philosophy of time maintains clear ontological differences between past and future. The past is already actualized, has a certain reality, and is capable of definite historical effects. The future, in contrast, is not yet actual and thus is necessarily indefinite. For Kline, the "fallacy of the actual future," encountered in numerous philosophers, importantly entails consequences that transcend purely philosophical or ontological discussions.[10] This fallacy, Kline argues, underpins the political theory and practice of tyranny and terrorism, and finds a hermeneutical correlate in the way history sometimes gets interpreted.

The hermeneutical approach found both in the later Hegel and in Foucault opposes the fallacy of the actual future. Foucault, like Hegel, eschews utopian projects, and turns to an analysis of historical actuality to develop a critical interpretation that remains tied to particular and local circumstances. The critical theorist, on this model, does not escape the particularism of his historical situation but remains, as Hegel puts it, "a child of his time." Access to the universal is given, not by a technical procedure that would allow for a utopian escape, but only by critically interpreting and working through the particular situations in which we find ourselves.

Alterity and Communality

The final part of this collection is united by a concern about another set of contemporary philosophical issues that revolve around questions

---

9. Michel Foucault, *The Final Foucault*, eds. James Bernauer and David Rasmussen (Cambridge, MA: MIT Press,1987), p. 18.

10. See George L. Kline, "'Present', 'Past', and 'Future', as Categoreal Terms, and the 'Fallacy of the Actual Future'," *Review of Metaphysics* 40 (1986), 215–235; and "Was Marx von Hegel hätte lernen Können . . . und sollen," *Stuttgarter Hegel-Tage, 1970.* Ed. Hans-George Gadamer. (Bonn: Bouvier Verlag Herbert Grundmann, 1974), pp. 497–502.

about alterity and the ethical status of the other person. One of the most famous and influential of Hegel's analyses—the dialectic of lord and servant found in the *Phenomenology*—continues to be the subject of ongoing controversy. The effect of his dialectical analysis finds its way into numerous influential thinkers, including Marx, Nietzsche, Sartre, Marcel, Buber, Levinas, and Gadamer.

Philip Grier introduces us to another thinker who offers a unique perspective on these issues: the Russian Hegelian, I. A. Il'in (1883–1954). With his help, Grier begins to explore Hegel's conception of rationality and its predilection to reduce otherness to sameness. Il'in is one of those scholars whose work has been obscured by larger historical events. Grier sets out to retrieve Il'in's overlooked interpretation of the Hegelian speculative concrete—a doctrine that provides a central organizing principle of Hegel's philosophy. From Il'in's reading it becomes clear that the proper context in which to delineate the general complexity of relations to 'the other' is found in Hegel's conception of the *concrete*, which he contrasts to the *abstract*. An abstract view of something is always a one-sided, partial, and underdeveloped view that overlooks mediating relations with the other in a fuller context. Only speculative reason can grasp the concrete, and thus, only speculative reason can grasp the true import of abstract alterity within a context of concrete communality. On Hegel's account, speculative reason entails "a unity of thinking subject and object thought," a unity that seems to overcome the difference between the one and the other.

Il'in traces the influence of Spinoza, Leibniz, and Fichte on Hegel's conception of speculative reason. Grier explains that Spinoza's notion of substance as a self-contained identity is the basis for Hegel's view that the speculative concrete maintains itself "in simple and immediate relation to itself." Leibniz and Fichte provide Hegel with the idea of the interior dynamic self-development of the concrete self-relation. Speculative universality becomes the stage for the inner drama of movement between subject and object, the one and the other, which issues in a relation of self to itself. The one and the other, from this perspective, are merely abstract moments of a fuller concrete unity.

Il'in argues that the concept of the speculative concrete is "the fundamental idea" of Hegelian philosophy. As such, however, it operates as a principle of Hegel's rationality rather than as a theme for his interpretation. If this is so, then it is easy to see why a number of important commentators[11] reach the conclusions they do about the

---

11. Grier cites a number of scholars who develop this critique. They include, William Desmond, Werner Marx, and Otto Pöggeler. The essays by Susan Armstrong and P. Christopher Smith in this volume further contribute to this critique.

inability of Hegel's conception of rationality to allow for genuine alterity. Grier acknowledges that this problem, which is also related to concepts of tragedy, suffering, death, and divinity, is probably the most fundamental one in contemporary debates concerning Hegel.

In this same spirit, Il'in had also concluded that on this central point Hegel's philosophy failed. In order to face up to the reality of tragedy, suffering, and death, even in the divine incarnation, Hegel would have to face up to the inadequacy of a rationality that would reduce otherness to unity. Il'in goes further, however, in order to show, first, that Hegel came to realize this inadequacy and as a result made significant compromises within his system, and, second, that these compromises cut across many of the themes that Hegel developed, including concepts like civil society and its multidimensional structures. The critical choice, then, both for interpreters of Hegel and Hegelian philosophers, is between preserving the system by insisting on the propriety of speculative reason, or recognizing that Hegel's compromises suggest a different conception of rationality—perhaps we could say a more hermeneutical rationality.

Michael Prosch explores this issue in Hegel's analysis of social relations and the full detail of associations found in the communality of civil society. Prosch focuses on the concept of the *Korporation* (corporation), a socioeconomic association that has as its principle of organization a common interest in a particular trade. Within civil society, the corporation is an institution that Hegel limits to those classes directly linked to commerce and industry. But this institution is not simply the expression of a set of economic ties; it constitutes an ethical identity, a way of moving beyond individual self-interests toward a more common interest. Although the existence of this interest is embedded in the particular and concrete economic purpose that defines the corporation's trade, it is also clear that it forms the basis for an ethical unity and universality. One might say, using terminology developed by Michael Oakeshott, that the corporation is a means for transforming a *societas*—a society united by civility but no common goal—into a *universitas*—an association united precisely by what Hegel calls a "conscious effort for a common end."[12]

How corporations are defined, and who is included or excluded from a corporation, can have practical import for the organization of society. If, for example, the ethical identity of a corporation includes only employers or self-employed artisans and professionals, and thus

---

12. *Philosophy of Right*, §254. See Michael Oakeshott, "The Voice of Poetry in the Conversation of Mankind," in *Rationalism and Politics* (New York: Methuen, 1975).

excludes workers and day-laborers, we might find a certain economic and political power invested in strict class-divisions. Prosch provides arguments which show that Hegel defined the corporation in a more inclusive fashion than a number of other commentators have suggested. Furthermore, he notes, Hegel identified corporations as important structures in the integrative organization of civil society. Like Rockmore, who indicates Hegel's concern about the persistence of poverty in modern society, Prosch points to Hegel's observation on the dismantling of corporate structure in England: it resulted in more poverty and unemployment, and it increased the moral degradation of its citizens. Surely Hegel's theoretical analysis of the role played by the corporation in civil society is not a detached interpretation of structures that already exist. It is, at least in part, a critical interpretation of the situation of poverty resulting from *laissez-faire* economic practices.

The corporation, Hegel judges, serves to protect its members against the contingencies of economic life, and thus plays an important role in maintaining the stability and welfare of civil society. At the same time the communality of the corporation elevates the isolated and immature individual to a new level of social relatedness. Inclusion in an "ethical whole" allows the individual to transcend the selfishness of mere personal well-being, but only in so far as he or she is a corporate member.

On one level the issue remains one of inclusion and exclusion. Who is included in such membership and who is excluded and thereby, as Hegel views it, deprived of the rank and dignity of a social class?[13] The issue, however, goes deeper still, as Grier and Il'ln suggest: does the propriety of speculative reason, and its celebration of incorporation, reduce the difference of individuality to a communal sameness. Does inclusion as much as exclusion rob the one individual and the other of ontological and social dignity?

P. Christopher Smith examines Kierkegaard's contribution to this discussion and suggests that Kierkegaard does a better job than Hegel at facing up to alterity. For Hegel, the issue of the other is tied to the idea that consciousness always thinks itself, even when it attempts to think the other. Otherness, then, is mere appearance, a positing of the infinite self which remains a mere aspect of self. Even if, in Desmond's terms, this constitutes an erotic fulfillment, Smith points out that Hegel fails to develop his analysis of social recognition explicitly in terms of erotic desire. Hegel thus misses the link between subconscious desire and the conscious requirement of recognition by another. Rather, he

---

13. See *Philosophy of Right*, §253

casts the analysis solely in terms of an asexual dialectic. Even when Hegel closes in on an experience of complete otherness—that is, the experience of *Angst* in the face of death, the complete otherness of existence—it gets immediately negated and reposited as a pure being for oneself. Hegel thus suppresses the otherness involved in sexuality and death. Likewise, the alterity involved in the opposition of lord and servant is reduced to the monological identity of one consciousness. Hegel's dialectic consistently dissolves otherness in order to reconcile itself, so that *Geist* always ends up as a self-contained experience, a self-possessed, and transparent consciousness.

In contrast to Hegel, Kierkegaard introduces a certain excess that disrupts the self-sufficiency of experience. Consciousness undergoes experience, suffers it as something that cannot be entirely self-contained. The despair, the fear and trembling, the *Angst* of consciousness is not a pseudo-dialectic of one-within-the-same, but an unresolvable and irreducible confrontation with alterity. Unlike Hegel, Kierkegaard does not ignore erotic desire. The erotic other, even in conquest, both exceeds and fails to satisfy desire. If resolution is possible in Kierkegaard's dialectic, it is not a synthesis of the one-in-the-other or the other-in-the-one, but a redemption that depends as much on the other remaining other as on the one giving itself up. The Hegelian reconciliation found within reason is here displaced by the possibility of redemption sought in a faith that remains outside of, other than, reason. The Kierkegaardian dialectic cannot be accommodated by the Hegelian one. Indeed, Smith suggests, experiences of desire, despair, and faith would necessarily disrupt the Hegelian dialectic with an irreducible alterity.

Susan Armstrong, in her feminist critique, deepens the analysis of Hegel's inadequacy in regard to otherness, and introduces a qualification to Smith's reading of Hegel and Kierkegaard. She contends that Hegel is no exception to the rule that governs most texts of Western philosophy, that the woman is always viewed as "the other." In Hegel's analysis of family life, the woman, "the other sex," is defined as biological and inactive in contrast to the male's mental and active life. This difference then takes on a rational and ethical significance, that is, men are ethically designed for political life, women for domestic duties. The mutual recognition involved in marriage remains limited because it is primarily based on natural passion and can only be fulfilled in the production of an other: the child. The child, however, who transcends the family and moves into civil society as the rational, autonomous individual, is construed as a male child, a brother rather than a sister, Eteocles or Polynices rather than Antigone. Hegel, we might say, remains a "child of his time" by embracing the ideology of the "sentimental family" as a way to legitimize the inequality of women.

Does Hegel's male-biased ideology invalidate his philosophy? Armstrong explores several conflicting answers to this question. One view is that this ideological prejudice is actually inconsistent with his basic tenets. Hegel's dialectic is motivated precisely by alterity and conflict. The other, the woman, is an essential and equal aspect of that conflict, and cannot be repressed without fear of contradiction. The other view, more in line with Smith's reading, is that Hegel's general philosophy actually forms the basis for his view of women, that is, that his dialectic systematically excludes "the other" by tracing out only the main story-line of history. Echoing themes explored by George Lucas, this view suggests that the others, the marginalized groups, become victims without history, or are totally absorbed in a dialectic and a rationality that is claimed to be universal, yet is clearly male and without remainder.

Armstrong circumscribes this conflict of interpretations with the suggestion that we develop a feminist hermeneutics. This would not only entail recognizing the philosopher, Hegel in this case, as part of a textual system beyond his control, but acknowledging that in most cases the philosophical author effaces *him*self in an attempt to provide impersonal, ahistorical, objective assertions—that is, assertions constructed in a male rationality. On this score, Armstrong suggests that Kierkegaard might be more promising than Hegel, since the former's concern is one with personal communication rather than objective reason.

On a closer look, however, Kierkegaard fares no better than Hegel with respect to the feminine other. Even if Kierkegaard places the personal author back into the text, and does this, not in spite of, but because of his use of pseudonyms, and even if, on the most general level, as Smith suggests, Kierkegaard provides for the irreducibility of the other, Armstrong still finds that Kierkegaard reduces the specific other, the woman, to insignificance. In all stages of existence— aesthetic, ethical, and religious—Kierkegaard portrays women as limited and incapable others, lacking "the full range of human achievement and awareness." So, even if in Kierkegaard we find a rationality that is less male, and a dialectic that is more open to alterity than in Hegel, we still find a double inadequacy. The woman is consistently the other, and this particular otherness is consistently devalued.

The essays contained in this collection suggest that Hegel continues to be an important source in ongoing contemporary discussions. In these essays his dialectical philosophy is kept alive through the transformations of hermeneutical dialogue and debate on such matters as the nature of rationality, the relation between ontological structure and ethical interpretation, the effects of historical existence and particularity, and their role in mediating the self-other relation. This volume thus aspires to honor the spirit of George L. Kline's suggestion: "We need, and shall continue to need, both Hegelian and un-Hegelian—even anti-Hegelian—studies of Hegel, though not of *every* kind. Looking ahead, we may anticipate that in the best of future Hegel studies the opposition between 'Hegelian' and 'un-Hegelian' approaches will, in good Hegelian fashion, be definitely *aufgehoben*."[14] Perhaps it would be accurate to say that not only does Hegel continue to be read, but that his work, (with all of its dialectical oppositions, but without clear consensus or synthesis) continues to be written; his spirit extended into texts such as those collected here.[15]

Shaun Gallagher
Canisius College

---

14. George L. Kline, "Some Recent Reinterpretations of Hegel's Philosophy," *The Monist* 48 (1964), p. 75.

15. In several recent works (see, for example, James P. Scanlan [ed.], *Russian Thought After Communism: The Recovery of a Philosophical Heritage* [London: M. E. Sharpe, 1994], p. xvi) references to the present volume of essays have been made listing the title as *Hegel and Hermeneutics*. This had been a working title when these essays were originally collected.

Part I
Hegel and Hermeneutics

1 The Hegelian Organon of Interpretation

H. S. Harris

I want to examine here the sense in which 'Spirit' is the 'compre-hensive' or 'absolute' category for Hegel. An influential school of Hegel interpretation has recently emerged in the Anglo-Saxon world which derives—through Walter Kaufmann, who was its most important leader—from Nietzsche. But it is appropriate to notice that a view very like theirs was first advanced by Croce (who was probably not—or not consciously—influenced by Nietzsche). According to this view, the Hegelian concept of Spirit can be (at least nominally) comprehensive, but all claims to absoluteness must be given up. The latest advocate of this view is Robert Solomon in his book *In the Spirit of Hegel.*[1]

It must be the case that the opposition of 'the Spirit' and 'the letter' is present in Solomon's mind, since he has little respect for what Hegel said he was aiming to do. According to this school's interpreta-tion, Hegel was a great creative interpreter of our Western culture, but his obsession with 'logical system' was a sham. Sometimes they seem to suggest that he was a conscious faker, that he was deliberately pulling the wool over everyone's eyes. But a more defensible form of their position (since Hegel put so much effort into his supposedly sham façade of logical system) would be the suggestion that one cannot do the sort of creative interpretation that Hegel did without a conceptual

---

1. Robert Solomon, *In the Spirit of Hegel* (New York: Oxford University Press, 1983).

framework; and that the conditions of acceptance created for Hegel by the rationalist tradition which he was actually overturning, forced Hegel to speak sometimes as if the framework he was inventing possessed a kind of absolute validity which he knew (and elsewhere stated clearly) no framework could have. Hegel is really Nietzsche— or to be more precise, he is Walter Kaufmann's Nietzsche—in disguise. (It is no accident that Solomon's book ends with a long quotation from Nietzsche.)

This will not do. Hegel himself began with the opposition between the letter that kills, and the spirit that gives life; and he did transform the Holy Spirit of his Lutheran upbringing into the non-denominational World Spirit. He himself would certainly have acknowledged Nietzsche as a later *Gestalt* (an embodied shape) of the World Spirit. Or in other words (since it is ultimately irrational to talk as if thinkers could make estimates of their successors), Nietzsche expressed his own time in a very significant way, and Hegel's philosophy was part of the substantial thought-fabric of that later time. But to take the spirit of Nietzsche's interpretation of his time for the Spirit of Hegel is not only unhistorical, but peculiarly unHegelian. It ignores precisely the fact that Hegel originated the non-denominational concept of Spirit that we are using. One can legitimately use the expression 'spirit of X' to indicate that one is concerned with the meaning and relevance of his achievement for one's own world, concerned with what he has inspired or may now inspire. But then one is using the conception of spirit that Hegel himself inherited, not the one that he originated.

Hegel himself is a limiting case for the taking of this liberty because he worked upon and transformed that traditional conception. His spirit therefore belongs to him in a peculiar way. He made the concept of Spirit into his absolute concept. In other words (I will say dogmatically) he claimed to be formulating for the first time a logically adequate concept of the World-Spirit. He may be right in this claim or he may be wrong. But if we are going to speak justly about the spirit of Hegel we cannot ignore the fact that this is what he claimed. If we believe that he was truly inspired, but he claimed too much, then we can properly write, like Croce, of "What is living and what is dead" in Hegel. But we must not designate the spirit of Nietzsche (or the social science of Marx for that matter) as the true spirit of Hegel. This sort of excess is unfortunately common. But it is radically anti-Hegelian.

I mean to defend here the thesis that Hegel did bequeath to us the logically adequate concept of the World Spirit; and that the logical adequacy of his concept of human existence in Solar time upon the surface of the Sun's third planet, is what he means (and *all* that he means) when he speaks of his philosophy as absolute knowledge, as

Science, or as Philosophy *simpliciter.* I shall focus attention first upon the word Science and particularly upon the expression 'Science of logic,' because attention to what the words Science and logic demonstrably *do* mean for Hegel fixes the boundaries of what more concrete claims and doctrines consistently *can* mean for him.

"The true shape in which truth exists can only be the scientific system of it. To make a working contribution to this end: that philosophy should come closer to the form of science . . . that is what I have set for myself as my goal."[2] So says Hegel in the Preface to the first systematic work that he published. Hegel's conception of Science (and especially of the "form of science") is methodically rational rather than empirical in its inspiration. Science means a body of propositions that are logically connected and interdependent. But this harmless truism only shifts the problem to the word logic; and the really original thing about Hegel is that where everybody before him (at least from Parmenides onwards) shared a severely rationalist conception of philosophical logic, his conception was empirically inspired.

What I mean by that is that he took an empirical view of the question of how logic is the "form of science." He was in perfect verbal agreement with everyone else about the propositions that "man is the logical animal" and "logical interdependence is the *form* of proper science." But the relation of form and content was not for him a matter of 'rational intuition' or 'intellectual sight.' That there are 'laws of thought' is obvious enough; and that there is a lawful order of things is equally obvious. But the relation between the two is not obvious; it is a matter for empirical investigation. The primitive assumption that 'the logical aspect of the world is its mathematical aspect,' whether made in conjunction with the empiricist postulate that 'there is a non-logical aspect of the world that is ultimately irreducible' or the rationalist postulate that 'there is no non-logical aspect of the world that is not ultimately reducible to reason,' is fundamentally mistaken, just because it is an assumption. No assumption ought to be made here. Instead, the history of the logical animal's attempt to make sense of the world must be examined without prejudice to see what sort of logical structure, what sort of necessary dependence, sequence, and totality, can be discovered in it by rational observation. The observation will be rational because the observer knows what formal logic is; he can follow an argument where it leads, and the argument will be controlled by observation because we agree that the record of the logical

---

2. Hegel, *Phenomenology of Spirit,* trans. A. V. Miller (Oxford: Clarendon Press, 1977), §5; hereafter cited as PhG.

animal's sense-making activity, of the quest for philosophical truth as the ultimate account of how the world makes sense, and what sense it makes, is there to be observed.

Hegel's philosophy is a philosophy without assumptions in the sense that he refuses to accept any intuitive presuppositions about the relation of thought to reality. In particular, he refuses to accept the identity of logic with arithmetic and geometry. If one retorts upon him that he does assume both that the human animal is a sense-making observer, and that the world of human observation does make sense, the answer is that in a very attenuated sense this is true. Hegel does make these assumptions in the not quite empty sense that he takes it to be a stupid waste of time to argue with someone who is prepared to deny them simply. But then he thinks it is a mistake to argue with those who maintain a different point of view at all. He is not making assumptions about the human animal or its world, but inquiring into what a certain *propositional hypothesis* that men quite generally assent to can consistently mean. He is not making an assumption but inter-preting a proposition that most people want to assume, to see what it means when it is truthfully maintained. If you do not want to maintain it, his work will lose its point for you. But if you want to maintain something else—for instance, that the existence of the world does not make sense, but is an unintelligible brute fact—you will find that position (or rather a whole set of positions that embody it) has its place (or their places) in Hegel's investigation; and if you can make sense of that, then you may become interested in the absolute sense at the end of Hegel's quest.

If, however, we are not to make assumptions about material truth, but are simply to *observe* what some of our fellows do now take to be true (as compared both with what others take to be true, and with what our predecessors have taken to be true), where should we begin and how should we proceed?

We begin where we are, with everything that we know. Having observed the tradition intelligently, we start with the common sense assumption that our senses are reliable. A "science of the experience of consciousness" (where consciousness means the knowing awareness of the world) is possible, Hegel claims, because if we proceed Socratically by laying down a hypothesis and comparing our definition of what is with our experience in applying the definition to the world that it is supposed to interpret, the way that our definition breaks down will provide us with the means to mend it, and so to replace it with a better one. Thus, in principle, the argument never needs either to stop, or to make a new beginning (such as we find very often in Plato's pictures of a Socratic conversation). Virtually no one has taken Hegel's claim seriously. The best book about Hegel's project that has been written in English—Westphal's *History and Truth in Hegel's Phenomenology*[3]—is exactly as bad as Solomon in that respect for they both reorder the argument in the same way, and yet if the phenomenology of Spirit is scientific in Hegel's sense, the order must be a necessary one. We may take it that this failure indicates that no one has managed to follow the argument. It is certain at least that no one has explicated the argument successfully. In my view, this is because those who do follow it in outward form do not take it empirically enough. But I am only concerned with the logical program at present.

The first thing that happens is that the simple assumption that our senses tell us immediately what is, has to be modified into the assumption that reality is a world of things that are only mediately known to us through the senses. That view, in turn, is modified into the hypothesis of the real world of Newton and Eddington, the world of an intelligible force that is phenomenally manifested as things in process. But now the puzzle is the duplication of this intelligible reality as a system of law in the mind of the observer. The observer now becomes the focus of interest as a practical (or free) activity. To observe this activity as a self-positing standard of 'what is'—or of the truth of life— involves the biggest (and the second most difficult) of Hegel's leaps; for we have to go from the highly sophisticated dynamic theory of matter, which the non-scientists Hegel and Schelling want to put in the place of the mechanical atomic or corpuscular theories of Cartesian and Newtonian physics, to a self-consciousness which has no scientific knowledge at all and no cognitive interest in the world. For what this self knows is not that "It (the world in which I am engulfed) IS," but rather that "I AM." What counts for it is not the world, but the will. True being is Lordship over the world. If we put it this way, we can see both the continuity and the progression in Hegel's Science. Each definition points to what is left out, and so to the simplest hypothesis that includes it.

The first experience of this lordly will is violent death. It does not matter whether one or both die in the conflict which the definition necessitates. Ideally the best model is Eteocles and Polyneices, the brothers who kill one another in a battle for the lordship of the City of Thebes (and so set in train the tragic conflict of their sister Antigone with Creon). This provides a theoretical transition to the concept of Spirit proper. For what the observers can see is that there cannot be

---

3. Merold Westphal, *History and Truth in Hegel's Phenomenology* (Atlantic Highlands, NJ: Humanities Press, 1979).

a 'lordly' consciousness without a subservient one. Thus it is the observer who is the spirit that unites these necessary halves of any really self-conscious will into one real self-consciousness. The lord and the serf have no spiritual consciousness at all, for they do not recognize that they are the complementary aspects of the single self-consciousness that they share. The lord does not even necessarily know that his consciousness is inadequate, because he is not forced to recognize, in the serf whose subservience keeps them both alive, his own essential subservience (and the subservience of his supposed absolute truth) to the needs and the bounds of natural life. The serf knows this because he gave up his will to save his life. But it is not he alone who is the necessary source of the next development in the concept of truth, because the unincorporated element is human mortality as natural rather than violent death; and "either on the throne or in fetters" (as Hegel puts it), one can become a Stoic in order to have a Self-Consciousness that is beyond that. I shall go with Marcus Aurelius rather than Epictetus, because by doing so I can skip 150 pages of Hegel's text and make a valid connection (which Hegel himself asserts) between Stoicism and the universal acceptance of the Roman Law. It is only by accepting the view that the world is governed by the rational will of the Stoic God (or Spirit) of which we are all sparks, that we can get a standard of truth as Self-Consciousness which has fully repossessed itself of the universe of scientific understanding. This Self-Consciousness knows not only that it is spiritual, that it involves a community of members, but that it is the Absolute Spirit, the universal community of rational selves who recognize the Reason that they all share in the absolute otherness of the order of Nature—or the fate which as good Stoics they must try to love.

But in regaining the world in theory, they have lost it again in fact. They have no insight into the operations of the Absolute Spirit at all; and the Emperor who ought to be the self-conscious will of this universal community, is simply the symbolic purple mantle wrapped around a life and death struggle of the legions. What begins as the universal justice of a Lord who is at least rational about his own interests, ends as the 'law of the stronger' in the Hobbesian state of Nature.

But, absurd as it may have been for the Roman Empire to identify itself as the civilized world (considering China of which they knew nothing, India of which they were vaguely aware, and the Aztecs of whom I myself know only the name), the conception of humanity as one universal community of rational agents was born in this Hellenistic culture. It became rational in the Stoic sense when the Gospel of the universal fatherhood of God, and the universal brother-and-sisterhood of man was preached, especially to those in servitude in this unified community.

Now, however, the absolute truth from which life gets its meaning was alienated. We are supposed to live our lives in this world for the sake of a knowledge, a freedom, and an equality that will be experienced only in a purely intellectual world beyond this life. Truth, however, is recognized to be a mode of experience. It essentially involves the knower, and is not supposed to exist as an object in the abstract. The standpoints of simple consciousness and Self-Consciousness are successfully integrated, and there is no room for a separation of theoretical from practical reason. It is the separation, or alienation, of what is from what ought to be (or of what is sensibly for consciousness, and what is intellectually for the self-consciousness of faith) that is here made absolute. The world of what sensibly is, is even declared to be radically irrational, to be lost and sinful, abandoned to the dominion of evil. This is empirically accurate because law and justice are not reliably to be found in this world. A few years before Constantine's accession there were six candidates wearing the Imperial Purple. Sixty years after his accession, the Empire was divided, and a hundred years after his accession Rome fell for the first time. Only in Heaven could one look for rationality and justice. But as the rational interpretation of the outwardly irrational proposition that Jesus our brother, the innocent victim of the universal law of the stronger, is the eternal Logos (the Son of God in whose body we are all members) and as such is sought and found, it becomes clear that Peter Abelard, the best logician of the twelfth century, and one of the greatest of all time, was right to prefer Paul to Aristotle, and the Christian doctrine of the Holy Spirit to both the realist logic that he overthrew and the nominalist logic that he put in its place. There can be no doubt that the enormous influence of Roman Stoicism (especially Seneca) in his mind was partly responsible for this—even though one cannot imagine any ancient Stoic who would not have been as sickened by the intellectual absurdity of the orthodox Christian faith as Plotinus was.

Hegel did not know more than a few useless scraps about Abelard. He knew the most significant argument of the only contemporary of Abelard who was his intellectual equal: Anselm. But the rational world of faith was interpreted for him by Dante, the poet who inherited and reconciled all that was best in its greatest flowering. Abelard's place is taken for Hegel by Luther—who was not a philosopher at all, still less a logician. Luther's return to the Pauline interpretation of the Resurrection resolved the practical absurdity of faith, and made an actual community of the faithful in this world possible. To make that community of faith rational was the task of the Enlightenment. This part of Hegel's argument almost every reader understands—except that Hegel seems perversely to be too sympathetic with what we call the wrong side (just as he seems too sympathetic with Creon in the confrontation with Antigone). He is positively gleeful about the way in which the triumph of the Enlightenment and the General Will of the rational community transplanted from Heaven to Earth leads only to the Terror, and he does not even try to interpret any social event after that. In the conceptual world that interests him, pure Reason and practical Reason are now sundered in the fully clarified form they have been given by the Enlightenment. This Kantian form of alienation is fairly easy to reduce to absurdity (most of us find it so absurd on its face that we act as if Kant's argument did not exist, although, of course, we regard it as a matter of the most elementary common sense that what is and what ought to be have nothing to do with one another).

The Hegelian resolution of the absurdity is the practical acceptance of the logical necessity of forgiveness. This is the first genuinely new element (except for paradoxes and puzzles which required a long process of rational interpretation) to be added to the concept of 'the absolute truth' since it was socialized in order to accommodate natural death. The achievement of a self-consciously rational community is a complex process which I have largely eliminated here because only the role of faith—i.e., of an apparently irrational element—is novel enough to deserve notice in this bird's eye view.

Forgiveness, through which the perspectives of rational agent and rational observer are reconciled, and the gulf between 'is' and 'ought' is closed, is the last element in the concept of finite spirit. It is in the forgiving consciousness that God becomes man. So Hegel can now deal with religious consciousness as the mode in which the community is consciously aware of its own unity as substance and self. The whole story has to be gone through again at the level of this communal self-consciousness in order to close the rift that Kant created between theoretical and practical Reason, or between critical knowledge and practical faith. When religious consciousness returns round its half of the circle to the rationally enlightened mode of the Lutheran community—that is, the community which knows that the Saviour resurrected as the forgiving and reconciling self-consciousness in every member is no object of faith, but simply the spirit of Reason itself—the Science of Consciousness is complete because the standpoint of Consciousness is transcended and we enter the sphere of Absolute Knowledge. We now know that we have reached the standpoint from which everything makes sense consistently with everything else. We know this, because 'truth' has now ceased to be 'correspondence' in any mode, and has become self-comprehension. There is now nothing outside of the concept for it to be compared with, nothing to conflict with it, to be found missing from it, and so cause further development. This absolute knowing is the conceptual context of all sense-making activity, because it is the concept of the human community interpreting both the world which is its naturally necessary home, and the historical record of the experience of its members.

The last thing that we discovered was why the very concept of free agency logically necessitates differing interpretations of everything that happens or is done. So the idea that troubles some interpreters (and leads to Marxian or Nietzschean rescue parties on behalf of 'the spirit of Hegel'), the idea that the dawning of absolute knowing must preclude the possibility of any significantly new knowing, doing, and interpreting, is the very reverse of the truth. It springs from the failure to escape from the 'standpoint of consciousness' (according to which truth is the correspondence between a concept and its object), and from the standard of certainty (according to which the touchstone of absoluteness is a mode of intuitive vision, and Reason is not understood to be a discursive process of interpretation). The imposition of either of these upon Hegel's Absolute Knowing makes nonsense of it. Most readers of Hegel take both for granted (often without conscious thought, because the very idea that an alternative is possible does not occur to them).

The concept of Absolute Knowing as the rational interpreting of human experience, is only the foundation stone of Philosophy as a science. I have left myself little space in which to say anything about this, but a few notes are worth having even if the end result is only the identification of a problem. If we look at Hegel's Science of Experience in the Kantian context of his time we can see that he has done two things. He has put the concept of actual experience (or the actual concept of experiencing) in the place of Kant's abstract concept of 'possible experience'. He has also reintegrated the whole of our actual experience within that single concept, whereas Kant's practical Reason postulates an intelligible realm beyond the bounds of 'possible experience.' That intelligible realm in Kant becomes the actual realm of Spirit in Hegel. We enter it whenever we talk to one another, although the decisive way in which we are bound to be aware of entering it is when we study the record left by someone who is dead. Then we are in a realm whose structure is constituted for us by pure thought. The concepts that structure the world in which rational beings truly exist are not concepts of the Kantian empiricist 'possible experience' at all; they are the concepts of our actual experience (of what the other speaker means, of Plato's world as comprehended by ours, etc.).

I do not want to leap over the Philosophy of Nature, and leave it out (as so many Hegel interpreters have done, because it was dead for the natural science of their time, and natural science was dead for them anyway). Hegel himself devoted an enormous amount of effort to the comprehending of the basic theoretical structures of the natural sciences of his time, and on that basis he constructed a unified concept of Nature within which the subconcepts were harmonized dialectically into a system. I have finally had to use the word *dialectic* because even the primitive concept of force—which Newtonian mechanics, the paradigm Science of the Kantian Understanding, already needs—is a dialectical concept. This shows itself in the enormous difference between the mathematical expression of force as a potential in a study, and its phenomenal expression as actual experience in the New Mexico desert (or as a Kantian possible experience in the nuclear winter).

Of course, I am cheating now, because this dialectical contrast between sense and intellect belongs to the science of experience and not to the science of logic. In the philosophical logic, which according to my view is the new organon for the unified interpretation of the world scientifically or in pure concepts—that is, theoretical constructs which are not Kantian concepts because they have no determinate instantiation in sense-experience—in that purely intellectual realm, the concepts must evolve logically first into self-opposition and then into self-transcendence through the emergence of a concept of higher generality, without any phenomenal intervention—any contribution from experience at all.

I do not want to try to defend or to explicate this higher dialectic here. I do not think that it has ever been understood in its proper context. It will be sufficient if I can say how the task of explicating it should be approached. Hegel's *Science of Logic* is the development in discursive scientific form of the very concept of actual experience that is the result of the *Phenomenology*.[4] At the beginning (in the empty concept of pure Being), and the end (the exposition of Absolute Knowing as logical method) it is directly determined by the concept of Absolute Knowing. So these termini are fixed. They participate in the absoluteness of the concept of rational interpretation which all who want to make objective sense of their life in the world must share. Objective sense means here a sense which relates their experience harmoniously to the experience of all the fellows they have ever had (living or dead) and a sense which will be accessible to all who will

---

4. See *Hegel's Science of Logic*, trans. A. V. Miller (New York: Humanities Press, 1969).

have them as fellows in the future. But in between these termini it seems to me that the Hegelian Logic must evolve with use. I will offer two contrasting examples of what I mean.

First, our concept of 'cause' is not now the Humean-Kantian concept from which the evolution of all this transcendental logic began. In this instance it is clear that dialectical development of what Hegel did with the Kantian concept must take place even if Hegel's deduction of cause is found to be valid for the Newtonian science of his time. But if that is once established, then there is no foreseeable possibility of that part of his Science of Logic being superannuated. For unless we cease to be animate organisms inhabiting the third planet of *Sol,* our lives will not cease to be bounded in important ways by the general theory of gravitation in its Newtonian form, and our balls and projectiles will behave as they always have done, no matter how non-intuitive that behavior may be (as Hume pointed out).

Secondly, the very same scientific revolution which made even the most enthusiastic of Hegel's disciples believe that his philosophy of nature was completely superannuated, can actually help us to recognize the enormous difference between philosophy of nature as he understood it, and philosophy of science as it has been understood since Descartes and Newton. Even in his own time, his attempt to frame the philosophy of physics in the context of the four elements of Pre-Socratic physics looked like mere folly. But Hegel took 'nature' to be the home-context of the human spirit; and we can now see how wise—and indeed how urgent—it is to set all of our world-transforming activities in the context of the meteorological process of 'the elements.' Ever since Bacon's time, experimental science—for which the elements are not elementary at all—has been the basis of more and more of those environment-creating activities. But the 'nature' which is the continuous background and extension of our human nature has always consisted basically of the three elements (earth, air, and water) which are media of life, and the one (fire) which provides our most vivid *Gestalt* of death. Man's mastery of fire was, arguably, the foundation-stone of the Spirit—if by that we mean (as we should) the environing frame of meaning that we humans create for our lives. Hegel, like everyone else in his time (except William Blake) thought Nature well able to take care of herself, and saw only a theoretical concern at the foundation of the human quest for natural science. We who can now see what a true prophet Blake was, ought by the same token to recognize both the tremendous imaginative achievement, and the crucial relevance and importance, of Hegel's recognition that the logic of nature must be framed in organic—and specifically in human-organic—terms.

To mediate successfully between my two examples—to link them dialectically—is the task of the future. But the task of elucidating Hegel's organon must first be done by studying Hegel's own uses of it (I am certain that it was developed in use in any case). Hegel used it in every science of a 'real philosophical' sort (that is, in every systematic interpretation of his world) that he produced. In the first place, and most obviously, it must be studied in connection with the comprehensive philosophy of nature and spirit which forms the direct application for which it was conceived and designed. But since it came to birth coevally with the Science of Experience (which is the critical first part of Hegel's System of Science, as he conceived it in 1807), the structure and sequence of Hegel's Logic must be compared with that also. It is quite evident that the transformation of the traditional concept of truth as substantial into a concept that is 'as much subject as substance' is the fundamental project of both, and both of them terminate with an exposition of absolute knowing. So the discursive routes of the two journeys must obviously be examined together.

Finally (as the *Phenomenology* shows) the properly scientific comprehension of any time is what is found in its prevailing philosophy. So Hegel's lectures on the history of philosophy provide the phenomenology of his Logic on the side of conceptual self-consciousness (the evolution of Religion being how the absolutely substantial Subject appears as an object of consciousness). It is to be expected that the actual historical sequence of thought—or what Hegel believed to be the sequence, for in the case of Parmenides and Heracleitus he gave a logical reason for what is fairly certainly a false belief—will help us to understand the deductive sequence of his logical theory.

When all this interpretive work (conceptual and empirical together, or as I should like to say hypothetico-deductive) has been done as well as possible, we shall know what to say about the radical criticism offered by the only previous student of Hegel's logic known to me, who saw it (I think) in more or less the same light as I do. C. S. Peirce—who is by far the greatest philosophical mind that the North American continent has produced—complained that the logical method that Hegel presented as the climax of the Logic in which it was employed is really not a method at all, but only a name for Hegel's own genius. If it were a method, said Peirce, others could learn to use it, but in fact no one has done so. I think it is true that no one has used Hegel's logical method in the way that he did. One good reason, as I have shown, is that almost no one understood what he was doing. Even Peirce, who concluded after many years of work that no satisfactory "long list" of categories was possible, may have been asking for an eternally satisfactory set, where Hegel's system itself demonstrates that only the comprehension of the actual science of the time as a dialectical system is possible.

If this view is correct, however, then Hegel's own estimate of the relative importance of the science of experience and the science of logic may be mistaken. I have spent many years working at the task of explicating the Science of Experience. So, when I declare that the *Science of Logic* is Hegel's most important work—as I always do, when I am asked point-blank—it is with the ironical awareness of propounding a paradox. I can hardly expect people to believe what I say, and yet I do believe that my declared judgement formulates the proper perspective in which to do what I am doing. It is the right perspective precisely because it is Hegel's own perspective. But when the work is all done, we may find that the right perspective for us to view Hegel's achievement properly comprehended, is that formulated by Peirce who said that the *Phenomenology* was "a work . . . perhaps the most profound ever written."[5] My own belief, however, is that in the perspective of Hegel's logical Absolute, the question itself is foolish. Both the science of experience and the science of logic are necessary to our comprehension of our time *sub specie aeternitatis,* and of logical eternity within the perspective of that time (that is, our time). In this respect, it was Spaventa who was right. The Absolute needs both "proofs" (as he called them).

---

5. C. S. Peirce, *Collected Papers,* 1903, Ms. 478, p. 27.

2 The End of Metaphysics and the Possibility of Non-Hegelian Speculative Thought

Robert J. Dostal

The contemporary debate concerning the end of metaphysics is closely tied to the question of foundations. Though some of the participants seem unaware of it, this debate has a long history. It is an outgrowth of the crisis of the philosophical tradition which accompanied the rise of the modern natural sciences in the seventeenth century. Philosophy defended itself from the usurper by insisting on its hegemony over the sciences by way of its role of laying and securing foundations for the sciences. The primacy of epistemology in the twentieth century in the schools of analytic philosophy or Neo-Kantianism is a recent expression of this same struggle. Overcoming epistemology and the abandoning of the question of foundations, however, is not tantamount to overcoming metaphysics. If we would disengage the question of metaphysics from the question of foundations, we could more fruitfully consider the question of metaphysics and speculative philosophy. A look at Kant's transcendental philosophy taken up in a non-epistemological, non-neo-Kantian way, might provide a rewarding avenue for thought. This way, I suggest, is the way of phenomenology. It leads first to Hegel and then to Husserl and twentieth-century phenomenology.

An Historical Introduction to the Question

One view of the history of philosophy finds metaphysics originating in the West simultaneously with philosophy in the thought of the

Pre-Socratics and their question concerning what there is. On this view the history of philosophy is essentially the history of metaphysics. The end of metaphysics in the sense of demise would mean the demise of philosophy and the end of an epoch of Western culture that stretches from the Pre-Socratics until today.

Metaphysics in this comprehensive sense is identified with philosophy as such and is, accordingly, difficult to define. We should note, however, that in this broad sense metaphysics need not mean foundationalism. Metaphysics is perhaps best exemplified historically by the lectures of Aristotle that were given this title, not because they concerned what is beyond the physical—so-called other-worldly metaphysical entities—but either simply because the archivist placed them after the lectures on physics or perhaps because they pursued further, in a separate series of lectures, the themes of the physics. These lectures present a series of loosely-connected themes: what there is, truth, possibility and necessity, and God, among others. They are concerned with the various *archai* of the world and our experience of it. But Aristotle's teaching of these matters is aporetic and loosely unsystematic. There are many meanings of being and they do not find a mathematicized analogical treatment.

An alternative narrower view that ties metaphysics closely to the notion of foundation is a much more recent development. Metaphysics as a systematic doctrine of first principles, from which the premises of the other branches of philosophy and the sciences might be deduced, arises only in the fusion of late scholastic and early modern thought. Such a view of metaphysics, inspired by the model of Euclidean geometry which was so important to both Descartes and Hobbes, found its culminating expression in the work of Christian Wolff in the first part of the eighteenth century. Late scholastics like Suarez and Fonseca, on the one hand, and early moderns like Descartes, Spinoza, and Leibniz, helped prepare the way for the systematic metaphysics of Wolff. Such a rationalistic metaphysics never took hold among the Anglo-Saxons and was radically challenged on the Continent by Kant toward the end of the same century.

Kant, of course, never rejected metaphysics as such—only dogmatic metaphysics. He set for himself the task of writing a critical metaphysics. A critical metaphysics would bring the history of philosophy to an end in the sense that the task of metaphysics would be completed and fulfilled. Though Kant never was able to accomplish this even to his own satisfaction, Hegel thought he had brought just such an end to philosophy and metaphysics. Though I suggest that Hegel was no more successful than Kant, Hegel does seem, from one retrospective view, to have brought about just such an end.

Hegel's very claim to have completed metaphysics evokes a chorus of voices that continue to ring and which argue that we ought simply to be done with it.

Just as metaphysics in this narrow foundationalist, deductive and/or dialectical, systematic sense is a relatively recent development, the proclamation of its demise is relatively old. In the chorus just referred to, we find Karl Marx, nearly 150 years ago in his *Introduction to the Critique of Hegel's Philosophy of Right*, speaking of the end of philosophy. His contemporary, Auguste Comte, dismissed metaphysics as belonging to an earlier age and affirmed the new age of positive science. Since then, the list of prominent thinkers who have held some version of a view of the demise of metaphysics might include among others Nietzsche, Dilthey, Husserl, Wittgenstein, Carnap, Heidegger, Adorno, Derrida, Habermas, and Rorty. Since the demise of metaphysics has been so long announced by the greatest thinkers of the last century and a half, why do we still concern ourselves with the question, the end of metaphysics? It seems a little late to still be writing the obituary or to be holding a graveside service.

Why the Question of Metaphysics Persists

We concern ourselves with the question of metaphysics because of the ineluctability of the questions with which metaphysics traditionally concerns itself. What the above list of critics of the metaphysical tradition have minimally in common is a rejection of a rationalism which is relatively innocent of experience and which presumes to be able to deduce all truth from some abstract principles or concepts, such as the laws of non-contradiction and sufficient reason (in the case of Wolffian metaphysics) or the concepts of Being and non-Being (in the case of Hegel). They reject a foundationalist metaphysics written from a god-like point of view which is no point of view at all. I would like to ask why a Kantian sort of response to the question of metaphysics has also largely been rejected.

The Kantian Transcendental Strategy and the Munchhausen Trilemma

Kant, as we all know, meant to replace the dogmatic metaphysics of the Wolffian school with a critical metaphysics based upon a transcendental philosophy that takes experience as its first premise and asks after the conditions of its possibility. This regressive and reconstructive mode of philosophical thought is able to avoid the commonly invoked Munchhausen trilemma attendant on any attempt to provide secure, systematic, and rigorously logical foundations for philosophical thought inasmuch as transcendental philosophy is not a version of systematic philosophy that attempts to establish first principles or axioms which serve as foundations. The Munchhausen trilemma asks us to choose among 1) an infinite regress, 2) logical circularity, and 3) the arbitrary breaking-off of the providing of reasons. My formulation of Kantian transcendental thought shows how Kant is appropriately challenged by this trilemma, for I suggested above that his transcendental philosophy takes experience as its first premise. Strictly speaking, this is a category mistake, for experience as such is not a proposition and cannot serve as a premise for any chain of reasoning. Rather than a mistake, I would like to argue that this is precisely the challenge and opportunity that the critical transcendental turn has offered contemporary thought. Its most promising development has been transcendental phenomenology, while its Hegelian speculative development brings it to a dead end.

The Objections to Kantian Transcendental Strategy

The narrow objection to Kant's theoretical work from any variety of other positions has usually centered on the inability to find Kant's arguments logically rigorous. In particular, the continued energetic discussion of the structure and aim of the Transcendental Deduction reveals both the appeal of the Kantian strategy and the dissatisfaction with its logical rigor.

The larger empiricist objection concerns, in the face of the failure of proof in this strict sense, the very possibility of establishing a synthetic a priori—one formulation that Kant took to be synonymous with his attempt at transcendental philosophy. For the empiricists, to put it simply and concisely, there is only logic and empirical science, only the analytic a priori and the synthetic a posteriori. Those a little more generous and less rigorous say that the need to distinguish between science and non-science, for example, between astronomy and astrology, calls for a meta-empirical reflection on science. Such a reflection should provide an epistemology (primarily a philosophy of science), though not a metaphysics. Dummett has not been the only one to observe that the strongest motivation of the logical positivists to establish the verification principle was not so much on behalf of what the verification was seen to enable and to support but on behalf of what this principle was taken to be able to exclude—

namely metaphysics.[1] As with Comte, empirical science is to replace metaphysics, indeed philosophy. An embarrassing aspect of this project is the need to argue for it in terms that were not exclusively empirical. Epistemology becomes first philosophy with the acceptance of this requirement, i.e., the argument on behalf of empiricism which was taken to be more than rhetoric or therapy. In hand with this project we find many readings of Kant as primarily an epistemologist—an epistemologist who all too often seemed to presuppose what had to be demonstrated.

With Quine's rejection of the two dogmas of empiricism, which include reductivism as well as the sharp distinction between the analytic a priori and the synthetic a posteriori, the framework within which epistemology had pride of place was undone.[2] As we all know, Quine argues that the foundationalism inherent in the epistemological attempts to justify empirical science cannot succeed. The epistemological project is to be abandoned. We should "settle for psychology."[3] Rorty, of course, develops this line of thought. The target of Rorty's attack, we should notice, is epistemology and an epistemological or Neo-Kantian transcendental philosophy. The Quinian/Rortian project is the overcoming of epistemology. There is to be no epistemology and, of course, metaphysics has long been abandoned. Rorty finds a place for philosophy not as a discipline as such but remnants of its history might be resources for "edifying discourse."[4] It is his taste for edification and politics that most distinguishes him from his teachers Quine and Carnap. With the Quinian and Rortian radicalization of the positivist project the Kantian critical and transcendental project is not further transformed. It is simply abandoned.

From Hegel to Contemporary Phenomenology:
The Appropriation and Development of
Transcendental Philosophy

On the non-empiricist side we find, of course, a different development. Kant's transcendental philosophy finds one kind of appropriation in the

---

1. Michael Dummett, "Can Analytical Philosophy Be Systematic, and Ought It to Be?," in *After Philosophy: End or Transformation*, ed. Kenneth Baynes, James Bohmann, and Thomas McCarthy (Cambridge, Mass.: MIT Press, 1987), pp. 189–215.

2. W.V. Quine, "Two Dogmas of Empiricism," in *From a Logical Point of View* (New York: Harper Row, 1963), pp. 20–46 (first published in 1951).

3. W.V. Quine, "Epistemology Naturalized," in *Ontological Relativity and Other Essays* (New York: Columbia University Press, 1969), pp. 69–90.

4. Richard Rorty, *Philosophy and the Mirror of Nature* (Princeton: Princeton University Press, 1979).

phenomenology and speculative thought of Hegel and another in the phenomenology of Husserl and the movement related to his work. Of the heirs of Husserl, perhaps Heidegger's work is, for our purposes, of greatest interest.

Though Hegel's critique of Kant is sharp, decisive, and influential in many respects, it is important to understand Hegel's own self-understanding of his project as the fulfillment of Kant's transcendental philosophy. On this account Hegel's *Logic* is the adequate transcendental deduction of the categories of the understanding, while Kant's remains deficient. Deduction here does not mean inference from first principles but dialectical speculation. The adequacy of Hegel's attempt rests importantly on the claims of completeness and totality. Hegel's claims in this regard are notoriously hard to accept. I would suggest that from a Kantian perspective, the unpersuasiveness of Hegel's completion of Kant's transcendental project rests in part on Hegel's not making good on a transcendental schematism, i.e., on relating his categories to intuition and experience. I would claim further that Hegel's attact on 'nature' as impotent and conceptless (*begrifflos*) is a correlate to this failure.[5]

In contrast to Hegel's speculative completion, the project of phenomenology as proposed by the early Husserl is precisely to stay close to experience while not being philosophically naive in its regard. Largely because in his intellectual setting the Neo-Kantians held sway, the early Husserl's own self-understanding sees phenomenology in opposition to Kant. But as his thought develops, Husserl's position comes self-consciously close to Kant. An important aspect of the project was the attempt to do better by way of a transcendental aesthetic than Kant's account in the *Critique of Pure Reason*. Thus his efforts to provide a phenomenology of temporality are of such crucial significance. Further, in contrast to Kant, Husserlian phenomenology, for example, does not tie the notion of experience as closely to the natural sciences. Nor is Husserlian intentionality representational in the way Kant's *Vorstellungen* are such that Kant must distinguish things in themselves from their representations. Like Kant, Husserl asks after the conditions of the possibility of experience but provides a richer notion of experience such that themes like the body, language, and history become fertile areas for phenomenological research, if not by Husserl then by his successors Heidegger and Merleau-Ponty.

As I suggested above, experience is the first premise for such a program. And though the Neo-Kantians developed Kant's philosophy

---

5. See *Hegel's Science of Logic*, trans. A. V. Miller (New York: Humanities Press, 1969), pp. 607–608.

into what some have appropriately called a *prinzipien-theoretisch* transcendental philosophy (i.e., a theory based on principles), the Husserlian transcendental philosophy is rather an *evidenz-theoretisch* transcendental philosophy (i.e., a theory based on evidence). Rather than seeking first principles or a categorical or dialectical scheme from which one might make sense of (perhaps even deduce) our experience, the reflective procedure of phenomenology claims to bring to *Evidenz* (intuitive self-evidence) the constituting intentional experiences. This is, I suppose, just the sort of thing that Putnam hopes to debunk when he says that the only way to save a correspondence theory of truth and an externalist realism is to postulate a special "magical" mental power, an intellectual intuition.[6] This, he thinks, takes us back to a pre-Kantian dogmatic metaphysics. That intuition is, in fact, no such magical and outlandish power for Husserl and for phenomenology in general, I can here only assert but cannot argue. By intuition Husserl means little more than the way things (in the broadest sense) present themselves to us.

The centrality of experience and evidence for philosophy is also why Dummett's proposal that a philosophy of language become first philosophy cannot on this view be adequate.[7] Experience is broader and less determinate than language, to be sure, but we ought not for the sake of intellectual convenience settle on the narrower and more determinate. Philosophy is just an attempt to bring to language the pre-linguistic and non-linguistic. Gadamer's claim in *Truth and Method*, that Being which can be understood is language, is a statement not about the linguistic character of Being but of the linguistic character of understanding.[8] Though Husserl himself did not contribute an adequate philosophy of language, significant phenomenological contributions have been made (most recently, for example, in Sokolowski's *Presence and Absence*) which ask us to consider the experience of language.[9]

First order descriptions of experience (the Göttingen phenomenology of some of Husserl's first followers) or first order descriptions of language (Austin's ordinary language philosophy) are not satisfying or sufficient. We inevitably want to know not only how things work or

---

6. Hilary Putnam, "Two Philosophical Perspectives," in *Reason, Truth and History* (Cambridge: Cambridge University Press, 1981), pp. 49–74. See also Putnam, "Models and Reality," in *Realism and Reason* (Cambridge: Cambridge University Press, 1983), pp. 1–25.

7. Dummett, "Can Analytical Philosophy Be Systematic, and Ought It to Be?"

8. Hans-George Gadamer, *Truth and Method* (New York: Continuum Press, 1975), p. 432.

9. Robert Sokolowski, *Presence and Absence* (Bloomington: Indiana University Press, 1978).

how to do things with words but why it is such and so and how it is that we can have a certain view or interpretation of things and language. A first order, merely descriptive, phenomenology would be merely empirical, and, in the end, could be best accomplished by the empirical sciences. The critical reflection on first order experience and the respective empirical sciences can be called transcendental. It is mistaken to assume that this title requires some non-experiential, perhaps solely introspective and subjective (and consequently 'mysterious') mode of reflection. It is a title that contemporary philosophers as various as Habermas, Gadamer, Taylor, and Putnam accept, albeit with hesitation. They hesitate because of the Neo-Kantian claim on it. It is a title decisive for Husserlian phenomenology. And it is a title, I would argue, that does not require one to reject the title of metaphysics, as for example, both Husserl and Habermas have done.

Though Husserl resists 'speculation' because it suggests somehow that thought has become unhinged from experience and intuition, it is telling that much of his later work concerning both temporality on the one hand as well as notions such as higher-order communities on the other hand is remarkably speculative, although not in a Hegelian sense. In the fifth Cartesian meditation, Husserl unusually accepts the title of metaphysics for his project.[10]

It is the understanding of phenomenology as metaphysics that characterizes the work of the early Heidegger, Husserl's younger colleague. A leading insight of Heidegger's early work is that to ask after conditions of experience and knowledge is, at the same time, to ask after what there is. Thus he writes in the Introduction to *Being and Time:*

> Every disclosure of Being as the transcendence is transcendental knowledge. Phenomenological truth (the disclosedness of Being) is veritas transcendentalis. . . . Philosophy is universal phenomenological ontology.[11]

The insight that the question of knowledge is at the same time the ontological question renders the subjectivist aspect of phenomenology objectivist and vice-versa—or, to put it another way, undoes any ultimate significance for the subjective-objective distinction. Phenomenology is not to be misconstrued as subjective idealism, despite the fact

---

10. Edmund Husserl, *Cartesian Meditations,* trans. Dorian Cairns (The Hague: Martinus Nijhoff, 1960).

11. Martin Heidegger, *Being and Time,* trans. John Macquarrie & Edward Robinson (New York: Harper Row, 1962), p. 62.

that both Hegel and Husserl, each in their own way, sometimes point in that direction.

Further, with Heidegger, any claim to certainty and apodicticity is clearly rejected. His notion of truth as disclosure (as a revealing that at the same time covers over) yields a phenomenology that keeps 'truth' as a central concern but which rejects any absolutist claims or any straightforward attempt to lay out "the furniture of the world." It does not assume God's point of view or the view from nowhere.

Heidegger, of course, was notoriously unsuccessful in completing the project of *Being and Time*. His seeming rejection of the project together with philosophy *in toto* on behalf of thought (*Denken*) has provided much encouragement for the second main movement which has rejected philosophy and metaphysics. The first movement, of course, was that of scientism: philosophy should give way to science. The other movement might be called (for want of a better label) poetism. Rather than claim that what philosophy aspires to do, science can do better, this movement has long claimed that what philosophy aspires to do, poetry can do better. Sometimes, as in the case of Rorty, these two camps conspire to divide the tasks. And this is why Putnam can appropriately say that Rorty is Carnap in Heidegger's clothing.[12] Heidegger, of course, never identified his *Denken* with *Dichten*. He only says that they are the closest of neighbors.

The later Heidegger, as we well know, did for a while call for the overcoming (*Überwindung*) of metaphysics—not the Hegelian completion but the being done with metaphysics (*Verwindung*). We do not require a commentator such as Derrida to notice how entwined Heidegger's later thought is with the metaphysical tradition. Heidegger himself explicitly affirmed his inability to be done with metaphysics. Similarly one of the most obvious features of Derrida's deconstructive project is its parasitism on this tradition. The force of both Heidegger's caricature of Platonism as the origin and fate of metaphysics and Derrida's notion of the 'transcendental signified' depends on the representational hypostatization of other-worldly principles. This Platonism lends itself to ready critique.[13]

---

12. A comment by Putnam at the 1987 Hegel Kongress in Stuttgart.

13. For Derrida's treatment of Plato see "Plato's Pharmacy" in *Dissemination*, trans. Barbara Johnson (Chicago: University of Chicago Press, 1981), pp. 61–171. For Heidegger's critique of Plato see his "Plato's Doctrine of Truth," trans. John Barlow in *Philosophy in the Twentieth Century*, vol. 3, ed. William Barrett and Henry D. Aiken (New York: Random House, 1962). For a critique of Heidegger's interpretation which is so important to Derrida, see my "Beyond Being: Heidegger's Plato," *Journal of the History of Philosophy* 23 (1985), pp. 71–98.

Conclusion

If, as I have suggested above, questions about the theory of practice and the practice of theory which have long been asked in the history of philosophy are still deserving of attention, and if these questions can be treated in a non-representational, that is, presentational manner such that the epistemology of foundations is no longer taken to be first philosophy, then perhaps truly speculative thought about a whole variety of questions can flourish. Such speculative thought cannot be a simple return to the ancients nor can it simply carry on the foundationalist epistemological project of so much of modernity. Insofar as it abandons the ideal of strict logical and systematic proof without abandoning the ideal of coherence, it can escape the Munchhausen trilemma by simply endorsing the inability to satisfy such criteria and by arguing the inappropriateness of presuppositions of such a trilemma, namely, a rigorously deductive system. Here too Kant's transcendental philosophy is a model inasmuch as Kant in the little read "Doctrine of Method" of the *Critique of Pure Reason* distinguishes philosophy sharply from mathematics and axiomatic geometry. On his view, for example, definitions, axioms, and first principles are not available to philosophy. From the Munchhausen perspective, such speculative thought will seem circular if not arbitrary. Here we find scientism and poetism in collusion. Scientism finds it does not meet rigorous standards, and poetism affirms its arbitrariness.

Speculative thought, in putting aside such criteria, must, nonetheless, coherently offer reasons and make distinctions. It must understand itself as fallible and in conversation with the tradition of thought that has elicited it. As a corrective to Hegel's logic, it must be attendant to our experience (and our experience of one another) and return us to experience. It can accept the titles: critical, transcendental, and even metaphysical. But such speculative thought might modestly hesitate to accept the title of first science while accepting the title of last science— that more comprehensive and reflective form of thought that must indeed come after physics, and whose 'end' is self-understanding.

3 Hegel, Heidegger, and Hermeneutical Experience

Walter Lammi

The legacy of Hegel's monumental philosophical system has proven to be a conundrum for many thinkers: impossible to accept in its totality, yet powerfully compelling. One's natural tendency is to pick and choose. Such a tightly-woven, all-encompassing system is not, however, a kind of candy store where one can select chocolate truffles but reject the marzipan. What criteria are appropriate for evaluating Hegel's philosophy?

Hegel's own emphatic answer is that the very concept of external criteria is in error. To comprehend his thought, there is no shortcut to avoid engaging it in its totality.[1] To engage means not merely to follow the course of his thinking with scholarly care, but to experience it in its fullness and depth. An indication of the special difficulty of this task is Heidegger's praise of Hegel, that he was the only philosopher (before, presumably, Heidegger himself) actually to experience the history of Western thought.[2]

This does not mean, of course, that Heidegger thought Hegel was fundamentally right in his interpretation of that history. It does mean that he thought Hegel was profoundly wrong—not dead wrong, but deeply wrong. There is for Heidegger, then, something interesting and challenging

---

1. See, for example, G. W. F. Hegel, "Preface" to *Phenomenology of Spirit*, trans. A. V. Miller (Oxford: Clarendon Press, 1977), §70; henceforth cited as PhG.

2. Martin Heidegger, "The Anaximander Fragment" in *Early Greek Thinking*, trans. David Farrell Krell and Frank A. Capuzzi (New York: Harper & Row, 1975), 14.

about Hegelian error, which is why he found it necessary to return time and again to Hegel. As Hans-Georg Gadamer has pointed out, it was in dialogue with Hegel, more perhaps than with any other philosopher, that Heidegger refined and continually reinterpreted his own experience of thinking.[3]

Gadamer has played a mediating role in Heidegger's encounter with Hegel. On the one hand, he bases his hermeneutical philosophy explicitly on the Heideggerian experience of thought, particularly the Heidegger of the "*Kehre*" (PH 50). On the other hand, in his own life-long dialogue with Hegel, Gadamer seems increasingly to lean toward the latter. In his "tension-filled proximity" to Hegel,[4] he ends up 'correcting' both Hegel and Heidegger to a point of sufficient fusion that Gadamer's Heidegger, far from exhibiting the radical break with tradition of the latter's reputation and self-understanding, becomes effectively reintegrated into the history of Western metaphysics.[5]

This opens Gadamer to the charge of syncretism. Again the question arises: According to what criteria can one legitimately reinterpret, dissent from, or pick and choose among philosophers' writings? How does one recognize philosophical error? One is reminded of Theodor Adorno's salutary warning that in every involvement with a great philosophy, "one cannot select what one likes. . . and reject what one finds irritating."[6] Dogmatic criteria are no less reprehensible than arbitrary or subjective ones.[7] To what criterion can Gadamer refer?

"Experience" is not a sufficient reply. More to the point is hermeneutical experience, which, despite Gadamer's attempt to universalize it, takes its bearings from a specific type of experience that is concerned with what has been transmitted in the language of tradition.[8]

---

3. See Hans-Georg Gadamer, "Hegel and Heidegger" in *Hegel's Dialectic: Five Hermeneutical Studies*, trans. P. Christopher Smith (New Haven: Yale University Press, 1976), p. 103, and *Philosophical Hermeneutics*, trans. David E. Linge (Berkeley: University of California Press, 1976), p. 230; henceforth cited as PH.

4. Gadamer, "The Heritage of Hegel," in *Reason in the Age of Science*, trans. Frederick G. Lawrence (Cambridge, MA: The MIT Press, 1981), p. 53.

5. See Robert Bernasconi, "Bridging the Abyss: Heidegger and Gadamer," *Research in Phenomenology*, 16 (1986), 5.

6. Theodor W. Adorno, "The Experiential Content of Hegel's Philosophy," in *Hegel: Three Studies*, trans. Shierry Weber Nicholson (Cambridge, MA: The MIT Press, 1993), p. 83.

7. This charge is made by Bernasconi in *The Question of Language in Heidegger's History of Being* (Atlantic Highlands, NJ: Humanities Press International, Inc., 1985), p. 2.

8. See, for example, Gadamer, "The Universality of the Hermeneutical Problem," *Philosophical Hermeneutics*, p. 10, and *Truth and Method*, trans. revised by Joel Weinsheimer and Donald G. Marshall (New York: Continuum Publishing Co., 1993), p. 358. All references to *Truth and Method* (henceforth cited as TM) will be to the second, revised edition.

It is not to commit a genetic fallacy, then, to suggest that hermeneutical experience derives from its origins a particularly useful perspective: understanding reading.

This suggests, to start, at least a provisional distinction between two kinds of experience: consciousness and the experience of tradition. Again provisionally, this seems to separate experience into one realm, of the 'personal,' and another, of the 'other' or, as Gadamer puts it, the "Thou" (TM 358ff). Thoughtfully to have experienced the history of thought may, then, be seen as a different order or kind of experience than that of one's own consciousness. The former requires the interpretation of historical texts; the latter, of something like introspection.[9]

There are some clear advantages to this line of demarcation. In the interpretation of texts, scholarly criteria such as accuracy of translation and textual fidelity become relevant. It is on these grounds that Hegel is generally spurned by professional historians, and Heidegger's own historical readings, especially of Plato, have been severely criticized.[10] In regard to the interpretation of personal spiritual experience, scholarship seems to have a less critical, more purely explanatory role.

Yet this distinction between criticism and explanation, while important, is of limited validity. The relevance of scholarly criteria is dependent on some degree of objectivity or textual fidelity in the interpretation of philosophic works. However, such historical works are far more than objects of study. Just as the Greek sense of 'theory' denoted an active interest and involvement in the matter at hand, so does hermeneutical theory require interpreters to bring themselves, the summation of their own experiences or what Gadamer terms their "prejudices," to the text.[11] Thus on the one hand, textual interpretation should be deferential to scholarly considerations of careful reading and contextual accuracy. On the other hand, interpretation cannot limit itself to a passive, if judicious, role. Gadamer points to the process of translation as paradigmatic for the combination of thoughtful care and creative thought necessary to all understanding of the world around us (TM 548). The good translator remains faithful to his text. As is the case with translation, however, there is ultimately no rule-governed method-

---

9. More accurately, 'retrospective introspection.' See Michael Allen Gillespie, *Hegel, Heidegger, and the Ground of History* (Chicago: University of Chicago Press, 1984), p. 78.

10. The history of this scholarly criticism is discussed in Robert J. Dostal, "Heidegger's Plato," *Journal of the History of Philosophy*, 23 (1985), 71–98.

11. See Gadamer, "Science and Philosophy," in *Reason in the Age of Science*, pp. 17f. Experience, strictly speaking, is not something we can have, but rather, as Heidegger puts it, something we "undergo." However, it is possible to speak of one's knowledge as the culmination of experience. See Quentin Lauer, *A Reading of Hegel's* Phenomenology of Spirit (New York: Fordham University Press, 1976), p. 4.

ology to hermeneutics.[12] Moreover, the distinction of hermeneutical and other experience becomes questionable when we look not to its original subject matter, but to the common ends of self-understanding and self-transformation. "All meaning," says Gadamer, "is related to the 'I'"; the nature of philosophical thought "consists precisely in recognizing oneself in other being" (TM 473, 346). To understand more clearly the relation of Hegel, Heidegger, and Gadamer, it seems necessary to deepen the discussion of 'experience'.

Among the many perplexing issues of the relationship among these three thinkers, perhaps none is more difficult to sort out than the concept of experience, which Gadamer has described as "one of the most obscure we have" (TM 346). Yet not only does it occupy a "systematic and key position" in his own thought (TM xxxv), but it is a key—perhaps *the* key—locus of both agreement and contention among these thinkers. At issue is neither the scientific concept of experience nor everyday experience, the kind that Hegel called "natural," and Heidegger, "fallenness," but experience in a more fundamental sense that philosophy seeks to investigate.

The first difficulty in talking about experience is that to Hegel, Heidegger, and Gadamer alike, it is not a thing, but a process or movement of consciousness that entails change of understanding, self-understanding, and the self that understands. Even a superficial definition of the term would require a recapitulation of its transformations, which is what Hegel provides in the "Introduction" to his *Phenomenology of Spirit*. Hegel views the *Phenomenology* itself as an immanent definition, as indicated by its original subtitle, "Science of the Experience of Consciousness." For the more limited purpose of sorting out the major contributions of Hegelian and Heideggerian views to the understanding of hermeneutical experience, what follows is (1) a composite sketch of experience that will emphasize agreements and similarities among Hegel's, Heidegger's, and Gadamer's views, and (2) a discussion of major differences. On this basis an assessment of Gadamer's "mediation" of Hegelian and Heideggerian experience will become possible.

Apparent Similarities

As a phenomenology, Hegel's science of the experience of consciousness is based on an observation of phenomena that refuses to theo-

---

12. See P. Christopher Smith, "Gadamer on Language and Method in Hegel's Dialectic," *Graduate Faculty Philosophy Journal*, Vol. 5 (1975), 53ff.

rize in the sense of "intrud[ing] . . . either arbitrarily or with wisdom obtained from elsewhere" (PhG §58). Phenomenology to Hegel is "not merely the reflection of the cognitive process" (§53). Heidegger and Gadamer also approach thought in ways that each has called phenomenological. Although the term covers a multitude of meanings, each of these thinkers tries to avoid dogmatism by going, as the phenomenological slogan put it, "to the things themselves" [*zu den Sachen selbst*]. Gadamer, no less than Hegel, stresses the importance of an active effort not to interfere with the inner necessity of thought's own movement (TM 464). To Heidegger as well, experiencing (*in Erfahrung bringen*) means "to let an opinion be confirmed by the matter itself."[13] Heidegger's "step back" is similar to Hegel's observer's stance in that it, too, requires thought to wait for the phenomena to appear or shine forth.[14] Experience is not a matter of intentional acts (TM 245); one does not create experience, one "undergoes," "suffers," "receives" it, as Heidegger says.[15] In order to observe the experience of consciousness, Hegel says, we must "surrender" ourselves to the movement of experience itself.[16] Heidegger speaks of the "event of Appropriation" [*Ereignis*] as that which also "surrenders" man to open a path to more "originary" experience.[17] "The thing itself" [*die Sache Selbst*] of experience requires this fundamental "letting-go and letting-be," which, far from implying detachment in the sense of disinterest, necessitates a depth of personal involvement that risks one's very sense of self.[18] This aspect of philosophical experience is reflected in a post-Hegelian terminological distinction between *Erlebnis* and *Erfahrung*. The former has connotations of an adventure from which one returns, while the latter indicates a way or path of discovery and self-discovery from which there is no return (see TM 60ff).

---

13. Martin Heidegger, *Hegel's Phenomenology of Spirit*, trans. Parvis Emad and Kenneth Maly (Bloomington: University of Indiana Press, 1988), p. 19.

14. This connection is supported by David Kolb's argument that Heidegger overemphasized the similarity of dialectical transitions in his interpretation of the *Phenomenology of Spirit*, reducing them to experiential unity as a single, repeated "step back" from natural consciousness to ontological awareness. David Kolb, *The Critique of Pure Modernity: Hegel, Heidegger, and After* (Chicago: The University of Chicago Press, 1986), p. 216.

15. Martin Heidegger, "The Nature of Language," in *On the Way to Language*, trans. by Peter Hertz (New York: Harper & Row, 1971), p. 57.

16. Hegel, PhG §53; see Heidegger, *Hegel's Concept of Experience* (New York: Harper & Row, 1970), p. 51: "[Phenomenology] follows the path of experience."

17. Martin Heidegger, *Identity and Difference*, trans. Joan Stambaugh (New York: Harper & Row, 1969), p. 40; henceforth cited as ID.

18. Robert D. Walsh, "When Love of Knowing Becomes Actual Knowing: Heidegger and Gadamer on Hegel's *Die Sache Selbst*," *The Owl of Minerva* 17 (1986), p. 160.

Philosophical experience always involves negativity (TM 353), something missing or incomplete, a lack,[19] disappointment (TM 75), doubt and despair (PhG §78). The "tragedy of hermeneutical experience" reflects a constant theme in the texts of Hegel.[20]

Not only is experience inescapable, but it exhibits a kind of progression, if not clear progress.[21] This progression holds regardless of whether it be towards spirit and Absolute Knowledge; deeper, more authentic or 'essential' thinking about the still unthought (ID 55); or the radical non-dogmatism of the fully experienced person (TM 355). The direction of movement is in each case, in Heideggerian language, from ontic to ontological. Gadamer mediates between Hegel and Heidegger by connecting the experience of the Absolute or the eternal with contemplation, communion, or 'tarrying' with the work of art (TM 101ff). This includes an overcoming of the "I" or subjectivity through moments of understanding in which Gadamer recognizes the fundamental experience of the Hegelian dialectic. Drawing from a phenomenology of play, Heidegger's (post-*Kehre*) essay *Origin of the Work of Art*, and the living conversation of language, Gadamer finds common philosophical ground between Heidegger's concept of experience and the inner nature of dialectic.[22]

Insofar as new experience emerges from negating, contradicting or even annihilating the old, it may be called dialectical (PhG §86). Dialectic entails a "reversal of consciousness" when consciousness achieves self-recognition in the other (TM 355), a reversal by which consciousness "realizes its own reality."[23] Whatever that reality may turn out to be, there is room for agreement over the path. Gadamer cites Heidegger's remark that "Hegel is not interpreting experience dialectically but rather conceiving what is dialectical in terms of the nature of experience."[24] Thought is immanent necessity, dialectic is a discovery rather than a conceptual tool.

---

19. Cf. Bernasconi, *The Question of Language*, p. 83, where he distinguishes this aspect of experience in Heidegger from Hegel's view of experience as a progressive development.

20. See Gerald L. Bruns, "On the Tragedy of Hermeneutical Experience," *Research in Phenomenology* 18 (1988), 191–201.

21. See Joan Stambaugh, "Introduction" to ID 16: "[T]hinking for Heidegger attempts to move *forward* by the step *back* into the realm of the essence of truth which has never yet come to light." (Emphasis in the original.)

22. See Gadamer PH 216ff. and "Hegel and Heidegger," p. 116: "[T]he language of philosophy, as long as it remains language, will remain a dialogue with that language of our world."

23. Heidegger, *Hegel's Concept of Experience*, pp. 116–117.

24. TM 354; Heidegger, *Hegel's Concept of Experience*, p. 119.

Gadamer's view is that the later Heidegger, after the *Kehre*, draws close to Hegel in two crucial ways: his recognition of the dependence of philosophy on history or historicity, and his attempt to transcend subjectivity.[25] These are both connected to the Hegelian dialectic, albeit in different ways.

Despite Heidegger's ultimate rejection of the dialectic, he retains, with Gadamer, its fundamental attribute of historicity. Experience is always historical in the sense that it is temporally particular (TM 353). Even if its dialectic is teleological or, as ontologically directed, reaches toward universal truth, experience remains rooted in finite, historical situations.

This implies that the way or manner of experiencing truth, and consequently our understanding of truth itself, may vary according to what one could call the worldviews of a given era—whether or not we follow Hegel in perceiving such worldviews as stages in the progress of spirit towards absolute knowledge. In any case, the experience of truth must be 'concrete,' reflecting its origins in "the earnestness of life in its concrete richness" (PhG §4). To Hegel it is a "principle of experience" that its phenomena must exhibit themselves as immediately present to the observer.[26] It is only a step further to describe the immediacy of this presence as an historical event or happening. To both Heidegger and Gadamer, the experiential moment is sudden and unique—even if what comes-to-presence in this moment is absence or the oblivion of Being. Thus the manner in which Being gives itself is historic or epochal, and, as Heidegger puts it, our only access to that experience is in the "sudden moment" of recall (ID 67). Gadamer views the sudden nature of experiential change (the existential moment) as indicative of a "mode of knowledge" that is a key to interpreting Heidegger's understanding of historical discontinuity; using the example of how "suddenly" the "mode of being" of a person changes upon our hearing of his or her death, Gadamer universalizes the experience of discontinuity expressed in tragic recognition.[27] The instantaneity or experiential discontinuity of the entry of the event of understanding into consciousness entails, according to Gadamer, a momentary loss of self. That is why it is only the past which allows us to be aware of the event (PH 58). This observation, which supports Gadamer's emphasis on the past over Heidegger's on the future, is

---

25. Gadamer, "Hegel and Heidegger," p. 104.

26. "Introduction" to *Hegel's Logic*, trans. by William Wallace (Oxford: Clarendon Press, 1975), §7.

27. Gadamer, "The Continuity of History and the Existential Moment," trans. by Christopher Wren, *Philosophy Today* 16 (1972), p. 237.

important to his interpretation, or "correction," of Heidegger.[28] Gadamer also applies the limiting or 'mediating' concept of an historical framework to a critique of Heidegger's thought. In the context of the rise of European nihilism and positivism's denial of the "true world," he suggests, Heidegger's "step back" does not escape metaphysical thought but actually illustrates historical continuity.[29]

Heidegger judged modern epistemology, insofar as it reflects Cartesian subjectivity in the sense of subjects gaining knowledge of objects, to be the true scandal of contemporary philosophy. His own view of Hegel is that he especially fell into this apparently solipsistic trap with his notions of God as Absolute subject and, consequently, the end of the experiential dialectic in Absolute subjectivity. Two points should be made about this assessment. First, as Gadamer points out, Heidegger's critique of modern subjectivity did not lead, as commonly supposed, to an existentialist denial of transcendence, but to new possibilities of experiencing Being (TM 99) or, as Heidegger put it in his *Letter On Humanism*, the holy. In this way Heidegger's opposition to Hegel led to a philosophical development that was carried on by Gadamer. Second, Heidegger's reading of Hegel on this central issue is highly suspect. Certainly Hegel's own argument is diametrically opposed to epistemological subjectivism (see e.g., PhG §76). Moreover, in the irreducibility of the Hegelian concept of objective spirit to individual consciousness, Gadamer also finds means of asserting transcendence in the experience of thinking. Again, Gadamer's hermeneutics effectively mediates Hegel and Heidegger.

Critique

One could continue to argue in this vein. In Heidegger's dialogue with Hegel, it may not be necessary to choose sides as though they were rivals.[30] At some point, however, it becomes difficult to ignore the mounting objections. If Gadamer is not pejoratively syncretist, he must take seriously Heidegger's radical, almost violent dissociation of his experience of thinking from Hegel's. Heidegger's objections may be summed up under three rubrics: the Absolute, the metaphysics of presence, and the dialectic. These topics are closely interrelated;

---

28. See Walter Lammi, "Hans-Georg Gadamer's 'Correction' of Heidegger," *Journal of the History of Ideas*, 52 (1991), 501–505.
29. Gadamer, "Hegel and Heidegger," p. 109.
30. Bernasconi, "Bridging the Abyss," pp. 21–22.

Heidegger is engaged not in eristics, but in a sustained encounter that enters into "the force and sphere" of Hegel's thinking (ID 47).

It is not difficult to see why Heidegger interprets Hegel's metaphysics as subjectivity. Hegel himself announces that everything depends on viewing the True or Substance as being just as much Subject (PhG Preface §17). If experience is Hegel's name for Being and the truth of Being is "absolute reflection," "the absolute self-thinking of thinking," subjective thought collapses into metaphysics and metaphysics, into subjectivity.[31] Heidegger means nothing arbitrary about the term subjectivity; he views it as the profoundest vision of Hegel's epoch.[32] He does, however, intend a critique of Hegel from his own standpoint, the gift of Being to thinking in his own time. From that standpoint, the constant presence or *parousia* of the Absolute is metaphysical illusion. Far from being omnipresent, Being has withdrawn to the point where we have even forgotten its oblivion. Insofar as the thinking of Being is connected with experience, this implies an entirely different meaning of Being for Heidegger, even if he is concerned with the same realm of Being and essence as Hegel.[33] For Heidegger in contradistinction to Hegel, essence means not grounding but the loss of any firm ground, an abyss.[34] As Heidegger himself puts it,

> For Hegel, the matter of thinking is: Being with respect to beings having been thought in absolute thinking and as absolute thinking. For us, the matter of thinking is the same, and thus is Being—but Being with respect to its difference from beings. (ID 47)

How is it possible to find 'essential' similarity in experiences whose 'essence' differs so profoundly?

At issue is Heidegger's *Kehre* and "step back" out of metaphysics and into new possibilities for thinking. Heidegger emphatically does not interpret his overcoming of the metaphysics of presence in terms

---

31. Heidegger, *Hegel's Concept of Experience*, p. 114, and ID 43.

32. Heidegger, "Overcoming Metaphysics," in *The End of Philosophy*, trans. Joan Stambaugh (Harper & Row, 1973), p. 89.

33. Werner Marx, *Heidegger and the Tradition*, trans. Theodore Kisiel and Murray Green (Evanston: Northwestern University Press, 1971), p. 44.

34. Bernasconi, *The Question of Language*, p. 78. See Otto Pöggeler, *Martin Heidegger's Path of Thinking*, trans. Daniel Magurshak and Sigmund Barber (Atlantic Highlands, NJ: Humanities Press International, 1987), pp. 129–130: "[For Heidegger] essence is no longer essence in the traditional way. The . . . ground of ground is thought as abyss. . . . Only slowly did Heidegger's thinking relinquish its wanting-to-ground. Experiencing the thrownness of the grounding projection had to be deepened to experiencing the abysmal character of the truth of Being."

of Hegel's dialectical overcoming or 'elevation' (*Aufhebung*) (ID 49). The experience of the "step back" belongs to preparatory thinking;[35] the dialectic, to the completion of thought. In this sense, Heidegger's thinking belongs to the future and Hegel's, to the past. Hegel's famous doctrine of the "owl of Minerva" seems to be untrue to Heidegger, and the experience of thought is radically incomplete.

The completion of the dialectic means for Hegel the end of experience, whereas Heidegger and then Gadamer decisively reject that possibility. Heidegger's preparatory thinking is preparation for a new beginning to the experience of thought, and his celebrated "end of philosophy," in the fulfillment of Western metaphysics, constitutes a resounding rejection of Hegel's end of experience in the fulfillment of philosophy. Gadamer, for his part, views the radical non-dogmatism of the fully experienced person precisely as openness to new experience (TM 355). On this issue there is no room for mediation.

Is the synthetic sketch of experience, then, ultimately syncretistic? By choosing Hegelian historicity over the Hegelian Absolute, does Gadamer mediate between Hegel and Heidegger by twisting the former— to provide intellectual legitimacy for twisting the latter? By tying Hegel's dialectic not to any ends but the endless openness of language, does he essentially misconstrue dialectical experience? And by interpreting Heidegger's *Kehre* and "step back" in terms of this dialectic, does he likewise misconstrue the Heideggerian experience of thought? In short, is Gadamer forcing Heidegger's 'preparatory thought' onto the procrustean bed of traditional metaphysics?

Doctrine and Experience

Let us look more closely at the oft-cited disagreement between Heidegger and Hegel over what it is that we experience. For Hegel it is fairly easy, if not to understand, at least to give names to the fundamental experience: the Absolute, the *parousia* of the Absolute, the self-certainty of absolute knowledge. This is not the case with Heidegger. Paradoxically, for Heidegger rather than Hegel, it is crucial that experience seeks expression in language; yet also for Heidegger, the language for primordial experience lacks words.[36] It is true that Hegel revised his language, notably by eliminating the very term 'experience' from the

---

35. Heidegger, "The Turning," in *The Question Concerning Technology and Other Essays*, trans. William Lovitt (New York: Harper & Row, 1977), p. 40.

36. Bernasconi, *The Question of Language*, 86–87: " . . . *Ereignis* is the word that arises from the experience of *the lack of a word* for Being." (Emphasis in the original.)

title of his *Phenomenology*. However, it was Heidegger who turned language revision into an art form. The experience of Being, Being as the difference between "beings" and "Being," the "turn," the "step back," the "unthought," *Ereignis* or the "event of Appropriation"—all attest to Heidegger's struggle to carry his experience to language beyond the traditional terminology of theology and metaphysics. This plethora of increasingly original expressions can lead to doctrinal confusion. Is Heidegger's "step back" into the "oblivion" of the "difference between Being and beings" (ID 50-51) the same as a "step back" to "retain the experience of the oblivion of Being"?[37]

In regard to the end or ultimate meaning of experience, Gadamer is clearly closer to Heidegger than Hegel. "It is of decisive importance," he says, "that 'Being' does not unfold totally in its self-manifestation, but rather withholds itself and withdraws with the same originality with which it manifests itself."[38] 'Truth' to Heidegger is to be found not in the progressive unfolding of the dialectic, but in a complex interplay of concealment and unconcealment. With Heidegger the central role of concealment is clear, which leads him to view fundamental experience more as the manner than matter of experience.[39] Truth is experienced as the revealing manifestation of light within its abysmal ground [*Grund*] in all-surrounding darkness. In this regard, Gadamer describes earth [*Erde*] as the "new and startling" element in Heidegger's post-*Kehre* thought because it asserts the primacy of concealment in the paradigmatic case of the experience of the work of art (PH 217). Like all experience, to Gadamer, this is ultimately self-understanding, although not in the sense of Hegel's self-transparency of absolute knowledge (PH 55). Gadamer argues that far from being self-transparent, we are dark to ourselves, and this darkness "co-constitutes" the truth of our being.[40] On the other hand, Gadamer finds an ambiguity common to Hegel's completion of experience and Heidegger's consummation of metaphysics, that both may be trapped within the "circle" or "inner infinity" of reflective thought.[41] What made Heidegger a thinker rather than a theologian was the passion and depth with which he experienced thinking, but the very strength of insight that made him so

---

37. Bernasconi, *The Question of Language*, p. 85.

38. Gadamer, "Text and Interpretation," trans. Dennis J. Schmidt, in *Hermeneutics and Modern Philosophy*, ed. Brice R. Wachterhauser (Albany: SUNY Press, 1986), p. 382.

39. Martin Heidegger, "A Heidegger Seminar on Hegel's *Differenzschrift*," trans. by William Lovitt, *Southwest Journal of Philosophy* 11 (1980), p. 28.

40. Gadamer, "Being, Spirit, God," in *Heidegger Memorial Lectures*, ed. by Werner Marx (Pittsburgh: Duquesne University Press, 1982), p. 69.

41. Gadamer, "Hegel and Heidegger," pp. 101–102.

powerful an interpreter of the tradition also proved, in Gadamer's view, to be his Achilles' heel. Seeking to recognize his own thought and being in every great philosopher of the past, he was able to enter into the power of their experience. Recognizing himself, however, also meant differentiating his experience of thought, and this concern for his self-profile led Heidegger, Gadamer says, almost willfully to distort Hegel's meaning.[42]

Gadamer's own critique of Hegel turns Hegel's concept of objective spirit against his Absolute.[43] Objective spirit as history and language is intrinsic to the Hegelian dialectic, yet irreducible to the dialectical experience of consciousness with itself. It points to an element of the concealed within Hegel's own thinking about truth. Moreover, Gadamer finds in the concept of the unconscious the possibility of limits to absolute knowledge from within consciousness itself.[44] According to Gadamer, then, the Heideggerian insight into the fundamental importance of finitude is also a hidden feature of the Hegelian dialectic.[45]

Perhaps we take the contradiction of Hegel's Absolute and Heidegger's abyss too much on the level of doctrine, and consequently too little on the level of a phenomenology of experience. Experientially speaking, what could they have in common? In fact Gadamer, in the passage just cited, affirms the Heideggerian insight on experiential grounds. The meaning of the work of art resists conceptualization, the meaning of history can only be understood retrospectively, and "the same basic experience" of limitations to human understanding applies to philosophic knowledge and the history of philosophy.[46] Although this leads to an emphasis on remembrance that sounds Hegelian, Gadamer credits the work of Heidegger for uncovering this "real historicity," which, "as the experience of oneself," sets limits to self-understanding (PH 49).

The Heideggerian-cum-hermeneutical experience of finitude thus denies the possibility of absolute knowledge via the Hegelian dialectic. As Gadamer puts it, the experience of finiteness "can remove the false claim of gnostic self-certainty from the self-understanding of faith" (PH 49). It does not, however, simply deny the Absolute. This experiential route does not entail a doctrinal shift from monotheism to atheism. Yet experience does lead to a desire, Heidegger says, to "remain silent

---

42 Gadamer, "The Heritage of Hegel," p. 62.

43. Merold Westphal, "Hegel and Gadamer," in *Heidegger and Modern Philosophy*, ed. Michael Murray (New Haven: Yale University Press, 1978), pp. 76–77.

44. Westphal, p. 81.

45. Gadamer, "Text and Interpretation," 380–381.

46. See Ibid., and context.

about God" when one is "speaking in the realm of thinking" (ID 54-55). This turns us from the question of the Absolute to that of language. The point of Hegel's speculative proposition, as he explains it in the *Preface* to the *Phenomenology of Spirit*, is that, as in the example "God is one," it throws the predicate of a sentence back upon its subject so that they mutually collapse in an infinite circle of inner reflection. Then everything depends on the explanation of this inner circle; without the explanation, the circle is a trap leading to the mystical night of oneness where, in Hegel's celebrated phrase, "all cows are black." Since the explanation is in language, everything depends on what words can and cannot do. The ambiguity that Gadamer finds in common with Hegel and Heidegger concerns language. To what extent was each of them liberated by language, and to what extent was each held captive to his linguistic usage?

Gadamer's answer in regard to Hegel is that in different ways he is both more and less captive than he seems to have been aware. More, in that he ignored the experiential inexpressibility of Spirit or the Absolute. Since Heidegger, says Gadamer, the "fundamental words of metaphysics"—Being, Spirit, God—are obsolete in the way they were traditionally read.[47] However, Gadamer believes that Hegel draws close to Heidegger when, despite himself, he successfully distances himself from his own method by virtue of the autonomous spiritual power of (the German) language.[48] This means that words, used well, do not capture experience so much as carry it forward into a spiritual freedom that ultimately distinguishes theological from philosophical thinking.[49] Adorno argues along similar lines when he harshly criticizes Hegel for a kind of theological dogmatism that confuses the conditioned with the unconditional and is consequently untrue to his own experience. However, even when Hegel "flies in the face of experience," Adorno adds, "experience speaks from him."[50] Language expresses more than an author's intent, perhaps even contrary to his intention, which ensures not only that we will understand him differently, but sometimes better.

The reason Heidegger prefers silence to the word 'God' is that the experience or historical destiny of Being does not come to words, including, Heidegger came to see, the word 'Being' itself. Indeed, the experience of the "event of Appropriation" (*Ereignis*), which signals

---

47. Gadamer, "Being, Spirit, God," p. 55.
48. Gadamer, "Hegel and Heidegger," p. 112.
49. See Gadamer, "Hegel's Philosophy and Its Aftereffects," in *Reason in the Age of Science*, p. 29.
50. Adorno, pp. 86–7.

Heidegger's "step back" out of metaphysics into the "essence of metaphysics," arises from this failure of language.[51] There is another way to look at this. Gadamer points out that the nature of the dialectic is such that, followed consistently, concepts become their experiential opposites. Abstract notions of justice, for example, have historically worked themselves out as crimes against humanity; the most complete justice is the greatest injustice (TM 468). One may choose, initially at least, not to jettison the words for such notions, but to hold to their expressive continuity through the reversals of experience and meaning, recognizing that fundamental concepts of thinking "often remain unthematic and exist only in their operative use."[52] This effort could lead either to a revitalization of the language of the tradition or to its rejection. Heidegger ultimately chose the latter in favor of a quasi-poetic means of expression that Gadamer considers "sometimes more expressive of a linguistic need than of its overcoming."[53] For himself, on the basis of hermeneutical experience, Gadamer chooses the former route.

This choice is at the heart of Gadamer's mediation of Hegel and Heidegger. Gadamer finds fault with Hegel's (and Plato's) dialectic insofar as it concerns the speculative development of the proposition, rather than the revealing-concealing self-transformation of language itself (TM 468). Gadamer is closer to Heidegger than to Hegel in viewing experience as constituted by the relation between language and the life-world.[54] However, he draws from Hegel's (and Plato's) dialectic its basic linguistic structure as the living conversation of question and answer. Heidegger too thought that language essentially belongs to conversation,[55] and in his *Letter On Humanism* he called questioning "the piety of thinking," although he later criticized this understanding in light of what he came to see as the more fundamental experience of "stepping back" and waiting. In Heidegger's words, "to think is before all else to listen, to let ourselves be told something and not to ask questions."[56] To Gadamer, on the other hand, questioning is "implicit in all experience"(TM 362). The "priority of the question" (TM 363), its 'mystery,' is what freed the

---

51. See Bernasconi, *The Question of Language*, pp. 86–7.

52. Gadamer, "Being, Spirit, God," p. 65.

53. Gadamer, "The Heritage of Hegel," in *Reason in the Age of Science*, p. 57.

54. See, Francis J. Ambrosio, "Gadamer: On Making Oneself at Home with Hegel," *The Owl of Minerva*, 19 (1987), p. 26.

55. See Kathleen Wright, "Gadamer: The Speculative Structure of Language," in *Hermeneutics and Modern Philosophy*, ed. by Brice R. Wachterhauser (Albany: State University of New York Press, 1986), p. 202.

56. Martin Heidegger, "The Nature of Language," p. 76. See also pp. 71ff.

hermeneutical experience from merely textual application to all knowledge and interpretation.[57]

The dialectic of continuity and discontinuity, revealing and concealing, presence and absence is illustrated in language. In language every word brings with its own singularity a multiple context of the unsaid. This linguistic context is a matter not only of intentional usage, but more fundamentally of the "unconscious of language," a theme that Hegel relegated to prehistory because of his understanding of history as the progress of freedom in self-consciousness.[58] In conversation, language itself is refined, and there Gadamer finds the living model for dialectic. One commentator has suggested that to Gadamer language may even be called the 'transcendental subject'; the self, individual consciousness, is merely "the vehicle of the tradition embedded in language."[59] Essential questioning and thinking do not own or use language, they answer to its historically mediated call.

It would, however, be a reductionist error to conflate language and experience. Heidegger points out that great poets and thinkers undergo an experience of renunciation with language, waiting for the word that lets a thing be present,[60] but renunciation and surrender are still experiences of oneself. As Gadamer puts it, "language is at the same time a positive condition of, and guide to, experience itself" (TM 350). Although it is an intrinsic part of experience to seek and find expression in language (TM 417), nominalism is precluded. Not all experience is linguistic, although it is language that above all reveals the world.[61] At the same time, however, the linguistic, as well as historical character of experience sets limits to that revelation.[62]

Conclusion: Mediation without Syncretism

Thus Gadamer coherently, if implicitly, answers the charge of syncretism from the perspective of hermeneutical experience. By finding his Archimedean point in interpreting the philosophical tradition, he is able

---

57. See Gadamer, "On the Problem of Self-Understanding," in *Philosophical Hermeneutics*, p. 50; and "The Heritage of Hegel," p. 47.

58. Theodore Kisiel, "Hegel and Hermeneutics," in *Beyond Epistemology: New Studies in the Philosophy of Hegel*, ed. by Frederick C. Weiss (The Hague: Martinus Nijhoff, 1974), p. 204.

59. Westphal, "Hegel and Gadamer," p. 70.

60. Heidegger, "On the Nature of Language," p. 65.

61. TM 547. See also Kisiel, "Hegel and Hermeneutics," p. 200.

62. Westphal, "Hegel and Gadamer," 79.

to wed a thoroughgoing respect for careful scholarship with independent philosophical thinking. By so doing it becomes possible, not to
pick and choose among thinkers' views as though philosophy were a
candy store, but non-syncretically to appropriate and mediate Hegelian
and Heideggerian interpretations according to defensible experiential
criteria. Hegel, like Heidegger, was engaged in the hermeneutical process of "building what is understood into his own thought," so the
central issue is less Hegel's or Heidegger's misunderstanding of past
thought than its reinterpretation and reintegration into their own experience of thinking.[63] Gadamer is alert to the experiential legitimacy of
thinkers' productive misuse of the history of philosophy, which is why
one should speak of his "correction" of Heidegger with quotation
marks. On the other hand, hermeneutics does entail a critical perspective that is informed by one's own thoughtful dialogue with the tradition. Tradition, says Gadamer, "is what is to be experienced" (TM 358).
From this perspective, Gadamer's mediation of Hegel and Heidegger
leads him to conclude that Hegel's concept of experience can be
rescued from the methodological compulsion from which he suffered,
and that Heidegger's break with the metaphysical tradition actually
represents an incomparable renewal of Western philosophy.[64]

---

63. Gadamer, "Hegel and the Dialectic of the Ancient Philosophers," in *Hegel's Dialectic*, p. 29 n. 20.

64. Gadamer, "The Heritage of Hegel," p. 46; and "Heidegger and the Language of Metaphysics," in *Philosophical Hermeneutics*, p. 230.

4 Firing the Steel of Hermeneutics: Hegelianized versus Radical Hermeneutics

John D. Caputo

The project of a 'radical' hermeneutics may be traced back to the attempt undertaken by Heidegger in the 1920s to forge what he called then a "hermeneutics of facticity."[1] What I mean by radical hermeneutics is nothing more than the attempt to adhere to the terms which were originally set for hermeneutics, to stay in the element of factical being, and to cut off the various escapes routes which hermeneutics has devised for itself in the meantime. In the development of hermeneutics subsequent to Heidegger's *Being and Time*—I am speaking of both Gadamer and Ricoeur—hermeneutics in my view has followed a decidedly Hegelian drift, the result of which has been a domestication of hermeneutics and a taming of facticity. Hermeneutics has been subverted by the comforts of metaphysics where metaphysics means precisely the resistance which philosophy puts up in the face of factical being in the world.

That is why, in the view which I defend under the title of radical hermeneutics, Derrida—one of hermeneutics' most outspoken critics—plays a more important role than Gadamer or Ricoeur, who are

---

1. Martin Heidegger, *Ontologie: Hermeneutik der Faktizität.* (Frankfurt: Klostermann, 1988), §§3–6. "Facticity" means the concrete historical experience of being-in-the-world as a matter of fact rather than not; it is opposed to a consideration aimed at analyzing the essence of human being. It turns on the Enlightenment distinction between fact and essence, but it takes 'fact' in a phenomenological sense.

hermeneutics' most famous guardians.[2] That is a perversity, I admit, but it is a perversity I am willing to defend. For Derrida's deconstructive critique is not, as its critics charge, a nihilistic levelling of meaning and truth, but rather a more merciless exposure of the factical constraints under which we labor. In the view which I defend deconstruction holds hermeneutics to the fire of facticity in a more pitiless way than either Gadamer or Ricoeur are prepared for. Deconstruction keeps hermeneutics faithful to its appointed path, to the way which is under-way in *Being and Time*, which is the truly essential thing in *Being and Time*, as Heidegger says on the last page of that work.[3]

I am in fact arguing two points at once: that hermeneutics never gets into motion, that its factical character is never faced up to until it is shocked into place by deconstruction. But, similarly, we do not see what is going on in deconstruction until we see that it operates within a certain hermeneutic framework. All of the charges of nihilism, rela-tivism, and scepticism that are hurled at deconstruction arise from a failure to see that deconstruction cannot and does not try to escape from a certain hermeneutic framework that is always already in place. If radical hermeneutics wants to fire the steel of hermeneutics with deconstruction, it is also interested in showing the place of deconstruction in the hermeneutic project.

Another way to put it is to say that radical hermeneutics is com-mitted to a double frame. On the one hand, it argues that there is a deconstructive frame around hermeneutics, that the hermeneutic situa-tion is always already penetrated by textuality and différance, that the hermeneutic host is always already invaded by the deconstructive parasite. On the other hand, it claims that there is a hermeneutic frame around

2. See John D. Caputo, *Radical Hermeneutics: Repetition, Deconstruction and the Hermeneutic Project* (Bloomington: Indiana University Press, 1987), pp. 1–7; 153–206. The classic work of twentieth-century hermeneutics is Hans-Georg Gadamer, *Truth and Method*, revised trans. Joel Weinsheimer and Donald G. Marshall (New York: Crossroads, 1989). The best commentary on this work is Joel Weinsheimer, *Gadamer's Hermeneutics* (New Haven: Yale University Press, 1985). The best overall introduction to contemporary hermeneutics is still Richard Palmer, *Hermeneutics: Interpretation Theory in Schleiermacher, Dilthey, Heidegger and Gadamer* (Evanston: Northwestern University Press, 1969), al-though a great deal has happened since this book appeared. The most readable-while-reliable introduction to Derrida is Christopher Norris, *Derrida* (Cambridge: Harvard University Press, 1987), although Norris tends to stress too heavily Derrida's proximity to transcendental philosophy. For a detailed study of the Gadamer and Derrida relationship, which is the principal challenge facing hermeneutics today, see Diane Michelfelder and Richard Palmer, eds. *Dialogue and Deconstruction: The Gadamer-Derrida Encounter* (Albany: SUNY Press, 1989).

3. Heidegger, *Being and Time*, trans. John MacQuarie and Edward Robinson (New York: Harper & Row, 1962), p. 488; hereafter cited as BT.

deconstruction, that deconstructive work presupposes the factical, hermeneutic situation, that deconstruction always has a context, that a parasite presupposes a host.

I will proceed thus in two steps: (1) I will try to show that there is a deconstructive frame around hermeneutics; and (2) I will turn the tables and argue that there is a hermeneutic frame around deconstruction.

Framing Hermeneutics

First, let us draw a deconstructive frame around hermeneutics. To do this, let us begin by recalling a point that has tended to be obscured by all the talk about anti-foundationalism, relativism, and fictionalism that deconstruction seems to provoke, and that is Heidegger's point that human Dasein is always and from the start in the truth (BT 263). Dasein constantly discloses the world, in one way or another. This is not the result of a decision that Dasein has made but arises from the very Being of Dasein; it is not so much what Dasein does as what Dasein is. There is truth by the simple fact, or facticity, of Dasein. We always and already presuppose truth; better still, truth is a presupposition that we cannot help but make. So from Heidegger's view, a merely logical refutation of scepticism is too weak. He thinks there is a stronger, ontological refutation of scepticism: "And if a sceptic of the kind who denies the truth factically *is*, he does not even *need* to be refuted" (BT 271). Only the desperation of suicide can put an end to truth.

Dasein cannot take leave of the realm of truth even when it falls into untruth. For untruth does not mean that truth and disclosedness get extinguished, or that Dasein fails to disclose anything at all. Understanding is not extinguished in untruth, Heidegger says, but uprooted, levelled off into commonplace and easily available understanding. Even untruth is a mode of truth, its flattened out, privative, and commonplace mode. The point is that factical Dasein is thrown into the truth, even in the mode of untruth, which means it is so beaten down by the truths it inherits that all it can do is repeat them lifelessly in dull, uninspired reproductions.

Dasein is always in the truth, in a historical, factical truth which never succeeds in twisting free of faciticity into either the absoluteness of eternal truth or the negative absolute of total scepticism. Dasein can never be absolved from the conditions of facticity, the conditions which frame it out and make it possible. It will never happen, so long as there is Dasein, either that truth will expire in the absoluteness of total closure or that it will come about in an event of total disclosure and unconditioned, eternal verity. We are always already forging some historical, factical, finite form of life for ourselves, letting historical truth happen in one way or another.

Truth is an incessant, factical event, and we do not know why: "'In itself', it is quite incomprehensibile why entities are to be *uncovered*, why *truth* and *Dasein* must be" (BT 271). Truth is a kind of *factum brutum*; it happens with a raw facticity. Truth happens because it happens, and we cannot say why. Truth thus is hallowed out by an abyss of untruth, a deeper inscrutability. We cannot explain the existence of truth; explaining is something we do in virtue of being in the truth. There is truth but there is no truth of truth. *Es gibt*: there is truth and that is all one can say.

That explains what has gone wrong with Gadamerian hermeneutics. There is no *Es gibt* in Gadamer but rather an adaptation of an Hegelian absolute in hermeneutic disguise. Gadamer dulls the edge of Heideggerian facticity. Gadamer was exceedingly good at showing how the factical-historical situatedness of Dasein is productive of understanding, not destructive; that the factical conditions under which Dasein labors do not merely limit understanding but also enable it. But Gadamer was out to put the brakes on facticity and to underwrite it with a Hegelian theory of the deep truth of the tradition. The happening of the tradition in Gadamer is a remarkably effective "postal process" (Derrida, *The Post Card* 64–67) in which the truth is always safely delivered.[4] It is true that Gadamer criticized Hegelian teleology and the notion that the absolute could ever reach an absolute form. But Gadamer was not denying the absolute so much as he was denying that the absolute could receive absolute embodiment. In the place of Hegel's history of absolute knowledge Gadamer put a history of understanding differently, a history of finite and ever diverse applications. But the whole thing turns on the most classical opposition of finite and infinite, expression and meaning, form and content. The result is a certain Hegelianism cut to fit the size of finite Dasein, a history of finite understanding of the infinite depths of the absolute spirit which is manifested in religion, art, and philosophy.[5]

Now that results in a rather domesticated idea of facticity. It is a facticity in which one is indeed thrown, but thrown into the infinite and ongoing life of the absolute and so enabled to assimilate—albeit in

---

4. Jacques Derrida, *The Post Card: From Socrates to Freud and Beyond*, trans. Alan Bass (Chicago: University of Chicago Press, 1987), pp. 64–67.

5. Mark Taylor does an excellent job of expounding and criticizing the Hegelianism of Gadamer in a chapter entitled "Paralectics" in *Tears* (Albany: SUNY Press, 1990). See also my "Gadamer's Closet Essentialism: A Derridean Critique," in *Dialogue and Deconstruction: The Gadamer-Derrida Encounter*, ed. Diane P. Michelfelder and Richard E. Palmer (Albany: SUNY Press, 1989), pp. 258–264.

finite gulps—its inexhaustible riches. It is a lot more like being born into wealth than thrown into the world. One can see the classical and reassuring metaphysical scheme in Gadamer that so effectively subverts facticity: inexhaustible riches/finite share; infinite meaning/finite understanding; infinite content/finite form. The history of understanding is the history of the endlessly different but always finite appropriation of the self-same truth. In the place of radical facticity Gadamer inserts a Hegelian process of the mediation and reappropriation of the deep truth of the tradition, a Hegelian facticity made safe by the cunning of reason.

Gadamer fails to stay in the element of facticity and instead lets it go up in Hegelian smoke. But in radical hermeneutics the whole idea is to stay with facticity, to see it through to the bitter end, to probe all the more searchingly the constraints which are imposed upon a factical being. And that is just what deconstruction has done for us. For once hermeneutics casts its lot with facticity, it cannot avoid the question of the frame, of textuality, of différance. The frame is always already in place. The frame is the place *of* the always already. *Immer schon:* that means nothing occurs without an antecedent, without coming into a place and a time which is already there, which has been prepared for it in advance. Dasein never gets a chance at a completely fresh start. We live always according to the terms of a contract that we did not sign and have to abide by terms that we did not negotiate. Things are always rimmed about with an edge and there is always something on the other side of the rim, and that goes on indefinitely. Texts always have contexts. Actions always have situations and situations have always evolved from a prehistory. Individual Dasein is always equiprimordially being-with others. Our discourse always emerges from a pregiven language of which we are not the authors but the heirs and which carves out in advance for us certain discursive possibilities. We are always already caught up in texts, contexts, language(s), history(ies), framed and reframed, framed in multiple, indeed framed in innumerably complex ways. What we insist upon in radical hermeneutics is that these contexts and frames cannot in principle be saturated, that they are insuperably dense, that they cannot be finally disentangled, that we are all once and for all laced about, strung up, framed. There is nothing outside the text, nothing outside the frame: that means, nothing ever occurs without a textual frame, without a horizonal enframing, no appearances without horizons, no beings with Being.

I am claiming that if you start out with a hermeneutics of facticity you get inevitably pushed into a deconstructive theory of texts and frames. In *Being and Time* Heidegger said that hermeneutics never involves trying to twist free of our presuppositions but rather penetrating them more fully (BT 358), and that the main fault of modernity has not been that it presupposes too much but that it presupposes too little. Hermeneutics proceeds on the assumption that it is precisely in virtue of the richness and complexity of the *immer schon* that Dasein manages to get anything done. In my view, *différance*, textuality, supplementarity, etc., are conditions to which we are subject, constraints under which we work and as such partake of the structure of Dasein's factical inheritance as described in *Being and Time.* Textuality constitutes the network of presuppositions, of frames, which always already precede our comings and goings. Textuality antedates any positing, lies under (*sub*) and before (*prae*) any position, so that we quite literally pre-sup-pose it. It is in virtue of its pre-sup-positional character, its quasi-transcendental anteriority, that Derrida refers to différance as writing before the letter, which is older than Being itself, because it is a condition for forming a unity of meaning like Being (and for de-forming it too).[6]

Thus in radical hermeneutics we do not think that good will can master the free play in textuality nor do we trust in the momentum of language to carry us into the true and the good.[7] We do not think we can glide into the truth by the power of conversational play because we doubt that most exchanges are fair. We think that dialogues are disguised polylogues; that who knows what is speaking through us. We worry about games that are played with a home team advantage, or about games that are not being played on a level field—unless it is the 'other' who has the advantage and the space is curved in favor of the 'stranger,' as in Levinas. We do not regard the tradition as the work of reason, as do Hegel and Gadamer, but we see in it at least as much exclusion and violence. Radical hermeneutics does not make everything turn on a model of assimilation and appropriation, of melting and schmelting horizons. It would rather give the absolute indigestion, make a little indigestible morsel, a Kierkgaardian fragment, a Derridean remainder, stick in the throat of *savoir absolue* so that it can't gulp it down.

But have we not then gone too far, we who insist on beginning with being-in-the-world, being in the truth, and with Dasein's inevitable implication in the truth, right up to the point of death itself? There is a delicacy needed in the operation that radical hermeneutics wants to perform. It wants to subvert the Hegelianizing of hermeneutics with a

---

6. Derrida, *Of Grammatology*, trans. G. Spivak (Baltimore: Johns Hopkins University Press, 1974), pp. 72–73.
7. See Michelfelder and Palmer, pp. 21–57.

deconstructive stylus. But it wants at the same time to draw textuality, framing, différance into a project of truth and being-in-the-world. Radical hermeneutics wants to put deconstruction to work to provide a more critical account of the factical limits which enframe human existence, a more incisive account of factical being-in-the-world. But it wants at the same time to frame deconstruction, to situate deconstructive analysis within being-in-the-world. There can be no question of a worldless play of signifiers, but rather a more radical account of being-in-the-world. Radical hermeneutics wants to situate this whole deconstructive critique, all this critical energy, in a factical being which is always already in the truth.

Now you see the trouble radical hermeneutics brings down upon itself. For by invoking deconstructive critique, by letting deconstruction into the heart of hermeneutics, have we not given the fox the run of the farm? Do we not lose all semblance of being-in-the-world and turn things over to the free play of signifiers? After all, Heidegger did not set out to deny intentionality but to found it upon care. But does not deconstruction deliver us over to signifiers chained to signifiers in a world endlessly deferred? Instead of being-in-the-world, do we not end up in deconstruction with what Rorty calls the world well lost?[8] And does not truth become a fiction in deconstruction so that human being in truth would just go up in smoke, like the last cloudy streak of the old metaphysics? Is not hermeneutic understanding scattered to the four winds by dissemination? If there is an undeniably Hegelian drift to Gadamerian hermeneutics, one has to wonder what we think we can gain by making straight away for Nietzsche.

You see all the trouble we have bought for ourselves.

Framing Deconstruction

That is why I want to try to frame deconstruction. I do not think the preceding objections hold water, either as defendable philosophical views in themselves or as interpretations of Derrida. They proceed from the assumption that deconstruction is something independent, something unframed, a philosophical view in its own right, a philosophical program with theories and position papers, with a kind of platform that it wants to sell or stand on. They fail to see that, however affirmative it may be, deconstruction is a practice not a program, a parasite not

---

8. Richard Rorty, *Consequences of Pragmatism* (Minneapolis: University of Minnesota Press, 1982), 1–18.

a host, more adjectival than substantive, an intervention not an original event, a disruption not something standing in place. Unless something is willing to serve as host, there can be no deconstructive parasite. Unless someone first says something, or does something, or tries to enforce something—and when have they not?—there is nothing for deconstruction to do. Deconstruction is always about something else, which precedes it, antedates it, something it means to release. To adapt the famous Husserlian definition of phenomenology, deconstruction is always the deconstruction *of* something—of texts, discourses, beliefs, practices, actions, institutions, works of art, of whatever there is. I do not deny that it is more than that, more profoundly affirmative, a deep *oui, oui* to language and the other, but this parasitical operation is essential to its affirmations.

Now it is my claim that the most general way to describe the sphere which is always already in place, which precedes and antedates deconstruction, is to call it the hermeneutic situation (See BT §83). The hermeneutic situation is the sphere of factical givenness, of our concrete comings and goings, of our commerce and communication with others, of our practices and beliefs. The hermeneutic situation is always already in place. It waits for us at the door when we are lost in thought; it waits for Descartes to finish doubting it, for Platonists to finish transcending it, for Hegelians to finish relieving it. It is the world that antedates philosophers and their philosophies, not only Platonists and Hegelians, but Gadamerians and, heaven save us, Derrideans. The hermeneutic situation is our first, last, and constant concern and nobody yet—from Empedocles to Frege, from Diogenes to Derrida—has succeeded in leaving it behind save by taking the extreme measure of dying in order to prove their point.

Dasein is always in the truth. It is in the truth whether it likes it or not; it is in the truth, even if that be in the mode of untruth. This is not anything Dasein has managed to do but something that happens as soon as it comes to be; it is a decision that is made for us by our very being-in-the-world. Deconstruction has not come into the world to deny being-in-the-world but to complicate it. Deconstruction does not try to undo it—how would it go about that?—but to show how much more dense and complex being, world, and 'in' are. Deconstruction does not spell the death of facticity but the radicalization of it. Deconstruction wants to take some of the steam out of all the rhetoric about 'life,' 'world,' 'the things themselves,' 'living presence,' 'givenness,' 'perception,' 'Being,' and all the other lures and comforts of philosophy. Deconstruction has been especially good at demonstrating how much the acutely critical phenomenological reduction leaves unreduced. Its aim in all this is not to deny that the perceived, lived world is in some sense there, but rather to get a more critical conception of just what its being there amounts to, of the conditions under which it is possible (and impossible).

Its more specific function, from which it gets the name of deconstruction, is to show that being and truth are historical and linguistic constructions which are possible only under conditions which make pure, ahistorical being or truth impossible, conditions that see to it that there is always a margin of undecidability surrounding being and truth. Deconstruction does not deny the world, but it insists on the mediated, constituted character of the world. Every time hermeneutics speaks of living dialogue or pure presence, deconstruction reminds us of the work of writing and mediation that rob them a little of their life and purity. This does not amount to a denial of communication or translation, of reality or knowledge, but simply an attempt to show how complicated it is to lay claim to objects of such hoary prestige. It is not out to undermine the hermeneutic situation but just to complicate it.

You see then the mutually enframing effect which hermeneutics and deconstruction have on each other. Each frames the other out in different ways, and one never escapes the frame or condition that is imposed upon it by the other. You might say that the hermenutic situation is first in the order of experience, of what we are always already in touch with, and that it provides our inescapable and irrepressible context. But textuality is first in another order, a certain transcendental order, a certain archi-conditionality, or quasi-transcendentality which imposes inescapable constraints upon our being-in-the-world.[9]

The critique that Derrida levels at Gadamer on the question of good will[10] is not meant perversely to take the side of ill will, as Gadamer thinks, but to delimit the attempt to make the will the master of speech. That is to insist upon the conditions of textuality which do not yield to individual wills, which is, it seems to me, nothing other than digging deeper into the facticity of Dasein than Gadamer is prepared to do.

But by the same token the hermeneutic situation provides the inescapably pregiven world within which deconstruction works. It is only because Derrida himself takes to heart the works of Hegel, Husserl, and Heidegger, of Saussure, Levinas, and Blanchot (and all the others), only because he has inherited these texts and not others, because he

---

9. See Rodolph Gasché, *The Tain Of The Mirror: Derrida And The Philosophy Of Reflection* (Cambridge: Harvard University Press, 1986), pp. 316–18.
10. See Michelfelder and Palmer, pp. 52–54.

has appropriated and applied them to his own concerns, and wishes to communicate a different view, a view of his own, to his colleagues and peers and students, it is only because of all of this, I say, and within this frame that Derrida took pen in hand and entered the world of French and American philosophy and criticism, that, years ago, he joined hands with his colleagues in G.R.E.P.H. to change the French educational scene.[11]

Deconstruction operates within a world which is always already in place, within the world of intentions, desires, motives, subjectivities, authors, histories, institutions, and every thing else which populates the historical world. Far from withdrawing into a worldless playing with signifiers, deconstructive critique moves about, always and from the start, within the concrete world of the historical, social, political, and institutional embodiment, let us say the worldly contextualization of signifiers. This can be shown in many ways, not the least of which is to read Derrida's works with more care than hysteria, not to mention the emphasis on openness to the other and making the other stronger, a point upon which hermeneutics is constantly congratulating itself!

There is a strong thematics of institutional critique that runs through Derrida's works.[12] Philosophy and literature are not for it pure or worldless writing, cut off from the concrete institutions and systems of power in which they operate, as in some forms of anemic, apolitical aestheticism. On the contrary, the whole of deconstruction strains against allowing this pure cut, this detachability and unlacing of the work—of art or of philosophy—from its enframing social and political context. Texts are always already enframed, by other texts of course, but also by political frameworks, by hierarchical systems which want to decide in advance who has the right to determine their value, whose voice has a right to be heard.

The deconstructive critique of logocentrism is not detachable from the critique of phallocentrism and ethnocentrism. The privilege of the logos has from of old belonged to fathers and sons and brothers, and the destiny of scientific rationality has always been the vocation of the West as opposed to the mysticism of the East or the primitivism of the

---

11. *Le Groupe de Recherches sur l'Enseignement Philosophique.* Founded in 1975 by Derrida and others to address the question of the connection between philosophy and the historical and political conditions under which philosophy is taught. The documents relating to Derrida's long involvement in the politics of education are now collected in Derrida, *Du droit à la philosophie* (Paris: Galilée, 1990).

12. On this point it is a mistake to oppose Derrida and Foucault for their aims are quite convergent. See Roy Boyne, *Foucault and Derrida: The Other Side of Reason* (London: Unwin Hyman, 1990).

African. The deconstructive critique of humanism has been in no small part a critique of the humanist desire to devalue the other-than-human, not only the other species, who also have a stake in our nuclear brinksmanship, but also the other human: the other sex, the woman who is defined by her lack of active reason or the phallus; the primitive or African who is defined by the failure to be born in Western Europe or North America. There is a long list in logocentrism of all those who do not share the logos, or do not share it fully, or who pervert it in the most unnatural way. The binary systems that are criticized by deconstruction are not worldless chains of signifiers for they assume the most brutal forms of worldly instantiation and institutionalization.

Derrida can find no other way to respond to the objections that deconstruction denies reference, or intentionality, or subjectivity, or that deconstruction locks us up in a kind of linguistic idealism, a sort of linguistic Berkeleyianism, than to describe such suggestions as "stupidities."[13] The denial of the transcendental signified is not the denial of every and any signified, but the denial that we ever reach some pure, unmediated, naked signified, that we ever make contact with the world so as to bring the chain of signifiers to a halt. What Derrida denies is that we can ever so inhabit the intentional momentum of a signifier into the world in such a way as to leave the signifier behind, to shed the chain to which it belongs and by which it is constituted, and to somehow savor naked presence. Signifiers are always tied differentially to other signifiers, joined by the very intervals which separate them from the other members of the same chain, so as to signify the world in just the way the particular linguistic chain permits. This is not to deny reference but to deny reference without difference. Derrida is simply denying what analytic philosophy denies under the name of "uninterpreted facts of the matter."[14]

In other words, deconstruction casts us back all the more forcibly into the world into which Dasein is thrown, submits us all the more mercilessly to the constraints under which we all along operate, takes all the more seriously the condition of facticity. That is why I think it pursues all the more radically the project of a radical hermeneutic. Deconstruction does not run hermeneutics into the ground or give the

---

13. Richard Kearney, *Dialogues with Contemporary Continental Thinkers* (Manchester: Manchester University Press, 1984), pp. 123–124.

14. It may be surprising to some to hear that a good deal of this Derridean project overlaps with Quine's thesis on the indeterminacy of translation, a point which is expounded quite nicely by John Llewelyn in *Derrida on the Threshold of Sense* (New York: St. Martin's Press, 1986). Graeme Nicholson makes a similar effort to relate Quine to Gadamer in *Seeing and Reading* (Atlantic Highlands: Humanities Press, 1984).

fox the run of the farm. On the contrary, deconstruction operates continuously on the ground of hermeneutics, of the pregivenness of the world, the only world we know, with all of its involute complexity or what the young Heidegger called "facticity."

Hermeneutics and deconstruction are involved in a mutual frame up. Deconstruction is ruthless about facticity; it will not break its bite; it is impossible to call it off. It lies in wait for some hermeneutic intention or other to transpire and then it descends upon it, scrutinizing the conditions and presuppositions which antedate and surround it, insisting upon the density of the context, the impossibility of cutting it off and drawing neat margins around it so as to allow for a clean and determinate analysis. Even so, deconstruction analyzes the world which is always already in place, the intentions and the transactions which never cease to transpire in the hermeneutic situation. Human existence is always in the truth, like it or not.

That is why I speak of radical hermeneutics. Hermeneutics occupies the place of the substantive, of the noun, of the host and so sets itself up for its adjectival nemesis, exposes itself to parasitic invasion. The radical here does not mean ground or foundational but rather that:

> . . . one always interweaves roots endlessly, bending them to send down roots among the roots, to pass through the same points again, to redouble old adherences, to circulate among their differences, to coil around themselves or to be enveloped one in the other. . . .[15]

Radical hermeneutics means that the transactions of factical life are always rooted in networks that we can never unravel, that our beliefs and practices spring from roots we cannot tap, that they reach down into depths we cannot fathom, far back into the past or the unconscious or who-knows-what.

Then are we locked without hope within a system that we cannot fathom, trapped by historical, linguistic, and institutional chains that are older than we know? On the contrary, the idea behind a radical hermeneutics is to restore life to its original difficulty, not to finish it off in a Hegelian-inspired regularity; to return philosophy to irregular shapes of concrete life and to cut off its escape into the smooth surfaces and evened corners of the universal. The weight of the world weighs heavily upon us, bending us towards lifeless repetitions of the past, inclining us to take the easy way out. But the task of a radical hermeneutic is to set out with a suspicious eye and a Derridean twinkle in search of something new.

---

15. Derrida, *Grammatology*, pp. 101–102

5 Rethinking the Origin: Nietzsche and Hegel

William Desmond

The Aesthetics of Origin

George Kline is well-known as a commentator on Whitehead, Hegel, and Russian philosophy. Less well-known is the fact that he has written very insightfully on Nietzsche. I refer particularly to his Presidential Address to the Hegel Society of America, entitled, "The Use and Abuse of Hegel by Nietzsche and Marx."[1] This offers a penetrating understanding of the instrumentalizing of time in Nietzsche and Marx, in train of a seriously flawed apotheosis of the world-historical future. Moreover, his documentation of Nietzsche's fetishization, not to say idolatry of futurity, is impressive.[2] Ultimately the rhetoric that

---

1. In *Hegel and His Critics: Philosophy in the Aftermath of Hegel,* ed. William Desmond (Albany: State University of New York Press, 1989). See also his Forward to *Nietzsche in Russia,* ed. Bernice Glatzer Rosenthal (Princeton: Princeton University Press, 1986). Also his articles " 'Nietzschean Marxism' in Russia" in *Demythologizing Marxism,* ed. F. J. Adelmann (The Hague: Martinus Nijhoff, 1969), pp. 166–183 and "The Nietzschean Marxism of Stanislav Volsky," in *Western Philosophical Systems in Russian Literature: A Collection of Critical Studies,* ed. Anthony M. Mlikotin (Los Angeles: University of Southern California Press, 1979), pp. 177–195.

2. Below I cite Zarathustra's lament that he walks among men as among fragments of the future. But Kline also draws our attention to Nietzsche's obsession with the ". . . man of tomorrow and the day after tomorrow *Mensch des Morgen und Übermorgen,"* and with the philosophers of the future. He cites Nietzsche: "In order to create [we need] liberation from morality and relief by means of festivals. Anticipations of the future! To

glories the future in instrumentalizing past and present is empty—a paean to a 'coming god,' call it Dionysus or the *Übermensch*, it hardly matters, a paean that seems to be as empty as the nihilism from which 'god' was to save us. The disastrous results for the human spirit in instrumentalizing time and idolizing futurity are now hardly debatable with respect to totalitarian Marxism, but the Romantic aura of a Nietzschean faith and hope still persists for many, not least due to the equivocating faith of some French Nietzscheans.[3] We owe a debt to Kline for helping us see that the ringing affirmation of a glorious transfigured future, somewhere over the rainbow, has about it the hollow ring of spiritual desperation.

Instead of focusing on futurity I want to think about the sense of origin. In fact, the empty apotheosis of futurity is not unconnected with a certain understanding of origin. Philosophical concern with origins, of course, has been excoriated by not a few commentators. Adorno will crudely dismiss philosophy of origin as fascism, though it is primarily Heidegger he wants to indict.[4] More generally, concern with a divine origin has been dismissed as ontotheology, just as concern with a transcendental origin is rejected as foundationalism or some form of nostalgia.

Nietzsche figures as an important influence shaping the caricatures of the philosophical concern with origin. He was concerned with origins in many ways. I will mention three: namely, his philological concern, his genealogical work in morals, and his metaphysics. The first two will be pursued in terms of a 'hermeneutics of suspicion.' The third will stop some in their tracks and cause them to throw up their hands in exasperation: What! we all know that Nietzsche had nothing but contempt for metaphysics; how dare you suggest that he was concerned with the metaphysics of origin! I will not recant. I will go further and align him with Hegel, that dread panlogical spectre which every postmodernist of the strict observance will quickly rush to exorcise with the sign of Dionysus. But both Hegel and Nietzsche offer us different variations on a metaphysics of what I call the erotic origin. I will explain this and the difference between the two variations more fully below.

---

celebrate the *future* not the past! To compose (*dichten*) the *myth of the future* ("The Use and Abuse of Hegel," p. 17). He notes (*ibid.*, p. 22) that Zarathustra speaks of "our great, far off empire of man (*Menschen-Reich*), the thousand year empire of Zarathustra (*das Zarathustra-Reich von tausend Jahren*)."

3. I think, for instance, of Bataille; or of Foucault's quest of Nietzschean excess in relation to sado-masochism and orgiastic revolutionary politics.

4. See T. Adorno, *Against Epistemology*, trans. W. Domingo (Cambridge: MIT Press, 1983), p. 20: "Fascism sought to actualize the philosophy of origins."

Recently perhaps the two most influential interpretations of Nietzsche have been the Heideggerian and the deconstructionist. The first sees Nietzsche as the last metaphysician, the second sees him as having transcended metaphysics in a new artistic philosophizing. I will not adjudicate between them, except to say that Nietzsche was as much a metaphysician as Plato, and to that extent Heidegger was right. Yet this metaphysics is intimately tied with the privileged place of art, and there is an aestheticist Nietzsche whose voice cannot be reduced simply to the voice of the last metaphysician. I am not endorsing either Heidegger's or Nietzsche's view of the tradition of metaphysics. I contest it. But metaphysics is inescapable, even when one claims to overcome or overturn it. Metaphysics is not the terrible prison house of mind we must destroy or deconstruct or whatever. Metaphysics is just what we need: honest thinking about the origin and the ultimate. There is no escape from metaphysics, and not because it is some kind of dialectical illusion *a la* Kant, unfortunate but inevitable. Honest, perplexed thinking about origin and ultimacy constitute the commission, responsibility, indeed the destiny of human mindfulness. To be metaphysical is the great privilege of the human being.

The Heideggerian interpretation rightly sees the hidden continuities of Nietzsche with previous philosophers. This is not to endorse the specifics of the continuities this interpretation claims. Heidegger certainly is not true to what I call the plurivocal nature of Nietzsche's philosophizing: there is the suffering, laughing Nietzsche who in all naivete would offer advice about the proper beverage to drink in the morning; there is the poetic Nietzsche, the playful Nietzsche, the buffoon. The Derridean interpretation of Nietzsche's styles does address something of this other Nietzsche. But we do not have to choose between the poet and the philosopher/metaphysician. Like Plato, Nietzsche was a poet-philosopher, and the poetry is not devoid of philosophical significance. A mere 'aestheticization' of Nietzsche is not enough, in the end trivializes him, as it would trivialize art.

Aesthetics and metaphysics are deeply interconnected: art has metaphysical significance, early and late, in the philosophical tradition, and in Nietzsche too. This significance is pervasive in Nietzsche's thinking. This is expressed clearly in the metaphysical aesthetic of the *Birth of Tragedy*: there the origin is called the primordial one, *das Ureine.* Here, I suggest, we encounter ultimacy as articulated under *the sign of unity.* The metaphysical may be dissimulated in later writings but it is still at work in the aesthetics. There we find ultimacy, as will to power, articulated under the sign of difference. Origin becomes the self-production of the many; the primordial one, under the sign of difference, is reformulated as the will to power as diversification.

Metaphysically the two sides are unavoidable, which is not to say that Nietzsche offers an adequate account of the relation of identity and difference, sameness and otherness, the one and the many. Quite to the contrary, he offers us an interpretation of difference which is reactive to an excessively univocalized sense of unity or identity. This interpretation tends to privilege an equivocal sense of difference. But if being is plurivocal, as I think, this does not mean that being is just equivocal. I cannot detail here some of the fuller implications of these statements, beyond saying that the plurivocity of being does suggest some exoneration of the poet-philosophers. This point also applies to the exoneration of Plato as a plurivocal philosopher. As such, he is not the first metaphysican in either Nietzsche's or Heidegger's sense, nor can he be deconstructed in Derrida's sense. No plurivocal philosopher fetishes an excessively fixated univocity, such as seems to be in question in relation to the so-called "metaphysics of presence."[5]

Where Heidegger underscores the same, Derrida puts emphasis on difference. The equivocity of Nietzsche allows both. Indeed his equivocal philosophizing sometimes allows almost anything. This can be a virtue, though not always, and indeed not frequently. His writings are, as the subtitle of *Zarathustra* says, for everyone and for no one, *für Alle und Keinen.* One might say that equivocal philosophizing allows everything and allows nothing.[6] Nor should we be fooled by Nietzsche's air of superior self-confidence. Quite simply, Nietzsche did not always know what he was talking about. He was trying out ideas, many of which he finally did not take seriously. Sometimes he is, as we say, just doing the fool. I am not insulting Nietzsche. He is quite happy to call himself a buffoon. He is often at his best when he is

---

5. The plurivocity of being and philosophy is taken up in a variety of ways in my works *Desire, Dialectic and Otherness: An Essay on Origins* (New Haven: Yale University Press, 1987); *Philosophy and its Others: Ways of Being and Mind* (Albany: State University of New York Press, 1990); *Beyond Hegel and Dialectic: Speculation, Cult and Comedy* (Albany: State University of New York Press, 1992); *Being and the Between* (Albany: State University of New York Press, 1995); *Perplexity and Ultimacy* (Albany: State University of New York Press, 1995). A succinct statement of the view is offered in my essay "Being Between," CLIO 20 (1991), 305–331. That issue of CLIO is devoted to discussion of the view I am developing.

6. The sometimes disastrous consequences of this equivocity are evident in the political legacy of Nietzschean thinking. Steven Aschheim in *The Nietzsche Legacy in Germany 1890–1990* (Berkeley: University of California Press, 1992) has very revealingly and dispassionately documented how Nietzsche could serve almost every shade of political and cultural opinion, including, of course, and perhaps especially, National Socialism. Nietzsche may say he writes for everyone and for none, but it seems that "everyone" has found some residence in his house of many mansions. Perhaps his house is for everyone and for no one because it is, we might say, hospitably empty.

doing the fool. Then he is a laughing philosopher. But when he puffs himself up in praise of his own genius, then there is something laughable, and not in Nietzsche's better sense either. There is something ever more laughable about the hagiography of his contemporary followers and the academic industry they have fabricated from his texts. One laughs with Nietzsche himself against the Nietzscheans, when he speaks of the scholars reading themselves to death, their heads smoking night and day.

If there is a community between philosophy and art, there is also a community between both and religion. Thus, relevantly to our theme, mindfulness of origin is bound up with religion, in that mythic stories image the sense of the ultimate origin or origins. Why is this important? Because if one philosophically understands the religious image or mythic story as one of the richest forms of human articulation about the ultimate, the affiliation of metaphysics and religion may be seen to redound to the credit of metaphysics. This tells against the debunking of both metaphysics and religion as alleged forms of ontological cowardice. To announce that religion and metaphysics are in flight from the truth of being as a dark condition on the other side of reason is not to escape metaphysics, but to be metaphysical again, just in the indictment of metaphysics as falsifying the truth of being.

Nietzsche gives the game away when he proclaims that only as aesthetic is the world justified: the only theodicy must be an aesthetic theodicy. But aesthetic here has nothing to do with aesthetics. Metaphysics, myth, and art intertwine.[7] This is something of which Hegel will not altogether disapprove. Hegel will locate art, religion, and philosophy at the level of absolute spirit. The role absolute spirit plays in Hegel is played by the aesthetic theodicy of will to power in Nietzsche. Of course, this is not to deny great differences between them. Yet

---

7. How can one avoid a certain affinity of Plato and Nietzsche when we think of the relation of art and metaphysics? "Plato versus Homer," Nietzsche said this was the fundamental antagonism, and claims to side with Homer. But what of the Plato of the *Timaeus?* In my discussion below I will suggest a move from self to art to world on an aesthetic model; nor is the artistic metaphysics repudiated in Nietzsche's later suggestion that the world is a self-birthing artwork. What would an aesthetic theodicy be without a world artist? Let us not forget Plato's *Timaeus* as picturing the world artist at work in fashioning the cosmos as a visible work of art, the most beautiful possible, even granting the recalcitrance and vagaries of the Errant cause. Recall Plato's philosophical art and the eikonic nature of the cosmos: "It is everyway necessary that the cosmos be an eikon of something (*pasa ananke tonde ton cosmon eikona tinos einai*)." (*Timaeus*, 29b1–2). Plato gives us, so to say, a kind of aesthetic theodicy. The cosmos itself is called a sensible god, an aesthetic god that images the intelligible (*eikon tou noetou theos aisthetos*) (*Timaeus* 92c).

Nietzsche's clear concern with the metaphysics of origin in, say, *The Birth of Tragedy* focuses on religious art and ritual: in a word, tragedy is sacred art. The cult of Dionysus is cult after all. It is, in a word Hegel uses, *Gottesdienst*.[8]

Obviously, the god served in this *Gottesdienst* is not the same for Hegel and Nietzsche. In the one case, we celebrate *Geist*, in the other Dionysus. But each offers a different articulation in terms of origin. We may call one the dialectical origin, the other the Dionysian origin. Let me paint the contrast.

In the case of *Geist* the origin is understood in terms of a dialectical self-becoming, self-mediation, and self-completion. Thus the Hegelian sense of origin points first to an indefinite beginning or indeterminacy. Hence Hegel will speak of the Idea in itself as initially an abstract universality. To be concrete and real in the proper sense this indeterminate origin must produce beyond itself. The theological language of creation may be invoked here, but it is clear that the creation at stake is not the bringing into being of something essentially other to the origin, but rather the self-externalization of the origin in the finite world. This self-externalization is the self-becoming of the origin. Moreover, it is the origin's dialectical self-mediation, in that the other produced is the origin itself in its own otherness. Hence in becoming itself as other, it is mediating with itself; it is becoming itself in its own self-othering. Finally, this self-becoming and self-mediation is teleologically bound to self-completion. It is in the end that the initial indefiniteness of the beginning is overcome. The end is the complete self-mediation, complete self-determination of the origin. The origin that is all but nothing in the beginning is only fully what it is in the final completion, the consummate self-articulation of what is only implicit in the beginning.[9]

In the case of Dionysus, the origin in itself is dark. Certainly in the younger Nietzsche we find the suggestion that there is a pain and suffering in the origin, to assuage which the Dionysian origin has to create beyond itself. There is an echo here of Schelling's view of origin in which the conflict and contradiction of conscious and unconscious plays a significant role, leading to the aesthetic resolution of conflict in the great art work. The darkness of the Dionysian origin is indicated by Nietzsche's use of the image of the maternal womb in the *Birth of*

---

8. For fuller discussion, see "Speculation and Cult: On Hegel's Strange Saying: Philosophy is God-service" in my *Beyond Hegel and Dialectic*, chapter 2.

9. See my "Art, Origins, Otherness: Hegel and Aesthetic Self-Mediation," in *Philosophy and Art*, ed. Dan Dahlstrom, (Washington: Catholic University of America Press, 1991).

Tragedy.[10] There is ontological pain at the beginning. For what is at issue in Nietzsche's sense of origin is the sundering of *das Ureine.* The primordial one is sundered into individuality. The primal guilt, as with Anaximander's *to apeiron*, is the splitting of the individual from the primordial one. There are suggestions here for Hegel's treatment of evil, which I have discussed elsewhere.[11]

Unlike *Geist* as origin, the point of beginning is not dialectical self-becoming and self-mediation. There is a rupture. And yet there is implied some return to wholeness and a certain mediation of self-becoming. Individuality and separation make us other to the Dionysian origin, but tragic vision comes to understand the truth of the origin, beyond every human rationalization and moralization of being. In celebrating tragic vision, the boundary that separates the individual from the primordial one is dissolved. The sin of separateness is purged, and there is exultation in the original energy of being in its indestructible surge of self-affirmation. It is very noticeable that there is a stress on self-dissolution, self-loss in a more ultimate original energy of being. The maternal womb takes back its separated issue. The Dionysian origin functions as what I have called an absorbing god, a principle of encompassing wholeness that in engulfing the individual assuages the pain and suffering of separateness, and most especially seems to overcome the sense of lack infecting the restlessness of human desire.[12]

Dionysian and Dialectial Origins

I know some commentators will immediately object that this is the younger Nietzsche still in thrall to Schopenhauerian metaphysics. The maturer Nietzsche was different. I promise to touch on this point again, but I think the differences between the younger and older Nietzsche are undergirded by a continuity deeper than is normally granted. For that matter, I think Nietzsche remained far more in thrall to Schopenhauer than he was capable of publicly acknowledging.[13]

---

10. This image of the mother giving birth recurs throughout Nietzsche's writing, particularly in relation to Nietzsche's sense of the pain of the creator. We also find the maternal image scattered through the writings of Schelling.

11. See "Evil and Dialectic: On the Idiocy of the Monstrous," in *Beyond Hegel and Dialectic*, chapter 4.

12. *Desire, Dialectic and Otherness*, chapter 1.

13. My own experience in reading Schopenhauer was the following. I had already read Nietzsche extensively before studying Schopenhauer intensively. I knew the official story that the mature Nietzsche had "transcended" Schopenhauer. Imagine my surprise to discover how astonishingly Nietzschean I discovered Schopenhauer to be! Of course, this

I suggest that there is a certain metaphor of aesthetic self that permeates the thinking of origin in both Hegel and Nietzsche. In Hegel's case, the understanding of origination is mediated through an appropriation of Kant's transcendental self. The Idea or *Geist*, of course, is not simply subjectified self, since it calls attention to an ontological and indeed historical power, as much as to an epistemic or categorial power. Yet the language of self—and again understood in no Cartesian or subjectivistic sense—informs the discourse. The Idea after all externalizes itself; the world is the self-externalization of the Idea; while the process of self-becoming is teleologically oriented to a self-determination and self-mediation, all the way to the absolute self-determination of the whole. Indeed, in the dialectical interplay of self and other, it is self that is offered the privileged position, in that the other is the self in its own otherness. Hence the return to self through the other is the culmination of the fulfilled dialectic.

The development of Hegel's dialectical origin can be thus described: first the moment of immediate unity; then the sundering, rather self-sundering of the unity into difference and opposition; then finally the mediation of opposition, and the reconstitution of unity in terms of a dialectically self-mediated whole. We can translate this into the metaphorical terms of the artistic creator as self. First we have the artist in his inarticulate unity and immediacy. The artist gives expression to what is implicit in the immediate, and brings to articulation difference and opposition. But in this difference and opposition the artist is finally mediating with self, bringing the inarticulacy of the origin to more explicit self-knowing. The end is the constitution of the mediated whole, the complete articulation which now fulfills the destiny of the origin to complete self-knowing.

This might seem very different to the Dionysian origin, but I do not think so. Nietzsche's own thinking owes an enormous amount to the Kantian turn to self, and its so-called Copernican revolution. He will not talk about the transcendental ego or idealistic *Geist*. Why? Just because the sense of origin implied by transcendental philosophy or idealism is not the dark beginning that Nietzsche himself, following Schopenhauer, divines. Dionysus is his mythic name for that dark origin. And yet the Kantian heritage lives on in Nietzsche's thought.

---

was all topsy turvy. A fresh reading of Schopenhauer rather reveals how Schopenhauerian Nietzsche always remained. When Nietzsche reminds us of the masked philosopher, this actually means we must always beware of what Nietzsche says about himself. We must beware of his self-presentation and self-interpretation. See my "Schopenhauer, Art and the Dark Origin," in *Schopenhauer*, ed. Eric von der Luft (Lewiston, NY: Mellen Press, 1988), pp. 101–122.

This is very evident in some of the more coarse idealistic epistemological utterances of Nietzsche: the knower imposes form on the formless; the strong philosopher indeed dictates or legislates the truth of being; will to power affirms itself in legislating the truth of being which in itself has no truth at all.

We might recall what Schopenhauer said: man is not a microcosmos, but rather that the world is to be thought of as a *makranthropos*.[14] Being is the human being writ large. Obviously, this can be given crude renditions. But any sophisticated version entails the recognition that we cannot avoid ultimate metaphysical metaphors when we ask the question of the meaning of being. All being is interpretation for Nietzsche; indeed all truth is 'my' truth. What is this but a less dissimulating projection of self onto the supposed formless chaos— less dissimulating than the idealistic projection, which would elide self in the projection, but projection nonetheless. With Nietzsche projective interpretation is affirmed even more virulently than in idealism. The metaphorical power of self, of creator, of artist is accentuated to an unprecedented degree.

When Nietzsche proclaims the *Übermensch* as the meaning of the earth, he will not be overt, that is to say, honest, like Schopenhauer, and say that the world is the *Übermensch* writ large. Nevertheless, he will suggest that apart from the extraordinary origination of the exceptional will to power the world is void of meaning, absurd, all but nothing. In the *Birth of Tragedy* there is no reticence about invoking the notion of the world artist as giving rise to the entire panorama of what is. This invocation of the artistic creator has ontological weight. Nietzsche may later become less explicit in his use of such a metaphysical metaphor, yet when he speaks of will to power, of all being as will to power, there will be ontological weight to this also. And the creativity of the *Übermensch* will not be at all divorced from this ontological weight, but rather will be the highest expression of the original power of being.

There is more to be said on this point, but for the moment we might say that the transcendental origin becomes orgiastic in Nietzsche where it is dialectical in Hegel. A sense of its excess to rational mediation or dialectical appropriation is proclaimed. It is in excess at the beginning, before reason comes into play; it is excess at the end, after reason has done its work to rationalize the world. The case is different with Hegel: the origin is implicit reason, and the self-becoming of the origin dialectically mediates its full self-realization as reason: there is no final excess to reason, not in the beginning, not in the end. Hegel may

---

14. See "Schopenhauer, Art and the Dark Origin."

anticipate Nietzsche when he says that truth is the bacchanalian revel wherein not a one is sober, and yet the revel is a state of transparent, unbroken calm.[15] We may say that Hegel's final emphasis falls on the calm sobriety of reason, whereas Nietzsche's falls on the intoxicated rapture of eros.

To say that in both there is a metaphor of self at work, whether conceived in terms of dialectic or in the name of Dionysus, is only one side of the story. For in both thinkers we find a certain tendency also to elide the self. This is an old philosophical proclivity, namely, to give finite selfhood over to a more ultimate power or principle or condition of being that transcends self. We see this in what we might call Hegel's selfless speculation. There is a surrender or sacrifice of self to the universal such that for Hegel it is an oxymoron to say 'my philosophy.' Nietzsche might seem entirely opposed to this, and in many respects he clearly is. Every philosophy is for him ultimately a confession or betrayal of the philosopher, and truth is said to be 'my' truth or truths, not the truth. And yet the highest moment of self-affirmation in Nietzsche seems also to be a moment of self-transcendence and self-dissolution. This is where Nietzsche speaks of *amor fati.*

We are reminded of the reversal in Schopenhauer from willful striving to will-less knowing, except that Nietzsche's *amor* is an accentuation of willing, not its extirpation. Nevertheless, there is a transcending release towards what seems beyond the will of self. There is a doubleness here that is full of tension. On the one hand, extreme self-affirmation; on the other hand, consent to the necessity of the course of being beyond the will of self. And does not the first block the second? Does not the second undermine the first? Can we have both together? Is there not something essentially equivocal, indeed disingenuous, about Nietzsche's position? Does he not end up, just like Hegel, singing hymns, now called Dionysian dithyrambs, to necessity, though Hegel called his hymns logic?

At his best Nietzsche is a philosopher of the equivocal; but he is also an equivocal philosopher. He does not always think through the equivocities; instead he celebrates them. I do not think he ever gives a satisfactory account of the togetherness of the above two positions. On the one hand, he was infected by the modern apotheosis of self, aesthetically expressed in the cultural elevation of genius, of which Nietzsche's *Übermensch* gives a masked version. The metaphysics of will to power is continuous with that apotheosis. On the other hand,

---

15. *Phänomenologie des Geistes,* ed. J. Hoffmeister (Hamburg: Felix Meiner, 1952), p. 39; *Phenomenology of Spirit,* trans. A. V. Miller (Oxford: Clarendon Press, 1977), p. 27.

there is something essentially unmodern about Nietzsche's deepest vision, which hearkens back to preSocratic cosmologies and tragic vision. He vacillates between these two, though wanting sometimes incoherently to affirm the two together. In the end, I think, the first wins out, and we find Zarathustra saying: "What returns, what finally comes home to me, is my own self . . . "[16]

Of course, even then Nietzsche could not escape his own passion for self-debunking. He will trumpet in *Ecce Homo*: Why I am a destiny. Perhaps this is a way of bringing the two together, though we are not entirely sure if Nietzsche has his tongue in his cheek when he proclaims himself as a destiny. He seems to be laughing at himself—lightly. But then there is no doubt but that the excess of a megalomania—laughable but no joke—is not far below the surface. It certainly breaks the surface in *The Anti-Christ* when he informs humanity in full seriousness that *Zarathustra* is perhaps the greatest gift ever offered to it. Moreover, he suggests, again in full seriousness despite the self-conscious bombast, that time is no longer to be measured from *anno domini*, and what he calls the *dies nefastus* that defines the beginning of Christianity. It should be measured from now, from the time of Nietzsche himself, as putatively breaking the back of history in two and inaugurating subsequent history, true, higher history. For not a few today Nietzsche is *the* philosopher, but how can one read such passages and not be embarrassed? Embarrassed not by Nietzsche, but for Nietzsche.[17]

It is interesting that when the 'modern' Nietzsche predominates, futurity receives main emphasis. Zarathustra puts the point in terms that indicate that without faith in a transfigured future, life would prove intolerable, unliveable. Thus Zarathustra laments that he walks among present human beings as among fragments of human beings:

> The now and the past upon the earth—alas, my friends, that is what I find most unendurable; and I should not know how to live if I were not also a seer of that which must come. A seer, a willer, a creator himself and a bridge to the future—and alas, as it were, a cripple at this bridge: all this is Zarathustra. . . . I walk among men as among the fragments of the future—that future which I

---

16. *Thus Spoke Zarathustra*, in *The Portable Nietzsche*, ed. and trans. W. Kaufmann (New York: Viking Penguin, 1976), p. 264.

17. George Kline ("The Use and Abuse of Hegel," p. 19) draws our attention to a letter Nietzsche wrote to his sister in his last lucid months (mid-November, 1888): "You haven't the remotest conception of the fact that you are closely related to a man and a fate in whom and in which the question of the millenia (*die Frage von Jahrtausenden*) has been decided. I hold the future of humanity, quite literally, in my hands."

envisage. And this is all my creating and striving, that I create and carry together into One what is fragment and riddle and dreadful accident. And how could I bear to be a man if man were not also a creator and guesser of riddles and redeemer of accidents?[18]

It is notable that the One here is not the origin as *das Ureine*, but the future One that will be created through Zarathustra's will to power. *Amor fati* ostensibly says its amen to all being, regardless of past, present, or future, but in practice Nietzsche was unrelentingly disparaging of the past and present, as the mostly sorry tale of the miserable miscarriage of human creativity. That is why the "It was" is such a heavy burden to bear for Zarathustra: it is other to present willing and a potentially debilitating weight on the pure openness of future possibility. Only by saying "Thus I willed it" is the relation to the past transfigured.

How transfigured? That is the question. There is rhetoric here which masks nonsense, and indeed a kind of cowardice before time's own recalcitrant otherness to our will to be future creators or creators of the future. The notion that the future will be, must be, the glorious realization of human creativity is the bombast of a groundless faith in future humanity. *Amor fati* is entirely incompatible with this glorification of a possible future about which nothing can be said, except that yes one knows, oh yes one surely knows, that it will be immeasurably great, yea my brothers verily it must be so. Well, it ain't necessarily so. Indeed, just the self-apotheosis of the human being may be an ontological degrading rather than elevation.

Do not accuse me of mocking Nietzsche. I am mocking Nietzsche. I also say: When he wants to offer us his Zaratustrian redemption—yes it is redemption that is on offer—*that* is how he preaches to us. No my brothers, do not stone me. Verily I say to you, out of their own mouths they stand convicted!

But perhaps I am too harsh on Nietzsche. Perhaps. But perhaps I am goaded to ire by the hurdy gurdy song, tunelessly ground out by the host of his contemporary acolytes. Perhaps.

Self-glorification and Fate

Be that so or no, let me return to philosophical sobriety. I suggest another possible approach to the tension of the above opposition

---

18. *Zarathustra*, "On Redemption," *The Portable Nietzsche*, pp. 250–251. See Kline, "The Use and Abuse of Hegel," p. 8.

between extreme self-affirmation and *amor fati*. Suppose we accentuate extreme self-affirmation; but suppose that just at that extreme what breaks forth cannot be called self in any straightforward sense; what breaks forth is will to power affirming itself; it breaks forth in inspiration. And Nietzsche himself—again without a blush—tells us that he has had experience of inspiration such as has not been had for millennia, perhaps never had. In other words, one tries to bring together the two sides by proclaiming that the creative, original self is the origin, is the breaking forth of the origin in its radical self-affirmation. One is reminded of the dialectical identity of the human and the divine in Hegel. The full self-affirmation of the human becomes identical with the creative self-affirmation of God or the absolute or will to power. It is hard not to think that something like this is equivocally at play in Nietzsche. In affirming self, Nietzsche affirms Dionysus, because he is Dionysus. That is why he is a destiny.

Consider Nietzsche's suggestion in relation to inspiration that there is a creating out of abundance. Does his description of will to power testify to what we might call a generous overflow of bestowing energy? I find the case again to be very equivocal. In my view creation is inseparable from the generosity of being. Origin is the giving of the other its otherness, and not simply for the self, or for the return to the self. Nietzsche has some equivocal intimations that there is a radical self-transcendence that gives beyond itself, that does not originate for a return to self at all. This too is a kind of selfless origination, even though the self is never more truly itself than when it gives out of its bounty to the other and for the other. It does not think of itself, or reckon on a return. Its originative being is its simple being for the other in radical self-transcendence.

To do justice to this possibility, we need to think in terms other than erotic origination. Nietzsche, and indeed Hegel, are here caught in equivocations neither escaped. Perhaps both might have wanted to think the meaning of original self-transcendence, but they could not properly do so while still captive to the metaphysical metaphor of erotic self-origination. We need to think of an origination from excess as abundance of creative being that gives other-being its being as other and for itself, and not for a return to the origin. This would be creation. We need to think of the origin as agapeic rather than erotic.[19]

---

19. The contrast of what I call the erotic and agapeic absolute is suggested in *Desire, Dialectic and Otherness,* but more fully explored in relation to Hegel in *Beyond Hegel and Dialectic*. The contrast is central to *Being and the Between*.

Without a proper sense of the plenitude of being as gift, we are tempted to define creative self-transcendence as an incessant vector to futurity. We are tempted by an instrumentalization of time and an empty apotheosis of futurity. Something of this is reflected in Nietzsche's concept of genius:[20] the explosion of a force that has been stored up over many generations. "The great human being is a finale" who squanders himself recklessly. Superficially, this might look like self-sacrifice, but really it is just the involuntary fatality of the outflow of stored forces. Nietzsche uses the image of the explosive (remember Nietzsche's ejaculation: I am not a man I am dynamite), as well as the river that floods the land. Genius is like all beauty—"the end result of the accummulated work of generations. . . . All that is good is inherited: whatever is not inherited is imperfect, is a mere beginning."[21] Superficially again this seems like a hymn to the past that is inherited, but when one remembers that Zarathustra walks among present and past humanity as among misbegotten fragments, and that futurity alone will redeem time, we quickly understand that past and present are to be instrumentalized to produce the cultural resources, themselves the necessary means for the end of unparallelled future creation.

In *Twilight of the Idols*[22] he recurs to the Greeks and his early view of Dionysus: Dionysus "is explicable only in terms of an *excess of force.*" Incidentally his discussion here gives the lie to the view that there is a significant departure in the later Nietzsche from the central notions of the *Birth of Tragedy*. He reiterates the orgiastic nature of the Dionysian and its relation to the tragic affirmation of life even in its pain and destruction. The image of the mother giving birth, the pain of birth pangs, also to be found in *Birth of Tragedy*, now named as his first effort at the revaluation of values, is repeated, indeed it is pronounced holy. The futurity of life, identified with its eternity, is experienced religiously in affirming procreation: procreation is the holy way to life. The Christian view is denounced for making sex unclean and casting "*filth* on the origin."

Does Nietzsche have a notion of agapeic creation? I think not. His expression of the overflow of fullness ultmately has an erotic modulation: it is an expression of self for self. As I have pointed out, even when Nietzsche speaks of affirmative will to power, such will to power affirms itself; it does not affirm what is irreducibly other to itself.

---

20. *Twilight of the Idols*, "What the Germans Lack," #44, in *The Portable Nietzsche*, pp. 547–548.

21. *Twilight of the Idols*, "What the Germans Lack," #47 in *The Portable Nietzsche*, pp. 551–552.

22. "What I Owe to the Ancients," #4, in *The Portable Nietzsche*, pp. 560–562.

Consider his "psychology of the artist" in *Twilight of the Idols.*[23] First frenzy is a necessary condition, sexual frenzy, frenzy in destruction, in cruelty, in daring, a frenzy that finally is "the frenzy of an overcharged and swollen will." Out of the feeling of increased strength and fullness, essential to this frenzy, "one lends to things, one *forces* them to accept from us, one violates them—this process is called *idealizing.*" Consider further:

> In this state one enriches everything out of one's own fullness: whatever one sees, whatever one wills, is seen swelled, taut, strong, overloaded with strength. A man in this state transforms things until they mirror his power—until they are reflections of his perfection. This *having to* transform into perfection is—art. Even everything he is not yet, becomes for him an occasion of joy in himself; in art man enjoys himself as perfection.[24]

This forcing, violating, glory in self is identified, believe it or not, with the Yes of Raphael!

There is something adolescent about this phallic psychology of self. The imposition of self is revealed in the passage from *Zarathustra*, reiterated to conclude *Twilight of the Idols: The Hammer Speaks*. What this says is "Be hard!" What is this? If one wants to be a destiny one must cut and cut like a diamond: "For all creators are hard. And it must seem blessedness for you to impress your hand on millenia as on wax, blessedness to write on the will of millenia as on bronze. . . ." Creative destiny is self-glorification. Indeed, for Nietzsche the whole point of the Greek festivals and arts was "nothing other than to feel *on top*, to *show* themselves on top. These are means of glorifying oneself, and in certain cases, of inspiring fear of oneself."[25] I fear we have here no twilight of the idols but the manufacture of a new idol, namely Nietzsche himself.

Erotic Origins

Let me elaborate on the significance of the foregoing in relation to erotic origination. An erotic origin is an origin that is its own self-becoming, and its self-becoming is thought according to the metaphor of a certain erotic self-surpassing. Eros is a dynamic movement of

---

23. "Skirmishes of an Untimely Man, #s 8ff, *The Portable Nietzsche*, pp. 518ff.
24. *Ibid.*, pp. 518–519.
25. *Ibid.* p. 559.

desire, a striving of self-energy that reaches out of itself to fulfill itself in appropriating to itself what is other to itself. Eros, out of its own original lack or incompletion, transcends itself towards the other. It thus transcends its own lack, but it relates to what is other by taking it to itself. In this taking to itself, it fulfills itself. The fullness, the fulfillment, properly speaking, comes in the end.

Hegel's dialectical origin certainly fits this description. In itself alone the Idea is a mere lacking indeterminacy. In order for it to be genuine and concretely real it must realize itself in time; this realization means its self-externalization and determination in becoming; it becomes itself in this process of determination, thereby transcending the putative lack of its original indeterminacy. But even though it necessarily must externalize or other itself, it discovers itself again in the otherness; for the otherness is simply itself again in the form of otherness; when this self-recognition occurs, the origin knows itself and knows itself as a process of self-determination. But it is in this end, not in the beginning, that the absolute is properly absolute; then it is the whole that entirely completes the intial lacking indeterminacy. The dialectical origin completely mediates with itself, completes itself in its necessarily self-unfolding trajectory from initial indeterminacy to complete, fullfilled concrete self-determination.

Hegel's dialectical origin has an ahistorical and historical side. This is also true of Nietzsche. Thus Nietzsche's *Ureine* fits the description of an erotic origin. For the beginning is dark and contradictory and incomplete. It is only in the end that the initial darkness is somehow redeemed, and the one reconciled with itself, even in its self-contradiction and suffering. One might say that the precipitation of individuals out of the primordial one generates times and history. But it seems that the primordial one must generate time in order to overcomes its own suffering and self-contradiction. Nietzsche speaks of the lust for life, the insatiable hunger for existence of the primal being. Time is needed to overcome the torment of the origin. Creation beyond self issues from such torment. It seems to me that from this tortured sense of the beginning comes Nietzsche's glorification of redeeming futurity. Very clearly in *Zarathustra* the past invariably is seen in the light of a necessity to be redeemed. Moreover, redemption is only thinkable in terms of a future transfiguration. Nausea at mankind's past and present can only be overcome by willing backwards, but not because there is an inherent good to be affirmed in past and present, but in order to release will from what seems beyond will and release it for what Nietzsche supposes is within will, namely the redemptive future.

But you will rightly raise the question: Did not Nietzsche in *Zarathustra* also say that he once did think, but no longer does, in terms of a God who suffered, and who because of suffering had to create beyond himself. Now that he has put away such ways of thinking, his song is a kind of lyrical Feuerbachianism: God and gods are projections of man's will to power out of a condition of weakness, projections that have to be reclaimed for man himself. Marx, Nietzsche, Freud are all Feuerbach's children here, and Feuerbach is only a deformed dialectical son of the father of modern dialectics, Hegel. Marx is a social Feuerbachian, Freud a psychoanalytical, and Nietzsche a poetic Feuerbachian.

But even when God is reduced to a projection of human power, a logic of erotic origination operates: out of initial lack, weakness, emptiness, and desiring man projects beyond himself; he transcends himself (externalizes himself) in religion towards an other that is not finally an other at all; the other is the self again; and the major trouble with previous religions is that they broke the circuit of self-appropriation on an unappropriated otherness, did not allow the return of the human being to itself. What do the sons of Feuerbach want? They want to close the circuit again, and allow the otherness of the human to return to itself. The truth of God is, or will be, man. The truth of creation is, or will be, human self-creation.

Of course, this circuit of self-creation is understood differently by each. And in Nietzsche's case there is an intimation that self is an abyss, and in truth beyond complete self-mastering. This sense of the beyond is deeply equivocal in Nietzsche, but I suggest that here emerges something significantly at odds with Zarathustra's claim, previously noted, that "what finally returns, comes home to me, is my own self." What emerges also throws light on the continuity as well as discontinuity between the earlier and later Nietzsche. What I mean is this.

Nietzsche's atheism cannot be assimilated to any normal species of humanism, precisely because there is a sense of excess to the human being that resists complete self-mediation. This excess opens up the human being to something other than the human. Hence the opening of radical self-apotheosis to what passes beyond self and *amor fati*. I suggest that there is still a concern with origin as other to the human but this is the shift. The *Ureine* conceived the origin under the sign of unity and identity; but the sign will be changed from unity to multiplicity, from identity to difference. Still named Dionysus, but more as will to power rather than *das Ureine*, the primordial one becomes what I will call the self-broadcaster, under the sign of multiplicity and difference. There is a reversal from identity to difference, and yet the will to power is still a self-broadcasting, in the sense of a self-scattering, a self-othering, and self-dissemination. Nietzsche praises himself for his acquired power in "the reversal of perspectives."[26] One might say that the One has now become Self-Othering. But even in this self-othering under the sign of difference, Nietzsche will still continue to say again and again: will to power affirms itself—itself and nothing but itself.

The devotees of Nietzsche will forgive me for again noting the affinity with Hegel, a master dialectician who could claim to reverse into its opposite any perspective you could conceive. Hegel's speculative thinking of the absolute one implies that the one is not truly absolute until it becomes self-othering: the one others itself into multiplicity and difference, and this is indeed its inherent nature. Why Nietzsche and Hegel are such brothers is because deep down their thinking is guided by a logic of erotic self-origination. Admittedly in Nietzsche's case, the logic becomes poetic, and in this ambiguously suggestive form, could be disguised and dissimulated—even to Nietzsche himself. It seems to me that the younger Nietzsche had not yet learned to mask his views as much as he did later. So there is a youthful ardour to the *Birth of Tragedy*: he reveals what he loves, recklessly—a love and recklessness that has to be seen through many masks later. In the reversal from the sign of unity to the sign of difference, I believe that one can still see the shape of what he loved as ultimate, relative to erotic self-origination.

You will object that Nietzsche in *Ecce Homo* describes the *Birth of Tragedy* as having something of the offensive smell of Hegelianism, as well as indicating his rejection of the artistic metaphysics. But why should we take anything that Nietzsche says at face value? Nothing he says can be taken at face value, on his own admission of being a masked philosopher. The mask cuts two ways. It may hide depth and profundity. It may also perfume the secret odour of Hegelian metaphysics that Nietzsche does not want us to smell, or smell out. But Nietzsche has taught us only too well how to smell out other philosophers. The nasal metaphor is one that he uses frequently, perhaps too frequently. I find no reason for accepting at face value Nietzsche's claim to have discarded the artistic metaphysics. This is where he revealed his deepest ardor as a younger man, an ardor whose youthful naivete he later sought to conceal. It is always hard to betray or confess one's deepest love, especially when age and the acids of skepticism have corroded one's more innocent faith.

Twilight of an Ideal

I do not forget the differences of Hegel and Nietzsche, in that erotic origin can be thought either in terms of an explicit teleology, or as

---

26. *Ecce Homo*, ch. 1, sect. 1, *The Portable Nietzsche*, p. 659.

ateleological. Clearly, erotic self-origination in Hegel has a teleological thrust—the goal is the self-mediating constitution of the completed whole. With Nietzsche, the self-othering of the origin seems to be without telos, hence we seem to have multiplicity without final unification, unrestricted differentiation without integration into a whole. This latter is the kind of understanding that informs the deconstructionist reading of Nietzsche.

There is much to the point about this, but I think there is more to be said. Explicit disclaimers to the contrary, Nietzsche does not avoid his own telos, a telos that is an equivocal *auto-telos*. Not surprisingly the aesthetic, as supposedly auto-telic, comes in again. What I mean is implied by statements like the following: "World—a work of art giving birth to itself!"[27] How does a work of art give birth to itself? Only if there is an ontological self-origination that is the very dynamic self-becoming of the process of being itself. We humans find it hard to think of a work of art apart from its origination by an artist. This was true of the early Nietzsche.

Hence I query: Why do some commentators breathe an audible sigh of relief that Nietzsche gave up, "mericifully," as Nehemas puts it,[28] the language of the world artist? What is the mercy, what is the relief? No explanation is offered. But of course, the embarrassment is the embarrassment of God. Strange shame at a god, when without the slighest chagrin one then continues to gas on about Dionysus. And one must query, given the seeming elision, where does the world artist go? What new form, more merciful, less embarrassing, does it take? Because it does take other forms, but now, as I put it, under the sign of difference rather than identity.

This is why the brotherhood of Hegel and Nietzsche in relation to the erotic origin is so revealing. One wonders if the artist has been elided for fear of falling back into the arms of a God. Can one avoid this? Even to say: a work of art giving birth to itself, one notes that it is to itself that it (whatever this *deus absconditus* is) gives birth. Self-origination is still self-origination, and as long as we try to make articulate sense, resort to some such locution seems impossible to avoid. One might say nothing, but that hardly helps. One might say: origin, or orgination; but then inevitably one asks, what kind of origin

---

27. *The Will to Power*, trans. W. Kaufmann and R. J. Hollingdale, ed. W. Kaufmann (New York: Random House, 1967), p. 419.

28. A. Nehemas, *Nietzsche: Life as Literature* (Cambridge: Harvard University Press, 1985), p. 91. I suppose that Nehemas' literary/textual model, applied to Nietzsche's metaphysics of the self-birthing artwork world, would make the world into a self-writing text, without any writer or author.

or origination. And then the resort to terms like identity and difference, same and other, is unavoidable. Nor will it help very much to write origin and then draw a line though it, as Heidegger does with being. There is no escaping the hard tasking of thinking of origin. The first jolt of the typographical gesture dissolves pretty quickly, and still we metaphysicians are perplexed—both about what appears and what is crossed out, even when it is crossed out.

The work of art that gives birth to itself tries to be its own father, mother and offspring. Is the idea intelligible? It is hard to make intelligible. It is as hard, or as easy, as some of the old ideas of God. This says as much for the old God as for Nietzsche's supposedly new god. And do not tell me that Nietzsche should not be subject to rigorous analysis, that to do this is ontotheology. This gives Nietzsche a very convenient bolt-hole whenever we ask about the intelligible coherence of his ideas. I cannot avoid thinking that his "god" dresses up in aesthetic/ontological form what metaphysicians of old spoke of as *causa sui*. I know that in one place[29] Nietzsche excoriates this notion as showing the deep fear of philosophers, fear of time and origins, their "Egypticism." But what Nietzsche denounces in others has often an uncanny tendency to haunt Nietzsche again, indeed to be resurrected in a different form. I suppose this is why Nietzsche had to continually leap frog himself, and why in the end, what finally returns is the old familiar, "my own self." It is a hard act to sustain the absolute originality one had proclaimed. His "madness," in a paradoxical enough reversal of perspectives, brings out the point with maximum lucidity. I refer to the penetration of one of his first mad letters (6 January, 1889, postmarked 5 January),[30] that poignant plea to Burckhardt: Bear with me please, for I am new to the business of being a god; "I would much rather be a Basel professor than God." And what is the pathetic destiny of this god? Sentenced to while away the next eternity cracking bad jokes!

Though Nietzsche is now presented as *the* philosopher of difference, it is the circuit of the same that is reconstituted in the work of art that gives birth to itself. The credentials he offers us for being the philosopher of difference are thus deeply equivocal. For there is no radical creation of the other as other, if all there is is the *causa sui* of the world/work of art that gives birth to itself. It is the same that is eternally recurring. I cannot enter into debate about the eternal recurrence of the same here, except that to say that it too is an attempt to

---

29. *Twilight of the Idols*, "Reason in Philosophy," *The Portable Nietzsche*, pp. 479ff.
30. *The Portable Nietzsche*, pp. 685–686.

close the circle and bring the two sides above together—extreme self-affirmation and *amor fati.*

Within the circle, or what is called the ring of eternity, the same might often look like the other or different. But that is within the circle. Moreover, Nietzsche is talking about the circle itself, not about what is in it. Plato returns. For Nietzsche is arrogating to himself all the powers of the Platonic philosopher as the spectator of all time and eternity. Nietzsche must in some sense, a sense he cannot explain, be able to see the circle of the whole, be somehow transcendent to it. Again here the evidence of a logic of erotic origination seems to me unmistakable in Nietzsche's vision, and again in a manner which makes Nietzsche a kindred of Hegel.

I identify a major source of this logic of erotic origination in a tendency to identify theogony and cosmogony in idealistic and pantheistic philosophies that appropriate Spinoza's notion of *causa sui*: it is necessary for God to become; indeed we cannot separate this self-becoming from the process of becoming of the world; ultimately the two are the same. This necessary self-becoming exhibits the character of an erotic absolute. How does one find this strain in relation to Nietzsche? One might think of Schelling's appropriation of Spinoza here, and of the fact that Schopenhauer reproduces a number of possibilities already fermenting in perhaps the more idealistic framework of Schelling. In other words, the dark other to idealism is present in this latter version of the erotic absolute, whereas in Hegel's dialectical origin it is the power of the erotic absolute to mediate absolute reason that is stressed.

Thus Schopenhauer speaks directly of the genital organs as the focal point of the Will, and what is Will but the dark striving energy that is the primordial ground of all becoming? Schopenhauer also says that all willing arises from deficiency and from lack; this is eros as a lacking desire struggling to overcome its initial lack. If this is the metaphysical metaphor that characterizes the process of being, then the primordial Will is nothing other than a dark, blind striving that must struggle to release itself from its own darkness. It does this in the will-less knowing of art, and for Schopenhauer more radically in the release from will of the saint. The erotic origin initially lacks peace, is in bondage to its own darkness; it strives for peace in an erotic struggle that seeks to transcend eros.

Interestingly, Nietzsche criticizes Schopenhauer for a melancholy attitude to sexual eros, and praises Plato for his "philosophic erotics" out of which developed a new art form of the Greek *agon,* namely dialectic.[31] Yet Nietzsche also continues Schopenhauer's sense of the

---

31. *Twilight of the Idols,* "What the Germans Lack," #'s 22–23, *The Portable Nietzsche,* pp. 527–529.

darkness of the origin but transforms will into will to power. We have already looked at a clear testimony to the erotic origin in *The Birth of Tragedy*, where through suffering and contradiction, creation and destruction, the primordial one seeks its own redemption in the process of becoming. In contrast to Schopenhauer, he seems to reject will-less knowing and the extirpation of will by the saint; he seems to accentuate the process of striving itself, striving without end, and erotic struggle without any peace at the end such as we find, say, in Platonic eros. I say he seems, for in fact the 'unselving' involved in this makes the extreme willing into a kind of will-lessness: willing everything in *amor fati* is consent to everything, and hence not just willing in the sense of asserting one's own will. The erotic absolute is absolutized under the mythic name of Dionysus. But this absolute seems to offer an orgiastic absorbing god which swallows us, deconstructs Apollonian individuation.

I think Nietzsche's description of the world as a "monster of energy"[32] is extraordinarily revealing:

> And do you know what the "world" is to me? Shall I show it to you in my mirror? This world: a monster of energy, without beginning, without end; a firm, iron magnitude of force that does not grow bigger or smaller, that does not expend itself but only transforms itself; as a whole, of unalterable size, a household without expenses or losses, but likewise without increase or income; enclosed by "nothingness" as by a boundary; . . . as force throughout, as a play of forces flowing and rushing together, eternally changing, eternally flooding back, with tremendous years of recurrence, with an ebb and a flood of its forms; out of the simplest forms striving toward the most complex, out of the stillest, most rigid, coldest forms towards the hottest, most turbulent, most self-contradictory, and then again returning home to the simplest out of this abundance, out of the play of contradictions back to the joy of concord, still affirming itself in this uniformity of its courses and its years, blessing itself as that which must return eternally, as a becoming that knows no satiety, no disgust, no weariness: this, my *Dionysian* world of the eternally self-creating, eternally self-destroying . . . my "beyond good and evil," without goal, unless the joy of the circle is itself a goal; without will, unless a ring feels good will towards itself—do you want a *name* for this world? A *solution* for all its riddles? . . . *This world is will to power—and nothing besides!* And you yourselves are also this will to power—and nothing besides!

---

32. *Will to Power*, pp. 549–550.

To any philosophically sophisticated reader, and Nietzsche has not been blessed with such readers often enough, it is impossible not to hear an echo of the Parmenidean One, the well-rounded circle of truth. Of course, this One has been dynamized by Heraclitean becoming in its eternal arising and dissolving. The self-becoming of the will to power closes into a cosmic circle. One hears in the background the voice of Spinoza's One—the Whole, fated, necessary, absolutely determined. One hears the voice of Hegel singing the dialectically self-mediating totality. Indeed since the human being is also will to power and nothing else beside, it seems impossible to distinguish the human self from the cosmic circle as will to power and nothing else beside. The beginning and the end is will to power and nothing else besides, and everything seemingly different and other is swallowed back into this orgiastic absorbing god.

In a word, Nietzsche is guilty of the sins he has charged to *messieurs* the metaphysicians. He is shameless about these sins, indeed seems to be hardly mindful of the fact that he is committing them. Alas, it is easier to take the speck out of Plato's eye than the beam from one's own. Do I exaggerate? Well, simply take note of the totalizing claim of Nietzsche's language. Nietzsche is recklessly totalistic. Hegel is supposed to be the totalizing philosopher *par excellence,* but his totalism is almost meek and dull compared to the reckless rhapsody of Nietzsche's totalism. You might say, as some commentators have, that Nietzsche was incautious in understanding will to power in cosmological terms, that he should have confined the thesis to human being. But when was Nietzsche ever cautious? He hated caution. Daring he loved—intellectual, spiritual daring. And can you seriously imagine him, like a good considerate scholar, or moderate analyst, saying: The world is will to power—for the most part. Or there is nothing else but will to power—but only here and there, and maybe now and then. Or: let me tentatively suggest the following empirical generalization: the world is will to power.

No. Nietzsche legislates. Nietzsche dictates. Not only is the human being mainly motivated by will to power, the world is will to power and nothing else besides. Making a total claim, one must even say, staking a total claim, Nietzsche is an extremist. It is all or nothing. And as it turned out, he had rightly divined that it was this lure of the extreme, not reason and argument, that would win him converts. Nietzsche does not deign to make a case but instead seeks to dazzle with his dancing at the edge. The dancing may begin in frenzy, perhaps even in divine madness, but because the dancer never resolves his equivocity towards the divine, because he can in no way distinguish between dancing full of God and dancing the idol of absolute self-glorification, that is, self-deification,[33] the dancing ends in mad madness. Nietzsche's song and dance continues to bewitch too many, but for us the spell is broken. We have ceased to be bewitched, we are no longer enchanted. The metaphysical magic that conjures away the otherness between God and man is black magic.

---

33. For Nietzsche's self-glorification is self-deification. Like the *causa sui*, Nietzsche wanted to create oneself. As he said in highest admiration of Goethe: he created himself (*Twilight of the Idols*, "What the Germans Lack," #49, *The Portable Nietzsche*, p. 554). Nietzsche willed to be his own mother and father and offspring all together. This is erotic self-origination, and like Hegel's absolute, in debt to nothing other, for there is no genuine other; what finally comes home, so spake Zarathustra, is the self.

Part II
History and Critical Reason

.

6

Recollection, Forgetting, and the Hermeneutics of History: Meditations on a Theme from Hegel

George R. Lucas, Jr.

> ...the dialectic of [consciousness] is nothing else but the simple history of its movement or of its experience, and [consciousness] itself is nothing else but just this history.... consciousness ... is always reaching this result, learning from experience what is true in it; but equally it is always *forgetting* it and starting the movement all over again.... The consciousness which is this truth has this path behind it [but] has *forgotten* it ... it merely *asserts* that is all reality, but does not itself comprehend this; for it is along that *forgotten path* that [each] immediately-expressed assertion is comprehended.
>
> —(G. W. F. Hegel)[1]

At several key junctures in the *Phenomenology of Spirit* (1807), one discovers Hegel making the rather startling assertion that acts of forgetting are what bring about the flux of historical events. Human consciousness, Hegel seems to be saying, consistently forgets what it has learned on the basis of its historical experience. Cultures and peoples are, as a result of forgetfulness, obliged to retrace painful steps on the road to the recovery of some forgotten truth. Forgetting thus seems to necessitate the various transitions between stages of consciousness in the *Phenomenology*, and, by implication, it generates the flux of time and the historical process itself.

Hegel does not tell us here or elsewhere, however, how or why this forgetting takes place, or what necessitates it. His account lacks an

---

1. *Hegel's Phenomenology of Spirit*, trans. A. V. Miller (Oxford: Clarendon Press, 1977), pp. 64, 141.

ontology of historical events and of the past itself, necessary to understand, for example, how an incident or occurrence might be forgotten, what becomes of it when it is thus lost to historical memory, and the manner in which that event might subsequently be recoverable to consciousness. In this essay, I will attempt to fill in these lacunae in Hegel's account of recollection and forgetting. In the process, I will want to explore the political ramifications of Hegel's intriguing but undeveloped suggestion about the nature of history and historical change. In providing Hegel with the missing ontology of past events sufficient to ground his assertions concerning the nature of history and historical change, my resultant neo-Hegelian account will address widespread contemporary concerns and confusions concerning the role of forgetting in political and cultural life more generally.

Erasing History

If it is the business of the historian to remember, Hegel reminds us that history itself consists largely of an ongoing and apparent loss to oblivion. In his introduction to the *Lectures on the Philosophy of History*, Hegel describes the "restless succession of individuals and peoples, who exist for a time and then disappear," and, in a famous metaphor, describes history itself as a "slaughter-bench at which the happiness of peoples, the wisdom of states, and the virtue of individuals has been sacrificed."[2]

In most instances the forgetting, the fading of immediacy, and the loss of intricate detail is inadvertent, and seems unavoidable. After all, no historical narrative can be all encompassing; even to attempt complete preservation of each and every detail would result in a narrative that was hopelessly complex and unintelligible. As a consequence, the welter of immediate detail that cannot be woven meaningfully (and selectively) into a subsequent historian's narrative must either be accorded a cursory treatment or else cast aside. This problem of perspectivalism in the hermeneutics of history is thoroughly familiar, and seemingly inescapable.[3]

---

2. Hegel, *Reason in History* (1837), trans. Robert S. Hartman (Indianapolis: Bobbs-Merrill, 1953), pp. 88, 26.

3. According to Karl Popper, who first coined the term "perspectivalism" for this problem now central to the hermeneutics of history (cf. *The Open Society and its Enemies* [London, 1945]): there is not, nor can there be, any one, single, Archimedian, observer-invariant account of past events. Rather, the most one can strive for in historical narrative is "perspectivalism": "objectivity" in this case refers only to the attempt to offer an unbiased and impartial or disinterested narrative account from the standpoint of some clearly-delineated and reasonably well-understood (cultural) perspective; i.e., "objectivity relative to a certain point of view."

Forgetting, however, is not always simply unavoidable or inescapable, it is often intentional. The forgetting of history in many instances occurs as the end result of deliberate actions. In this vein, a retired former Soviet army officer, Colonel Vladimir Malinin, related how he and his first wife, Yevgenia, first learned for themselves of how the Soviet state dealt with political prisoners:

> Yevgenia, an archivist for the state prison system, accidentally discovered a secret report written to Soviet leader Nikita Khrushchev by the director of the camps administration in the Far East. The report recited a litany of horrors that shocked the couple out of their previous unquestioning devotion to the Soviet state. According to Mr. Malinin, the report recounted that 17.5 million people had been imprisoned in a sprawling network of labor camps for political prisoners in the Kolyma River valley north of Magadan between 1933 and 1952. Of those, the report said, 16.3 million had died of exhaustion or illness and another 85,877 had been shot to death. Having stumbled upon such forbidden knowledge, Mr. Malinin said, he agonized over it for months, then finally shared his secret and sought advice from a friend named Ivan Chistiakov, who held a high position in the Magadan regional administration. "He told me, 'It's better you *forget all about it*,'" Mr. Malinin said.[4]

This might be described as a strategy of suppression of the past, in which a powerful political elite seeks to prevent the dissemination of historical information that would threaten or undermine its current political status. There are other, active (rather than inadvertent) kinds of forgetting that operate in history. Recently, at the relatively advanced age of seventy-six, a former Japanese army physician decided to break a longstanding code of silence and denial and speak out for the record concerning Japanese military atrocities during World War II. At issue were allegations, never acknowledged by the Japanese, that army doctors had conducted a variety of cruel and scientifically unwarranted experiments on Chinese and Korean prisoners of war. The physician, Dr. Ken Yuasa, remarked:

> I must confess, with embarrassment for myself and the country, because I strongly believe everyone should know the truth. If I don't tell my story, what the Japanese military has done will be *erased from history*.[5]

---

4. *Newsday* article on Soviet prison camps, reprinted in *The Baltimore Sun*, "Photo helps ex-Soviet officer recall U.S. prisoner." Monday, September 20, 1993, p. 3A. My emphasis.

5. Dr. Yuasa, imprisoned for three years as a war criminal at the conclusion of WWII, as quoted in a recent Associated Press article on Japanese war crimes: *The Baltimore Sun*, Tuesday, September 7, 1993, p. 7A. My emphasis.

Somewhat in contrast to the case of Soviet suppression cited above, Dr. Yuasa finally refuses to condone repression, a conspiracy of silence and denial concerning unsavory medical and pseudo-scientific activities. Some Japanese and German physicians and concentration-camp *capos* would prefer that their misdeeds be forgotten, hoping that their own repression, combined with collective cultural amnesia, will ultimately lead to what Dr. Yuasa describes as the erasure of history.

Attempts like these to force people to forget all about the historical record constitute the stock in trade of tyranny. Czech author Milan Kundera maintains, in his *Book of Laughter and Forgetting*, that "the only reason people want to be masters of the future is to change the past."[6] Tyrants often see the need for this social or cultural amnesia, this need "to change the past" (in Kundera's terms), either to hide what they have done or to disguise or distort what they propose to do. Ultimately, the loss of the past brings on a kind of amnesia, a psychological malaise in which the very being of a people seems to have evaporated. Writing in the aftermath of the brutal repression of the "Prague Spring" of 1968, Kundera reflects that

> Prague . . . is a city without memory. It has even forgotten its name. Nobody there remembers anything, nobody recalls anything. . . . Time . . . is the time of a humanity that no longer knows anything nor remembers anything, that lives in nameless cities with nameless streets or streets with names different from the ones they had yesterday, *because a name means continuity with the past* and people without a past are people without a name.[7]

In response, Kundera proclaims that "the struggle of man against power is the struggle of memory against forgetting."[8] The fruits of victory in this struggle are the preservation, intact, of the lives and the experiences of ordinary people—or rather, of the events out of which those lives and precious individual identities are constituted. Eyewitnesses, even participants in historical events may decide after decades of silence and denial to speak out, as did Dr. Yuasa, committing their testimony to some sort of enduring record. Guilt by the perpetrators or by compliant witnesses, or anger and desire for vengeance on behalf

---

6. Milan Kundera, *The Book of Laughter and Forgetting*, trans. Michael Henry Heim (London: Penguin Books, 1983), p. 22.

7. Kundera, p. 157; my emphasis. The author is here glossing on Franz Kafka's description of Prague in order to assess the effects on the culture of Soviet-instigated suppression of history.

8. Kundera, p. 3.

of victims, provokes individuals to commit themselves to the cause of recollection.

The principal insurrectionists, the chief guerrilla warriors in this struggle against forgetting, are historians. Throughout the 1980s a debate raged in the academic field of twentieth-century Russian history between what was characterized as an older generation of conservative political historians, led by Robert Conquest of Stanford University, and a newer generation of social historians, led by J. Arch Getty of the University of California and Shiela Fitzpatrick of the University of Chicago. The lengthy and acrimonious debate between these two factions over methodology in fact concealed a larger conflict between memory and forgetting.[9]

The social historians accused the older political historians of having developed an overly-dramatic and personalized view of Russian history. This view, based upon what the social historians characterized as subjective and anecdotal testimony of dissidents and victims, tended to focus on and demonize the role of Stalin and his henchmen in carrying out the terrible purges in Russia during the 1930s, and downplay or ignore the role of other factors that might have contributed to the magnitude of the widespread party purges that culminated in the Great Terror (ca. 1938–1939).

The revisionist social historians, by contrast, were suspicious of the narrative that anecdotal eyewitness accounts yielded, and argued that this ought to be corroborated and supplemented by the more objective and impartial data derived from official records and archival sources. The political historians responded that the official records of

---

9. Robert Conquest's magisterial study of Stalinism, *The Great Terror*, was first published by Oxford University Press in 1968, and has since been revised, enlarged, and translated into a number of languages (including Russian). His study of forced collectivization and the Great Ukrainian famine under Stalin, *The Harvest of Sorrow*, was published by Oxford in 1986.

J. Arch Getty's doctoral dissertation at Boston College in 1979, represented the first venture of social historians into this period and these topics, heretofore the exclusive domain of political commentators, political scientists, and economists. Getty attacks the reliance of Conquest, in particular, on what he defines as "the totalitarian model" of history, and accuses him of "demonizing" Stalin: cf. *Origins of the Great Purges: The Soviet Communist Party Reconsidered, 1933–38* (Cambridge University Press, 1985).

Conquest and Getty are among the participants in a symposium devoted to the revisionist history of Stalinist Russia in *The Russian Review*, 46, no. 4 (October, 1987). That symposium, in turn, was prompted by extremely sharp and negative reactions to the lead paper in a previous year's issue of this same journal by Sheila Fitzpatrick: "New Perspectives on Stalinism," *The Russian Review*, 45, no. 4 (October, 1986), 357–374. In addition to these lengthy exchanges, two issues of *The Slavic Review* (Spring, 1983; Summer, 1986) also featured discussions of revisionist social history and Stalinism.

tyrants could hardly be regarded as impartial and reliable; that often, such records were Orwellian instruments of forgetting—airbrushed, sanitized, and falsified in order to hide the truth.[10]

This bitter debate on historical methodology sputtered mootly to a halt, however, when the social historians were finally able to obtain full access to the sorts of hitherto-restricted archival materials to which Colonel Malinin also refers, following the collapse of the Soviet Union in 1991. Bureaucrats are nothing if not meticulous in their attention to detail, beyond, it seems, even the power of the tyrant to corrupt. In the newly-opened "Center for the Preservation and Study of Documents of Contemporary History" (formerly the Central Party Archives of the Communist Party) in Moscow, Professor Getty himself discovered neatly typed records like those Colonel Malinin had accidentally encountered earlier—chilling, impersonal, objective government records providing unmistakable documentation of atrocities of at least as great a magnitude as Professor Conquest's numerous witnesses and scholarly allies had envisioned.[11] Airbrushed photographs, official silences, campaigns of disinformation, and surreptitious warnings "to forget all about it" could not, in the end, obscure or cast into the oblivion of forgetfulness the sheer historical massiveness of the Stalinist purges, of the Ukrainian famines, or the terror of the Gulags.

Japanese medical atrocities, the European Jewish Holocaust, Stalinist gulags, and the Ukrainian famines are, however, all world-historical events of massive proportions, involving millions of people. These events generated widespread anguish, pain, suffering, and anger. It would be a monumental task to attempt to erase such events from history—perhaps, owing to their dimensions, therefore impossible in practice. There is always someone left, someone willing to speak out.

Even so, the threat of historical oblivion carried in these stories seems all too real. Physical records are themselves, after all, merely historical artifacts with a finite lifetime. Individual eyewitnesses die; their memories are lost to us, and they are themselves forgotten. Their

---

10. In his acclaimed novel, *1984*, British author George Orwell vividly described the manufacture of "memory holes," in which the historical record—newspapers, etc.—are systematically re-written on a daily basis. Archival documents which cannot be rewritten are "vaporized."

11. Getty discovered, for example, a report prepared by the Ministry of Internal Affairs in December, 1953, documenting the numbers of persons repressed by state security from 1921 to 1953, prepared using KGB archives housed at TsGAOR archive. The charts for each year provided orderly records of the number of persons arrested, the reason for sentences, the numbers executed, and by whom they were sentenced. These documents are forthcoming in a multi-volume series, *Annals of Communism*, initiated by Yale University Press.

archives, diaries, books, and other written records likewise fade and crumble with a temporal measure only somewhat longer than that of their authors. This casting aside, this loss to oblivion that Hegel describes so effectively seems to constitute the larger process and the wider backdrop of history against which the historian's memorial task forms a modest, or even an insignificant foreground.

Yet there lurks an intractable conceptual confusion—I would term it an ontological confusion—inherent in the strategy pursued by all who seek, for their own purposes, to effect such erasures from the historical record as described in the cases above. The forgetting, which is the warp and woof of history, it seems, is always a subsequent matter. Forgetting is not simply the failure to remember; it is not merely an omission. Forgetting is the cessation, or the active prevention, of an act of transmission of memorial data from preceding to subsequent moments of consciousness. What the intellectual terrorist may be able to achieve (if entirely successful) is totally impeding transmission of even the slightest trace of a given moment, or sequence of moments, to the next—a termination or discontinuation of a series of events.

But such a cessation or active discontinuation of the transmission of the legacy of a thing, or of a related series of things, is rather obviously not the same as a retroactive obliteration of the thing itself. Our intellectual terrorist will have succeeded only in preventing or preempting the possibility of memory or later recollection. Contrary to science-fiction accounts, he would not thereby also have been able to work backwards in time and unmake the original existant, the very being of the thing thus forgotten.

Forgetting as the essence of history is confined entirely to subsequent history. Forgetting affects the transmission of the past, which in turn grounds our conscious assignment of meaning to the past; but it does not thereby affect the being of the past itself. Our failing to pay attention in the 1990s to records and memories of past medical atrocities, for example, does not mean that those events themselves somehow failed to occur as they did occur to those who were victimized by them in 1937 or in 1941—let alone does it mean that such past events are themselves reversible or unmakeable.

All that forgetting can accomplish, either inadvertently or deliberately, is that what once was, or what was once achieved, is subsequently unrecollected by consciousness. Past events do not cease to be; rather, they can only cease to be consciously remembered. This result holds true for the commonplace as well as for larger, so-called world-historical events: this conclusion is thus not a matter of magnitude, but of fundamental metaphysical principle.

The Ontology of the Past

What sorts of entities are past events themselves? Temporal passage from the present to the past is usually understood to involve the cessation or completion of [present] concretizing activity, once this activity has resulted in the achievement of determinateness or closure. But does the attainment of determinateness also necessarily entail that the completed and determinate event and its objective achievements thereupon literally disappear into oblivion? If not, then where do past events go? What becomes of them? In particular, does the subsequent existence or being of such past events depend solely thereafter upon their being remembered? Virtually every instance of forgetting discussed above—and in particular, the strategies of forgetting pursued by the tyrant—presuppose that, so far as the past is concerned, to be is nothing more or less than to be remembered. Thus it seems possible in principle for events literally to be erased from history by bringing about a complete failure of collective memory.

But can it be true that the very existence of events in the past ceases-to-be, or that past events somehow lose the ontological determinateness they once possessed, when they are totally forgotten? And if so, by what means are they recollected—as dead, gone, and forgotten events sometimes seem to be?

These questions represent more merely than idle philosophical curiosity. Something about our commonly-held views of the past makes it conceivable to the tyrant that a forgetting of history is possible, that the past can be undone and cast into oblivion. Kundera suggests, in fact, that actual loss of the past is possible partly because of the sheer welter of detail, the relentless and oppressive weight of subsequent events crowding out the prior ones, perhaps aided by weariness, complacency, or despair. He writes:

> The bloody massacre in Bangladesh quickly covered over the memory of the Russian invasion of Czechoslovakia, the assassination of [Chilean Marxist President Salvadore] Allende drowned out the groans of Bangladesh, the war in the Sinai Desert made people forget Allende, the Cambodian massacre made people forget Sinai, and so on and so forth *until ultimately everyone lets everything be forgotten.*[12]

Something about historical recollection, however, calls this common presupposition into question: the past is not merely memory

---

12. Kundera, p. 7; my emphasis.

and interpretation, nor does the being or actuality of past events depend solely upon their being remembered. Rather, the past itself may comprise something else, something external to conscious acts of memory, as well as something beyond the kin of deliberate or unconscious acts of forgetting. The past, in and for itself, consists of a set of what the British-American philosopher, Alfred North Whitehead, called "stubborn, irreducible facts"—determinate, fixed episodes of experience-that-was, each of which is itself unaltered by inclusion or omission in subsequent episodes of experience. In that ontological sense, every past event possesses an internal integrity, a being which is beyond any subsequent act of forgetting—be it loss of memory, suppression, or distortion—to erase. In that case, we would be forced to conclude that this ontological past must itself reside somewhere, so as to be capable of being recollected. The moral rectification of the tragic effects of tyranny, cited above, seems to necessitate or legitimate this odd metaphysical view of the ongoing existence of an unalterable past as a kind of meta-archival record of events 'as-they-were-in-and-for-themselves,' as a kind of Kantian *Ding-an-sich*, providing an objective ground or warrant for our knowledge and our memories.

A distinguished American Hegel scholar, George L. Kline, employs insights drawn from his study of both Hegel and Whitehead to argue that we must distinguish between the being and the meaning of the past.[13] The being of the past—what past events were in and for themselves—is fixed, determinate, and unaffected by inclusion or exclusion in subsequent events. By contrast, Kline argues, the meaning of the past—that is, the myriad ways in which a past event can be included (or excluded) in a subsequent event—is never fixed, never finished, and always, in principle, open to subsequent reinterpretation. Meaning is always (in Heidegger's phrase) "on the way." Illustrating the complexity and importance of this subtle distinction, Kline writes:

> I do not deny that there are cases—especially those which bear significantly on the history of human culture—in which the relation between the being and the meaning of past events is complex and even opaque. For example, a day, a year, or even half-a-dozen years after the births—on particular days in 1265, 1756, and 1879— of Dante, Mozart, and Albert Einstein, respectively, it would *not*

---

13. "Form, Concrescence, and Concretum," *Explorations in Whitehead's Philosophy*, eds. Lewis S. Ford and George L. Kline (Bronx, NY: Fordham University Press, 1983), pp. 104–146; and "'Present', 'Past', and 'Future' as Categoreal Terms, and the 'Fallacy of the Actual Future'," *The Review of Metaphysics*, 40 (1986), 215–235.

have been possible to state that the author of the *Divine Comedy* (or even "a great poet," or even "a poet"), or the composer of *The Magic Flute*, or the formulator of the Special Theory of Relativity had been born on those particular days. The *being* of these recently past or "ex-" events did not yet have the meaning which they later came to have. One could say only that male infants of a certain description had been born in such-and-such places, of such-and-such parents, etc.

The *meaning* of all such cultural events is cumulative and slow to emerge, requiring decades in ordinary cases and centuries in extraordinary ones. In a sense, it is never completed: there is no end to the valuing "up" and the valuing "down" of the contributions to human civilization even of such geniuses as the three just named. But the *being* of ex-events such as these three births, I insist, is not affected by accretions, erosions, or other changes in their *meaning* (evaluation, interpretation).[14]

This philosophical *aporia* regarding the ontological status of the past thus presents us with two clearly distinct alternatives. (1) The past is ontologically grounded, as symbolized but not limited to the examples of archives and artifacts that persist independent of conscious acts and are available and amenable to subsequent recollections and reinterpretations. The past consists of determinate and fixed events-that-once-were, each of which has its being, its facticity *an und für sich*, regardless of our subsequent conscious memories of it. Our interpretations of the past affect us, but are utterly powerless to affect it. We cannot go back in time and unmake, or remake, what once was and ever shall be, world without end.

(2) In decided contrast, the past consists of nothing more or less than our collective memories in the present of earlier events. Those events themselves, in Whitehead's technical metaphysical terminology,

---

14. "Form, Concrescence, and Concretum," p. 131. This discussion does not appear in an earlier version of this essay, published in the *Southern Journal of Philosophy*, 7 (1969–70), 351–360. In the subsequent paper, the text of Kline's Presidential Address to the Metaphysical Society of America in 1986, Isaac Newton, Jane Austen, and Igor Stravinsky are substituted for Dante, Mozart, and Einstein in the present quote. There Kline concludes: "Clearly, the meaning of past existents within the history of human civilization is cumulative and slow to emerge, requiring decades in ordinary cases and centuries in extraordinary ones. Strictly speaking, it is *never* completed; the reinterpretation and reassessment, the *Verwertung* and *Entwertung*, of the contributions to human civilization of even such geniuses as the three here named is a continuing and unending process. Still, the *being* of such past existents as those three births, at given times and places, is *not* modified by changes in their *meanings*." (Cf. "Present, Past, and Future as Categoreal Terms," p. 223).

"perish;"[15] they live, then die, and once dead are themselves gone forever, except as their determinate outcome is included as a datum in some subsequent act of memory and recollection. The past thus exists only as memory. When recollection fades or ceases, then past events pass utterly into oblivion and are forgotten forever.

If the first alternative is correct, then the tyrant's strategy of forgetfulness is conceptually flawed in principle, and rests upon a mistake. Memory can be managed, but the past is always available independently somewhere for recollection. The past persists, somehow, somewhere, awaiting full disclosure.

If, by contrast, the second alternative is correct, then the tyrant's ploy is foiled only by contingent circumstances: by a failure of effort, a lack of thoroughness, or perhaps just plain bad luck. But the tyrant's ploy is not flawed in principle; indeed, it is always in danger of succeeding. We are thus perpetually haunted by the ever-present danger of becoming, in Kundera's phrase, "a people without a name."

The Hiding Places of Memory

Toward the end of his novel, Kundera has the heroine, Tamina, taken by a friend into the countryside, many miles from Prague. There, in a scene reminiscent of Proust, a walk on a muddy hillside awakens lost

---

15. Whitehead adopted a phrase from John Locke to describe time itself as "a perpetual perishing." The flux of experience which gives rise to temporal passage is quantized, according to Whitehead, into discrete episodes or distinct occasions of experience. Each such active episode or occasion eventuates in its own determinate result or outcome, after which its own, internal, self-constituting activity ceases.

On one interpretation of his Lockean variation, these "ex-events" or finished episodes then perish—that is, they pass out of existence altogether, into oblivion—except and unless they are "positively prehended" and included as data in the self-actualizing activity of some subsequent occasion of experience. Their ultimate loss to oblivion is also prevented by their being caught up as an element in the ongoing divine experience—what Whitehead terms "the Consequent Nature" of God.

On another interpretation, held by Professor Kline, myself, and some others, the perishing of these past or ex-events [Kline defines these as "concreta"] does not entail their utter loss to oblivion. Rather, their objectified determinateness or being persists indefinitely as potential data for subsequent (future) acts of becoming. This latter interpretation offers, to my mind, a more satisfactory account of Whitehead's central notion of causality and "causal efficacy" as the ground of experience, avoids the reliance on a *deus ex machina* to account for the persistence of the past, and yields a more nuanced meaning to Whitehead's oft-quoted Principle of Process, that "being is *constituted by* becoming" (Alfred North Whitehead, *Process and Reality*, Corrected Edition, eds. David Ray Griffin and Donald W. Sherburne [New York: The Free Press, 1978], p. 23).

memories of a similar walk taken with her husband, whose death she now grieves.

> Yes! Yes! Now she understood. Finally! We will never remember anything by sitting in one place waiting for the memories to come back to us of their own accord! Memories are scattered all over the world. We must travel if we want to find them *and flush them out from their hiding places*![16]

Where do memories hide? In this sense, the observation of Hegel about forgetting in history which prompted this examination has a venerable history. From its very beginnings, philosophy has concerned itself centrally with the problem of recollection and forgetting. The ancient Pythagoreans engaged in daily rituals of recollection, believing that by developing a perfect capacity to hold everything in mind all at once, they would thereby attain immortality. The "Myth of Er" in Plato's *Republic* describes forgetting or a sense of forgetfulness as endemic to the human condition. The philosopher is one who responds to that absence, recognizing and lamenting this perceived loss, and willing to spend a lifetime in the quest to recover those lost, primordial memories. Heidegger described the whole of Western culture as *Seinsvergessenheit*, the forgetfulness of Being, and set himself the task of recollecting, behind centuries of tradition, custom, and linguistic practice, the unmediated acquaintance with Being that humankind once possessed, but has now lost. For Augustine and for Whitehead, perfect recollection and the overcoming of forgetfulness—and, for Whitehead, the final achievement of the Pythagorean's objective immortality— are finally attained in an ongoing act of divine recollection. God, Whitehead writes movingly, "is the poet of the world . . . sav[ing] the world as it passes into the immediacy of his own life [as] the judgment of a tenderness which loses nothing that can be saved."[17]

Hegel, as we noted, figures prominently in this Western philosophical preoccupation with the problem of forgetting and recollection. Like Plato before and Heidegger after, we observe in the *Phenomenology* that loss, absence, and the sense of something missing or incomplete impels consciousness on its historical journey—on what Hegel, in the Preface to this great work, dramatically terms "its highway of despair."

The cessation of suffering, the metaphorical end of consciousness's journey on this historical highway, the rectification of injustice, by contrast, lie in recollection. At the conclusion of the *Phenomenology*—

---

16. Kundera, p. 167.
17. Whitehead, *Process and Reality*, Corrected Edition, p. 346.

on its final page, in fact—Hegel suggests that philosophical wisdom lies less in the attainment of some new, undiscovered truth than in the recollection and full retention of all that consciousness has already learned—like the ancient Pythagoreans, holding the Whole all together simultaneously. This full internalization of what Hegel terms philosophical or comprehended history is characterized, in an interesting and poignant metaphor, as "the Calvary of absolute Spirit"—an image of an end that is also a beginning, of suffering that is also triumph through suffering.[18]

The recent confessions and acknowledgements of Japanese war crimes, delving the depths of Stalinist terror in the newly-accessible archives of the former Soviet Union, and the opening of the United States Holocaust Museum in Washington, DC in 1993, all likewise signify that historical recollection—recovering, retaining, and reweaving what was forgotten, suppressed, and distorted by the tyrant into a full and complete narrative of the present—alone can bring us to closure, to reconciliation, and to some measure of peace with ourselves. All of these memorial events are instances of moral closure, of ends that are simultaneously beginnings, of narrations of suffering, the final and full narration of which is simultaneously a triumph over suffering. Our earlier awareness of absence, of loss, of incompleteness, even in the absence of a full knowledge of the forgotten details, is what prompts and prods historical consciousness, in these instances, not to rest, not to remain content with indifference and forgetting, but to press on along the highway of despair toward a full understanding of what actually occurred and why.

The very sense of absence that partial forgetting engenders—that gap or space in the airbrushed image of our collective experience— seems to guarantee the final triumph of recollection over forgetting. This absence, this sense of loss or incompleteness, awakens in us the discomfort that Plato characterized as *eros,* the desire to know, to recover that which was lost. It is almost as if a society or culture functions like a vast analogue of a Freudian personality in such instances: its memories of trauma and tragedy having been forcibly suppressed or repressed, the society itself suffers the kind of widespread malaise: the psychological disorientation and disorder that Kundera so masterfully narrates in his native Czechoslovakia. Like an individual patient in psychoanalysis, moreover, the social malaise can only be set right by a full and therapeutic recollection of, and by a coming to terms

---

18. Cf. *Hegel's Phenomenology, loc. cit.,* pp. 492–493; see also Donald Phillip Verene, *Hegel's Recollection* (Albany, NY: The State University of New York Press, 1985), pp. 111–114.

with, the original tragedy or trauma. The loss of memory amounts to a loss of self; and these lost or partial selves, like Kundera's Tamina or Plato's philosopher, wander the earth in search of the hiding places of memory.

Of the two alternative accounts of the ontological status of the past that I outlined above, the first alternative represents a commitment to a form of historical realism, delineating an ontologically independent past—a meta-archival, objective record independent from memory. Certainly the enormity, the monstrosity, the sheer extensiveness of the crimes committed in the German-Jewish Holocaust, in the Stalinist Great Terror, in "the deportation of a million Lithuanians, the murder of hundreds of thousands of Poles, the liquidation of the Crimean Tartars" insures somehow that these events "will remain in our memory" even when no photographs or records any longer exist, and even though the State subsequently proclaims the events themselves "a fabrication."[19] Here the tyrant's ploy fails in circumstance because the massiveness of the events, and the psychological weight of their memory, is simply too vast and extensive to obliterate.

Novelists like Kundera and George Orwell, strangely enough, seem committed to the second alternative account of the past. In denouncing tyranny, they seem nevertheless to grant the tyrant's implicit premise that the past consists entirely in what is encompassed within conscious memories in the present. Thus, if it is possible to impede the recollection of certain events so that historical interpretation is ever thereafter impoverished by their absence, then forgetting triumphs. Tyrants may well succeed in their desire, as Kundera characterizes it, to be "masters of the future in order to change the past."

Yet, as we noted in the previous section, the physical or material rooting or grounding of life-experiences in some sort of permanent historical record is not merely a matter of size and magnitude, but of fundamental metaphysical principle. It is recollection of the ordinary and of the limited—and likewise, the failure of forgetting even in these instances where it should practically succeed—that supports the first alternative of an ontologically-grounded past, independent of memory and interpretation.[20]

---

19. The phrases in quotation are from Milan Kundera, *The Unbearable Lightness of Being*, trans. Michael Henry Heim (London: Faber & Faber, 1984), p. 67.

20. Kline cites this problematic character of his stubborn distinction between the being and the meaning of the past in his Presidential Address for the Metaphysical Society of America: "I recognize that this distinction, and this claim, generate theoretical difficulties. One of these is the risk of reducing the *being* of the past, in its immunity to present changes in the *meaning* of that past (as one historical present after another

In defense of that first alternative, I maintain that we can give a straightforward account of the existence of an ontologically distinct past, immune from the mutability of Orwellian tyrants and postmodern historical-hermeneutical constructivists, and preserve intact the complete meta-archive of our collective experience, including the ordinary and the mundane, as well as the world-historical. Moreover, such an account need not rely on implausible claims regarding other possible worlds, such as a realm of the Forms or a distinct repository of the past; neither do I rely in this account on the *deus ex machina* of an Augustinian divine mind or a Whiteheadian "Consequent Nature of God" as perfect knowers. If one desires to fasten upon analogues and antecedents of the view I shall adumbrate, I would suggest—in addition to Hegel and Whitehead, already cited—the "holy and despised" Spinoza, or perhaps the Bergson of *Matter and Memory*.

The key to our dilemma is to recognize, not merely that past events never cease to exist, but that they never cease to be with us as material ingredients in the present. In memory, there is the act of remembering, and the thing remembered, as in perception there is an act of perception and the object or content of that perception, the thing perceived. Neither thing ceases to be, simply because of a subsequent failure to include it in a memory or perception.

Against an earlier generation of scientific, methodological hermeneuticists who thought of the past as something incredibly distant and alien that we had to de-mythologize and think our way back into, Hans-Georg Gadamer objected that the past is not to be thought of as something distant, alien, and separated by a vast gulf of time and incommensurability. Rather, in language reminiscent of Whitehead's account of repetition and prehension of every aspect of the past in each element of the present, Gadamer maintained that the past is what is handed down to us, it is literally in the present,

---

values the past "up" or "down"), to a kind of historical analogue of the Kantian *Ding an sich*, unknowable to such finite and fallible knowers as ourselves, although "there" to be known in fine detail by a Perfect Knower. Still, it seems to me that to give up this distinction and this claim is to run the greater risk of lapsing into a kind of historical *constructivism* which, in the end reduces the historical past to an artifact and instrument of each successive historical present. Such a reduction and such instrumentalizing carry with them not only theoretical difficulties of their own but moral and political risks which I find unacceptable" ("Present, Past, and Future," p. 223).

Agreeing fundamentally with Kline's position, I am trying in the present essay to offer a detailed account of the theoretical difficulties of the constructivist position, while giving an account of the 'where' of Kline's 'there' of the past-in-itself, which I will hold to be knowable in principle by less-than-perfect knowers like ourselves, without relying on the *deus ex machina* of divine memory, as in Augustine and Whitehead.

with us now.[21] This, in turn, is an interesting restatement of the Hegelian philosopher R. G. Collingwood's principle of the "insuscitation" of the past in the present.[22] The past, according to these thinkers, is the material ground, and its 'ex-events' are the ingredients, of present experience. Our problem of forgetfulness in the present is thus not an utter loss to oblivion of what once was, but rather, an inability to recognize and to decipher or interpret the past in our midst.

But just what is this material past that persists in our midst in the present? Physicists now routinely remind us that each one of us contains within our own bodies quite a large number of atoms and elementary particles—stardust, if you will—left over from the primordial cosmic Big Bang. The effects of this primordial event are evident in the present in many other ways—in, for example, the universal background radiation at a temperature of 3° Kelgrade that pervades the known universe. Radio astronomers recently mapped this radiation, creating what they describe as a pattern of ripples in the space-time fabric left over from that primordial generative event, billions of years ago.[23] The cosmos itself is thus literally a vast memory of the details of the event of its own genesis. The very physical details of this cosmic history are woven indelibly into the present fabric of the universe.

There is, for the physicist and the astronomer, no vexed metaphysical or ontological question concerning the whereabouts of this determinate past. That past is present; it is in the present, and it constitutes the present as the material cause of the present. Our cosmic past has always been with us, and indeed, has always been us: presumably, Socrates and Phaedrus gazed out wonderingly at the same heavens with the same background radiation as do we now, and their bodies were likewise presumably composed of the same percentage of stardust as are ours. We have, however, only comparatively recently recognized the presence of this past within us, and even more recently begun to learn how to read and to decipher these texts. Bergson, in *Matter and Memory*, was fundamentally on the right

---

21. Gadamer refers to this feature of the past and of our interpretation of it as "phenomenological immanence;" see the Foreword to the Second Edition of *Truth and Method*, trans. J. Weinsheimer and D. G. Marshall (New York: Continuum, 1993), p. xxxvi; also pp. 264–265.

22. Collingwood, *The Idea of History* (Oxford: Oxford University Press, 1946); see also *An Autobiography* (Oxford: Oxford University Press, 1939).

23. Interviewed at length on this discovery in the *Chronicle of Higher Education* in 1992, the chief astronomer of the project described his computer-generated "photograph" of these space-time ripples (somewhat hyperbolically) as akin to "gazing upon the face of God."

track:[24] matter is in truth a kind of vast hologram, enfolding the details of its own past; the very physical stuff that we are and that surrounds us is nothing more or less than a record of its—and of our—past.

The being of our determinate physical past, the narration of our origins, is thus now, and always has been, present, determinate, and ready-to-hand. That presence has, until comparatively recently, gone unrecognized. Once recognized, moreover, the meaning of that past is still unclear. What is clear is that the physicist and the astronomer have become, in this case, historians, working to uncover and to provide interpretations, narrations, of that cosmic past.[25]

It is likewise with our biological and cultural past. We do not for a moment doubt that we had human ancestors long before the dawn of written records. Indeed, quest for greater knowledge of ancient peoples—of their lives, of the rise and fall of their civilizations—constitutes the principal focus of research in physical anthropology and paleolithic archaeology. The memory of their names, if they had names, and the details of their lives, are largely lost to us, forgotten to consciousness. Yet we do not doubt that these people without a name once existed, nor can we reasonably doubt that their lives and experiences had as much determinateness and authenticity for them as do our own for us. They live in our present consciousness more in imagination than in conscious memory. But that does not imply that they themselves were fictitious, or that their former being is in any way altered by our inability to recollect and to interpret their lives.

In fact, we have discovered only recently that these people without a name dwell in our midst in the present more readily than any of us might have imagined possible only decades ago. Genetic biologists inform us that, alongside the physicist's stardust, we carry the living biological material, the genetic inheritance, of these ancient peoples and their civilizations. Anthropologists remind us, in addition, that our gait and gestures—raised eyebrows, smiles, salutes, and handshakes—enfold millennia of cultural history stretching back into prehistoric

---

24. Henri Bergson, *Matter and Memory*, trans. N. Paul and W. S. Palmer (New York: Macmillan, 1911), ch. IV: matter and mind are both forms of duration; matter is in fact wave-like, consisting of pulses of energy of extreme brevity, bound together by a thread of memory. This corresponds to Whitehead's notion of an enduring object, constituted of serial societies of actual entities, each inheriting from its predecessors a common element of subjective form. This "serial inheritance" corresponds to what Bergson means, and what is meant in the present essay, by physical memory.

25. It is thus no accident that Professor Stephen Hawking of Cambridge University entitles his widely-read, popular, and highly speculative account of mathematical astrophysics, *A Brief History of Time* (Cambridge: Cambridge University Press, 1989).

antiquity. The past is biologically and culturally, as well as physically, present in our midst.

We ourselves are thus constituted out of the 'legible texts' of those nameless ancestors. Those temporally distant events, and those ancient peoples are within each one of us; we are literally as well as metaphorically constituted (or, more accurately, reconstituted) out of their previous lives and experiences. As we are, each one of us, physically constituted out of the first galactic stars, so each of us carries within us a genetic code which is a complete historical text, describing in minute detail every previous connection of ourselves to one another and to those who have gone before us, down to the distant beginnings of time itself. Once more, this physical fact about what we are did not begin to be the case yesterday; rather, persons (and objects and states of affairs) in the world have always been thus constituted. The new development is that we have begun to recognize the presence of the being of the past in our midst only during the last few decades. And, once again, we are far from knowing how to read these texts fully and accurately in their entirety. But were we able—and indeed, insofar as we are becoming increasingly able—to read them, we could recover the details of those ancient prehistoric lives as reliably as we now infer the details of more recent cultures and peoples from the written texts and material cultural artifacts they have bequeathed us.

In the case of primordial pre-history, the genetic biologist, the physical anthropologist, and the archaeologist must serve as our historians, attempting to recollect and interpret what has always been present within us and among us, even though unrecognized, unnamed, and unknown. Every bit as much as the more conventional historians, these scholars are engaged in revealing (in Willa Cather's beautiful phrase) how "we possess together the precious, the incommunicable past."[26]

Hegel's concluding observations on History at the very end of the *Phenomenology* are thus far more accurate in every literal sense than even he himself could have imagined:

> *History* is a *conscious* self-*mediating* process—Spirit emptied out into Time . . . [History] presents itself as a slow-moving succession of Spirits, a gallery of images, each of which, endowed with all the riches of Spirit, moves thus slowly just because the Self has to penetrate and digest this entire wealth of its substance. As its fulfilment consists in perfectly *knowing* what *it is*, in knowing its substance, this knowing is its *withdrawal into itself* in which it

---

26. This phrase is the concluding line from Ms. Cather's famous novel, *My Ántonia* (Boston: Houghton Mifflin Co., 1918).

abandons its outer existence and gives its existential shape over to recollection . . . [which is] the *Er-innerung* [the *inward-izing*] of that experience.[27]

The past has its being in the present; it is not located in some mysterious elsewhere, or solely in the Mind or in the Consequent Nature of God. Rather, the past is with us, and is us, in the present. We cannot say and as yet we do not know what other artifacts from the past are present among us—a "succession of Spirits" from the past which are ready-to-hand, whose presence we do not yet recognize, and whose historical texts we do not begin to comprehend. This much, however, we can safely conclude: the past is not merely our legacy, one prized possession among many belongings. Instead, the past is the cumulative totality of Being itself. It is all that endures, and all that matters. The past is all we have, and it is literally what we are in the present.

---

27. *Hegel's Phenomenology of Spirit*, p. 492.

7 Hegel and the Social Function of Reason

Tom Rockmore

I t is hard to think of any philosophical issue more important or less discussed than the social function of philosophy. Although Hegel has often been held to change his view in a way that invites criticism of his later understanding of the relation of philosophical theory to practice, this issue is rarely examined. I will show that his view of this theme remains constant early and late, and the criticisms raised against it are misguided.

Is Philosophy Useful?

Philosophers, who routinely focus on the most minute concerns, most of which are interesting to no more than a small group of other philosophers, but not to the general public, rarely devote any sustained attention to the wider utility of what they do. Yet philosophers build no bridges, bake no bread, and do not cure the sick, or even provide services to the halt, the lame, and the blind. Despite claims to the contrary, it is not obvious that philosophy is intrinsically worthwhile. It is not obvious that philosophy does more than respond to a sense of wonder, or that, if this is what philosophy does, that it is socially important to do so.

The general theme of the social function of philosophy has been under desultory debate for many centuries, at least since Socrates claimed that the unexamined life is not worth living. But we do not seem to be any closer to a consensus about how philosophy relates to society. Whereas it once seemed obvious that philosophy was central to society, according to Plato the condition of the good life, that idea no longer seems obvious at all. The rather dismal performance of some well-known philosophers in this century calls into question the very idea that philosophy has privileged access to truth and casts doubt on the proverbially unshakeable link between knowing the truth and doing the good.

Arguments supporting a positive reading of the utility of philosophy are mainly lacking. Hegel also makes a version of this familiar claim, although in a weaker form. The question we will be concerned with here is simple enough, although it is anything but simple to respond to: what does Hegel contribute to the idea of the social relevance of philosophy? In particular, we will want to determine not only what Hegel claims on behalf of philosophy, but also what resources can be marshalled to defend his analysis. I will argue that both Hegel's understanding of the social function of reason and the main objections against it can be understood against the background of Kant's theory, and further argue that, on a reasonable interpretation, Hegel's view successfully answers its critics in surpassing the critical philosophy.

Philosophers have never been shy about making claims for the usefulness of what they do. The theme of the social utility of philosophy is constantly invoked, but often in a confused, unsupported, even dogmatic way, such as through the supposed link between reason regarded as socially useful and philosophy regarded as the highest form of reason. If this link holds, then philosophy is supremely useful, even indispensable. An example is the later Heidegger's inconsistent assertion that what he calls thinking, as distinguished from philosophy, is not practically relevant but that being, the theme with which it wrestles, directly engages the future of all humanity.[1] There is an obvious inconsistency between the modest quietism of his claim for thinking beyond philosophy and the rather less modest, in fact immodest claim for the importance of the topic.

Heidegger's later view provides a straightforward, but wholly unsupported reformulation of the traditional philosophical conviction of its importance for the good life. His claim, although clear, is clearly not accompanied by any argument. It is as if it were self-evident, as Plato

---

1. Martin Heidegger, *Basic Writings,* trans. David Farrell Krell (New York: Harper and Row, 1977), p. 240.

seemed to think, that philosophy is the highest, most useful pursuit. Yet some two and a half millennia later, what once seemed obvious, and what to Heidegger may still have seemed so, is not likely to win general assent without discussion, perhaps not even likely to do so after discussion. Certainly, few observers are now willing to grant Heidegger's contention that the problem of being that apparently led Heidegger to turn to National Socialism is central for human being.

Heidegger may have overestimated the importance of his preoccupation with being for human being. His conflation of what he believes is philosophically important with what is important for all people is not an isolated phenomenon. Yet it is typical of philosophers who tend to take themselves and their concerns all too seriously, as if the whole future of the human race depended on them, in Heidegger's case on correcting a wrong turn on the high road to being a couple of thousand years ago. Others, including some philosophers and many non-philosophers, think this is a vast exaggeration that requires discussion and demonstration. Philosophy may once straightforwardly have seemed indispensable, although we recall that Socrates was continually put in the position of needing to argue for this point. But the period in which this argument seemed intuitively plausible is now past.

We now live in a period when philosophy seems less than indispensable, not only to others, but even to philosophers; and what philosophers do fails to inspire confidence in their wisdom or insight. There is widespread scepticism, not about knowledge per se, but about the uses of philosophy. The premature conclusion of the Young Hegelians that philosophy had reached an end made such important later thinkers as Kierkegaard, Marx, and Nietzsche understandably reluctant to refer to their own theories as philosophy. For the same reason, distinguishing between philosophy and science, Marxists depicted Marxism as science and endeavored to resolve the unresolved and philosophically unresolvable issues through Marxist science.

A variant of the view that philosophy is no longer useful appears in analytic philosophy in at least four ways. One is the view associated with the early Wittgenstein that the resolution of philosophical problems is philosophically interesting only, but rather uninteresting for everyone else since there is no practical payoff.[2] Then there is the scientistic conviction of the Vienna Circle thinkers that truth can only come from natural science and, for that reason, philosophy has no

---

2. See Ludwig Wittgenstein, *Tractatus Logico-Philosophicus*, trans. D. F. Pears and B. F. McGuinness (London and New York: Routledge and Kegan Paul, and Humanities, 1963), proposition 6.52, pp. 148–149.

other legitimate role than as philosophy of science. From another angle of vision, Whitehead defends a related view in his conception of philosophy as the critique of scientific abstractions. Yet these thinkers at least held that the logical empiricism they favored was socially progressive, in tune with historical progress. Third is the view of contemporary analytical thinkers who have been turning in record numbers to such fields as biomedical ethics to recover content, in order to give meaning to philosophy that, when it takes the form of mere technique, as has increasingly happened in analytical philosophy,[3] loses its human interest. Finally, there are the others, not all of whom are concerned with issues of social relevance, who, apparently convinced that analytical philosophy, which has dominated the philosophical thought of this entire century, is finally on the decline, have been turning to pragmatism in record numbers, including Rorty, Putnam, Quine, perhaps Davidson, and so on.

Rorty provides a special case if only because his stance, like that of Heidegger, one of his intellectual heroes, is so inconsistent. Like Heidegger, he combines at least a continued verbal concern with social relevance with a supposed turn away from philosophy. His initial willingness to take the linguistic turn[4] eventually led to the conclusion that if analytical foundationalism fails, as he argues, then philosophy fails and only edifying conversation remains.[5] His later effort to draw the consequences of that view,[6] in particular his more recent concern with what he calls liberal irony, is a clear effort to determine a useful role for such conversation.[7] Yet it is unclear why the mere concern with suffering, or the willingness to discuss it, should be regarded as contributing to its alleviation. We are right to be skeptical about the practical consequences of Rorty's version of the utility of reason in an extraphilosophical setting.

Skepticism about the practical usefulness of philosophy further follows from the actions of its practitioners. The view that philosophy is peculiarly useful, even indispensable to discern reality and guide our actions is threatened by the ways philosophers tend to act, particularly

---

3. William Barrett, *Illusion of Technique: A Search for Meaning in a Technological Civilization* (Garden City: Anchor, 1978).

4. Richard Rorty, *The Linguistic Turn: Recent Essays in Philosophical Method* (Chicago: University of Chicago Press, 1967).

5. Richard Rorty, *Philosophy and the Mirror of Nature* (Princeton: Princeton University Press, 1979).

6. Richard Rorty, *Consequences of Pragmatism* (Minneapolis: University of Minnesota Press, 1982).

7. Richard Rorty, *Contingency, Irony and Solidarity* (Cambridge: Cambridge University Press, 1989).

recently. It is pretty obvious that philosophers have rarely been true to their self-described calling to examine and to defend reason. The philosophical record in our time tends to confirm the suspicion that philosophy is irrelevant or worse. When faced with the rise of National Socialism, Husserl's call to defend reason may appear inadequate, even a typical intellectual misunderstanding of the gravity of the situation that seemed beyond all reason.[8] But in his appeal to independent reason, Husserl is light years ahead of Heidegger's identification with Nazism,[9] and Lukács's with Stalinism, without even considering the sordid actions of such more minor figures as Paul de Man.[10] It should be a sobering thought that during the dark years of National Socialism there was no organized philosophical protest at all.[11] It is significant that the Nazis, who dealt with their opponents in the harshest way, rarely needed to turn against philosophers. Astonishingly, only a single philosopher, Kurt Huber, lost his life for actions undertaken against Nazism that were directly related to philosophy.[12]

Philosophy's View of Itself

If doubts are widespread about the social role of philosophy or about why so many philosophers have behaved badly, it doesn't follow that philosophy itself is socially useless. Perhaps philosophers have simply been unequal to the demands of their calling, unable or unwilling to respond to the commands of reason. If that is the case, then philosophers but not philosophy itself are at fault.

The belief that philosophy is socially relevant is solidly rooted in the philosophical tradition. Historically, the conviction that philosophy can and in fact does play an important social role is linked to the philosophical concern with knowledge. Socrates's reported insistence that the unexamined life is not worth living was immediately transformed into the Platonic claim that philosophy is a necessary condition of the good life. This claim has had a long but checkered

---

8. Edmund Husserl, *The Crisis of European Sciences and Transcendental Phenomenology*, trans. David Carr (Evanston: Northwestern University Press, 1970).

9. Tom Rockmore, *On Heidegger's Nazism and Philosophy* (Berkeley: University of California Press, 1992).

10. Tom Rockmore, "Philosophy, Literature, and Intellectual Responsibility," *American Philosophical Quarterly*, vol. 30, no. 2, April 1993, pp. 109–122.

11. George Leaman, *Heidegger im Kontext, Gesamtüberblick zum NS-Engagement der Universitätsphilosophen* (Hamburg: Argument Verlag, 1993).

12. Ibid.

career in later thought, where it has been restated by numerous philosophers, in our time perhaps most prominently by Husserl and
Habermas.[13] They are representative of the widespread but widely
unexamined conviction among philosophers over centuries, characteristic of the Platonic tradition, that philosophy is the only source of
knowledge in the full sense, and that such knowledge is socially useful,
even socially indispensable.

Since neither of these points is obviously true, each requires
discussion. Philosophers have traditionally devoted more attention to
making out the claims for knowledge than to examining the suggestion
that philosophical knowledge is indispensable or even necessarily useful. The treatment of the Cartesian theory is a good example. The
debate about the theory of knowledge is the major theme in modern
philosophy at least since the seventeenth century. For the most part,
this discussion has focused on Descartes's foundationalist strategy, the
preferred philosophical approach to knowledge in modern times. Generations of philosophers have scrutinized the perceived consequences
of the Cartesian epistemology and its alternatives.

Like many other philosophers, Descartes takes a quietistic perspective on society. He explicitly maintains that it is better to change
oneself than fortune, although he also insists on the limitless social
utility of his perspective.[14] He famously devotes careful attention to
making out his claim for knowledge. But he makes no or almost no
effort to argue for its social utility, something that he takes as a given.
So far as I know, this aspect of his theory has also not attracted
sustained attention in the large Descartes literature.

In this respect, Descartes is typical of the assumption for the
social relevance of philosophy that is less often discussed than assumed, and mainly discussed through the effort to demonstrate that
philosophy is the source of knowledge whose utility is intuitively obvious.
The generally critical reception reserved for the Cartesian claim to
know and the generally uncritical acceptance of his idea of the usefulness of his discussion illustrate the modern disinclination to provide
careful examination of assertions for the relation of philosophy to
society. Few writers devote sustained attention to working out the link
between philosophy and society. Even fewer of the claims are scruti-

---

13. Tom Rockmore, "Penelope's Web: Reconstruction and the Relevance of Reason," *Journal of Speculative Philosophy*, vol. 7, no. 2, 1993.

14. In a gloss on his method, Descartes claims that through its proper application
there is nothing so remote that it cannot be discovered. See *The Philosophical Works of
Descartes*, trans. Elizabeth S. Haldane and G. R. T. Ross (New York: Cambridge University
Press, 1970), I, pp. 47, 92.

nized in the discussion. Yet this is not the case for Hegel, whose understanding of knowledge is rarely discussed but whose view of the social utility of philosophy has attracted criticism that is not always founded on a secure knowledge of his thought.

The Kantian Background

Hegel's view of the social utility of philosophy can be regarded as an effort to think the Copernican Revolution through to the end from a perspective arising after the French Revolution. Similarly, his view of the social utility of philosophy can be regarded as a response to the claims of the Kantian theory. Many philosophers exhibit a variant of Descartes's disinclination toward political involvement. But a commitment to society, and to the social interest of philosophical reason, is a constant theme in the German tradition. Both Kant and Hegel think of philosophy as practical. Kant's view of the social utility of theory depends on an inconsistent reading of reason as both independent of and subordinate to practice, arising out of his reaction to the theories of Plato and Aristotle. With respect to the social use of theory, Hegel's reaction to Kant, and his own, rival conception, can be understood as a selective reading of one strand of Kant's theory against another.

The view of philosophy as a socially indispensable science goes all the way back in the tradition to Plato, who advanced this normative conception in the *Republic*, that great source book of Western philosophy. The well known Platonic understanding of philosophy amounts to the claim that pure theory is practical. This view attracted immediate resistance. Aristotle, his most famous pupil, quickly distinguished between pure and practical forms of reason in order to draw a completely different conclusion. He clearly insisted that pure theory, or knowledge of the unchanging, is without practical relevance.[15] According to Aristotle, only practical theory, which provides merely approximate knowledge about the world in which we live, what Plato stigmatized as the grasp of the despised *doxa*, is practically relevant or socially useful.

The dispute between Plato and Aristotle with respect to the social utility of philosophy is only the first installment in a debate about the relation of theory and practice that traverses later philosophy and that is still with us. In the German tradition, this dispute takes the form of an ongoing effort to understand the relation of philosophy to society

---

15. Aristotle, Metaphysics 982 b 27–28, in *The Complete Works of Aristotle*, ed. Jonathan Barnes (Princeton: Prineton University Press, 1984), II, p. 1555.

by subordinating theory to practice. This effort reaches its peak in Marx's "Theses on Feuerbach." Yet despite what Marxists may think, Marx neither invents nor discusses the issue of the social worth of theory for the first time, since this venerable concern reaches back into Greek antiquity.[16]

Like his entire critical philosophy, Kant's understanding of the relation of theory and practice lies at a crossroads of the modern discussion. It is both traditional, reformulated in ways consistent with his concerns about the main doctrines of the philosophical tradition, and profoundly innovative. One of Kant's innovations is his steady concern with human being. Descartes, it is well known, defends a passive, spectator theory of subjectivity. In ways consistent with his critical philosophy, Kant takes an anti-Cartesian, active view of human being. It is known that he lectured on anthropology for over twenty years.[17] In a letter from the critical period, he remarks that nothing is more useful than the problem of man if only progress can be made in this direction.[18] In his study of anthropology, he examines what man can make of himself.[19] In the *Critique of Pure Reason*, he famously describes three questions that circumscribe philosophy. In his study of logic, he adds a fourth question: what is man?[20]

Despite his interest in human being, Kant's understanding of the social use of theory is unsatisfactory. It inconsistently combines the traditional philosophical emphasis on theory as independent of, but indispensable for, practice with the nascent effort to subordinate theory to the practice it is intended to illuminate. The result is an unresolved tension, in Kant's language an antinomy, literally a violation of law, at the heart of his view.

On the one hand, Kant retains the traditional philosophical view that theory subsumes, or wholly includes, practice, as in Plato's conviction that the knowledge that allegedly only philosophers possess is socially indispensable. Kant argues in this way because of his belief in the necessary utility of theory as such, for instance in his conception of philosophy as a *conceptus cosmicus* necessarily interesting for all

---

16. Nicholas Lobkowicz, *Theory and Practice: History of a Concept from Aristotle to Marx* (Notre Dame: University of Notre Dame Press, 1967).

17. See his letter to Stäudlin, from 4 April 1793, in *Briefe von und an Kant*, in *Immanuel Kants Werke*, ed. Ernst Cassirer (Berlin: Bruno Cassirer, 1923), X, p. 205.

18. See his letter to J. S. Beck dated 27 October 1791, in *Kants Werke*, X, p. 98.

19. Immanuel Kant, *Anthropologie in pragmatischer Hinsicht*, in *Kant-Werke*, ed. Wilhelm Weischedel (Darmstadt: Wissenschaftliche Bibliothek, 1975), X.

20. *Kant's Introduction to Logic*, trans. Thomas Kingsmill Abbott (New York: Philosophical Library, 1963), p. 15.

mankind.[21] Kant's Platonic attitude is apparent in his argument, the basis of his moral theory, that what we should do can be determined on a wholly theoretical level. For Kant, the principle guiding any particular action must be derived from universal moral principles independent of any particular situation. The resorption of theory into practice that is the obvious result is clearly apparent in Kant's analysis of their relation, where he rebuts the very idea that theory could fail to be practical.[22]

This traditional approach to the relation of theory to practice is obviously unsatisfactory. Kant only claims to but does not demonstrate that theory is relevant since he fails to prove that an analysis meant for any and all situations is useful for any particular situation. Hegel correctly points out that the Kantian criterion of general law applies everywhere and nowhere.[23] He further points out that universal and binding principles cannot even be formulated without taking on the contingent aspect they refuse.

On the other hand, Kant's profoundly innovative, non-traditional side appears in his effort to subordinate theory to practice. Kant makes two successive efforts to think the primacy of practical over theoretical reason. To begin with, he subordinates pure reason to its practical counterpart on the grounds that all reason is ultimately practical and even speculative reason is complete only in its practical usage. The weakness of this solution is, as he notes, that although it enables us to understand the coexistence of both forms of reason within a single subject, we cannot understand how practical action is possible. As early as the first edition of the *Critique of Judgment*, Kant indicates that this solution is doomed to failure.[24] But in the second edition, he relates the two forms of reason through the newly introduced third faculty, or judgment. Here he shows that practice is independent of reason that in turn depends on it. This insight influences later German philosophy. Fichte, for instance, holds that the role of philosophy consists in the solution on the theoretical level of problems arising in the social context. This general attitude is obviously

---

21. Kant, *Critique of Pure Reason,* B 864, p. 655.

22. "On the Proverb: That May Be True in Theory But Is Of No Practical Use," in Immanuel Kant, *Perpetual Peace and Other Essays,* trans. Ted Humphrey (Indianapolis: Hackett, 1982), pp. 61–92.

23. G. W. F. Hegel, *The Phenomenology of Spirit,* trans. Arnold V. Miller (New York: Oxford University Press, 1977), p. 259.

24. Immanuel Kant, *Critique of Judgment,* trans. J. H. Bernard (New York: Hafner, 1951), Introduction, part III, pp. 12–15.

a later form of the Aristotelian assertion that theory is not independent of, but rather limited by, its object.

Kant's conception of the utility of reason is obviously contradictory. For it cannot be the case that theory contains practice and also depends on it. Although he is interested in human being, and concerned to relate theory to practice, his repeated efforts to analyze this link conflict among themselves. He fails to provide an acceptable analysis of the practical use of theory, or to justify the social utility of philosophy.

Hegel Elaborates Kant's View

Hegel shares Kant's conviction about the practical relevance of theory, a theme that concerns him throughout his career. This theme that looms large in his last book begins to emerge much earlier. It clearly has roots in his early, but quickly-tempered enthusiasm for the ideals of the French Revolution, quickly tempered by his criticism of its excesses, and in his early hopes, at a time when he was more sanguine than he was later about the prospects for social change, for a revolution of ideas in Germany. As a young man, he believed in the practical relevance of Kantian theory. He even seemed to anticipate a social revolution as a likely consequence of philosophical theory. In an important early letter to Schelling, detailing his philosophical hopes, written in April 1795, the young Hegel writes that "From the Kantian system and its highest completion I expect a revolution in Germany."[25] Some five years later, in another letter to Schelling, from November 1800, he couples his drive toward philosophical science in the form of system with the concern to intervene in the life of men.[26] This attitude raises two problems that can be formulated as questions: how does Hegel understand theory as practical? How does the view he later held, after becoming a famous philosopher in Berlin, relate to its initial formulation? The first question concerns the relation of theory to society, and the latter touches on the unity of his theory over time.

We have already noted that Kant has not one but two inconsistent ways of understanding the relevance of theory through his analysis of the relation of theory and practice. Hegel's understanding of the relevance of reason is closely linked to his selective reading of Kant. In

---

25. Letter to Schelling, dated 16 April 1795, in *Hegel: The Letters*, trans. Clark Butler and Christiane Seiler (Bloomington: Indiana University Press, 1984), p. 35.

26. Letter to Schelling, dated 2 November 1800, in Hegel, *The Letters*, pp. 64.

rough terms, he rejects the Kantian reformulation of the traditional, Platonic view that philosophical theory as such is practical in favor of the more innovative Kantian subordination of theory to practice. His own contribution can be regarded as an attempt to show how theory can be subordinate to but also influence practice, roughly the same problem that Marx later took up. We recall Marx's early concern to realize philosophy that he identified with the speculative philosophy of right, hence with Hegel's theory that, in his view, remained unrealized.[27]

Marx's conviction that Hegel's theory remains theoretical only, that it is finally impractical, reflects a widespread suspicion that, and despite his best efforts, Hegel's theory fails to grasp practice. According to this view, Hegel is no more successful than Kant in bringing theory into relation with practice, in demonstrating the social relevance of philosophy. No one denies Hegel's youthful interest in social change, although there is debate about whether it survived the later evolution of the theory. Hegel's critics argue that his conception of the relevance of philosophical reason was either incoherent, later became politically reactionary, or both. His theory, especially his later theory, has come under attack for tending to promote social stasis rather than social change when change is indicated. For such critics, Hegel's theory is part of the problem rather than part of the solution. Yet Hegel's understanding of the way reason relates to the social context derives from a view of reason that develops but otherwise remains constant in his theory early and late.

Hegel on the Social Utility of Philosophy

Hegel's conception of the social role of philosophy is both a constant concern in his writings and difficult to grasp. He frequently comments on the link between philosophy and society in a way that some have seen as problematic. The problem his remarks seems to raise is focused in two famous passages in his writings: a letter to Niethammer written immediately after the appearance of the *Phenomenology*, his first great work, and a passage in the preface to the *Philosophy of Right*, his last book. In the intervening period, and after publishing the *Phenomenology*, Hegel was obliged to leave the university because of his chronic lack of money and the closing of the University of Jena when the town

---

27. "The Critique of Hegel's Philosophy of Right: Introduction," in *Karl Marx: Early Writings*, trans. T. B. Bottomore (New York: McGraw-Hill, 1964), pp. 41–59.

was occupied by Napoleon's troops. After a period as editor of a local newspaper in Bamberg and director of a Gymnasium in Nuremberg, he returned to the university by accepting a chair in Heidelberg and later another chair in Berlin. It is often held that the two passages, from writings at opposite ends of Hegel's career, reflect very different, even inconsistent angles of vision on the social role of philosophy.

The letter to Niethammer was written from Bamberg, prior to Hegel's arrival in Nuremberg. The passage in question is both a defense of philosophy as well as of his decision, as one concerned with political issues, to remain committed to the kind of theoretical work undertaken in the *Phenomenology* that, Hegel implies, is practically significant. It is further meant to reassure his friend Niethammer, who earlier provided the financial guarantee for the publication of Hegel's great treatise. Hegel means to suggest that when his friend, who in the meantime has taken on ministerial functions in the government, later gives up organizational activity to return to science, the practice of science will be practically important. With this in mind, Hegel writes: "I am daily ever more convinced that theoretical work accomplishes more in the world than practical work. Once the realm of representation [*Vorstellung*] is revolutionized, actuality [*Wirklichkeit*] will not hold out."[28]

Although he does not repeat his earlier allusion to the critical philosophy, Hegel does insist on the practical results of philosophical theory. His reference to the revolutionizing of representation refers to his technical understanding of the difference between religion, or the realm of picture thinking, and philosophy, which is conceptual. In the *Phenomenology*, he argues for philosophy as the highest point of the cultural process and the truth of religion through its capacity to substitute concepts for images. He now seems to be saying that religious ideas remain merely that, without practical effect, but that when religion has been transformed into philosophical dress, its ideas tend to put themselves into practice, even to realize themselves.

Hegel often stresses the practical force of ideas. A favorite example is the idea of freedom whose slow realization, he maintains, is the central theme and work of human history. So in the *Phenomenology*, in a famous passage, he analyzes the French Revolution as the result of an abstract theory of morality, in effect as a kind of Kantianism, that is self-stultifying in practice.[29] In *Reason in History*, where he identifies the essence of spirit as freedom, he suggests that history is

---

28. *Hegel: The Letters*, p. 179.
29. Hegel, *Phenomenology*, "Absolute Freedom and Terror," pp. 355–364.

the progress of consciousness of the idea of freedom and that the actualization of freedom is the purpose of the world.[30] And in the *Philosophy of Right*, he discusses ethical life as the realization of the idea of freedom.[31]

The concept of freedom illustrates Hegel's conviction that philosophical ideas have practical consequences. Hegel further develops this conviction in a remark on the historical moment following the French Revolution. In its wake, despite important reservations about political events in France, Hegel's optimism about the real possibility for basic social and political change was immensely encouraging to others, who sensed his enthusiasm and shared his hopeful diagnosis of the period. In a famous passage, he assesses the concrete situation in the post-revolutionary period: "Besides, it is not difficult to see that ours is a birth-time and a period of transition to a new era."[32] Yet Hegel was careful to distinguish between the concept and its realization, the very problem illustrated by the failure of the French Revolution to fulfill its promise. In the very next paragraph, he writes:

> But this new world is no more a complete actuality than is a new-born child; it is essential to bear this in mind. It comes on the scene for the first time in its immediacy or its Notion [*Begriff*]. Just as little as a building is finished when its foundation has been laid, so little is the achieved Notion of the whole the whole itself.[33]

Does Hegel's View Later Change in This Respect?

Hegel's understanding of the relation of philosophy to the social context is a constant in his theory early and late. Yet for many observers, his view of the relation of philosophical theory to society later seemed to change in a way that has often made it a target for criticism. In the period of the *Phenomenology*, his optimistic view of theory as practically relevant stressed philosophy as the epitome of culture and the role of theory in bringing about social change. Later, when he arrived in Berlin, he continued to insist on the cultural primacy of philosophy

---

30. Hegel, *Reason in History*, trans. Robert S. Hartman (Indianapolis: LLA, 1953), pp. 22–25.

31. Hegel, *Philosophy of Right*, trans. T. M. Knox (London: Oxford University Press, 1967), §142, p. 105.

32. Hegel, *Phenomenology*, §11, p. 6.

33. Hegel, *Phenomenology*, §12, p. 7.

while silently reducing its practical role even as he appeared to approve the present social situation. So in the course of *Lectures on the Philosophy of World History* he gave five times from 1822/23 to 1830/31 during his period in Berlin, he argues that only the German peoples realized through Christianity that man is free,[34] and further argues that the world is as it should be.[35] Although there is clearly a self-satisfied air in such claims, one should not infer that Hegel thinks that the stage reached in the Germany of his day represents the final stage of history or that what is is not susceptible to further improvement. For Hegel, who remains critical of the society of his day at a time when he is thought to have abandoned his earlier liberal attitude, continues to see philosophy as important in bringing about social change.

In the "Talk to his students on the occasion of the beginning of his Berlin lectures," for instance, he stresses the social role of philosophy as significant for culture and as the manifestation of human capacity in its highest form without mentioning its practical effect.[36] To comprehend his view in this text, it is important to distinguish between Hegel's obvious satisfaction in being called to a chair in Berlin, as he says by the grace of his majesty the king;[37] a certain nationalistic tone in the cited passage, as in Hegel's unsupported claim that at present philosophical science lives only in Germany;[38] and his view of the relation of philosophy to society. In a clear reference to the Prussian state that has honored him, aware that the present time follows on a more difficult situation when intellectual work was impeded by more pressing, material concerns, he writes:

> Here culture and the fulfillment of science is one of the essential moments in the life of the state. In the present university, the university of the middle point, must also find the middle point for philosophy, all spiritual culture and all science and truth, as well as its role and care.—Not only is it however spiritual life in general that constitutes a basic element in the existence of this state; but more precisely the great struggle of the people in league with its princes for independence [*Selbstständigkeit*] through the destruc-

---

34. Hegel, *Reason in History*, p. 24.
35. Hegel, *Reason in History*, p. 47.
36. "Anrede an seine Zuhörer bei Eröffnung der Vorlesungen in Berlin" [1818] in Hegel, *System der Philosophie. Enzyklopädie der philosophischen Wissenschaften*, in *Sämtliche Werke*, ed. H. Glockner (Stuttgart/Band Canstatt: Friedrich Frommann Verlag, 1964), VIII, pp. 31–36.
37. Hegel, *Sämtliche Werke*, VIII, p. 31
38. Hegel, *Sämtliche Werke*, VIII, p. 34.

tion of foreign unfriendly tyranny [*gemüthloser Tyranneî*] and tyranny in the mind [*im Gemüthê*] has made a good beginning.[39]

The problem of human rights, especially as concerns freedom of thought, was obviously placed on the agenda through the French Revolution. The second article of the famous "Declaration of the rights of man and of the citizen" ["*Declaration des droits de l'homme et du citoyen*"], promulgated in 1789, guaranteed the right to resist oppression, which can be interpreted as the right to revolution, and the tenth article guaranteed the right freely to hold and to express all opinions. This document immediately evoked a philosophical debate that, more than two centuries later, is still underway. Kant, who was impressed by the idea of the realization of human rights, nonetheless clearly condemned the concept of revolution considered as a right to resistance or to revolution against the existing state. In the last completed work of the critical philosophy, *The Metaphysical Principles of Virtue*, which appeared in 1797, hence after the French Revolution, he typically argues that it is never justified for the people to rebel against the government[40] and that every effort to amend the constitution through force is punishable.[41] This did not prevent his followers from taking a more militant stand. Johann Benjamin Erhard, a left wing Kantian, explicitly approved the right to revolution.[42] Fichte, a slightly more moderate Kantian, wrote a long defense of the French Revolution.[43] He also explicitly defended freedom of opinion in 1793 in a speech directed against the European princes who, he claimed, repressed it.[44]

Hegel was of course aware of this and other precedents. More moderate than the Jacobin Fichte, consistent with his tendency always to acknowledge progress by separating the wheat from the chaff, he finds something good in the present government. He acknowledges the political progress brought about through the Prussian government. Yet he does not identify philosophy as such, or even his own philosophy, with the state of his time. For he remarks on the need to determine

---

39. Hegel, *Sämtliche Werke*, VIII, p. 32.

40. *Metaphysische Anfangsgründe der Rechtslehre*, in *Kant Werke*, VII, pp. 439–440.

41. *Kant Werke*, VII, p. 463.

42. "Über das Recht des Volks zu einer Revolution" [1795] in Johann Benjamin Erhard, *Über das Recht des Volks zu einer Revolution und andere Schriften*, ed. Helmut G. Haasis (Frankfurt a. M.: Syndikat, 1976), pp. 7098.

43. "Beitrag zur Berichtigung der Urtheile des Publicums über die französiche Revolution," in *Fichtes Werke*, ed. I. H. Fichte (Berlin: de Gruyter, 1971), VI, pp. 37–288.

44. "Zurückforderung der Denkfreiheit von den Fürsten Europens, die sie bisher unterdrückten, Eine Rede," in *Fichtes Werke*, VI, pp. 1–35.

the place of philosophy in that state. And in another place in his talk, he draws an implicit, but clear distinction between what is and what is possible, by writing:

> A still sound heart has the courage to demand truth, and the realm of truth is that in which philosophy has its house, which it edifies [*erbaut*] and which through its study we partially realize [*theilhaftig werden*]. What is true in life, great, and godlike is through the idea; the goal of philosophy is to grasp it in its true shape and generality.[45]

Although Hegel is aware of social change, his view of the relation of philosophical theory to society remains constant. Now as before, he continues to insist that philosophy has a social role to play. Although he feels that times have changed in a way that benefits philosophy, he no longer thinks that change is in the air. This does not mean that he identifies with the present situation, or finds his own goals and aspirations as more than imperfectly reflected in the contemporary state. Rather, consistent with his interpretative practice—without speaking of the possibility of basic social change that, at present, does not seem to him to be a real possibility—he calls for recognition of what has in fact been accomplished.

Hegel's commentators have noticed a difference, perhaps more a difference of emphasis than of doctrine, between his early activist turn of mind and his later apparent quietism. It is as if Hegel, grown rich and famous, officially acknowledged in the Prussian State, had silently altered his philosophical view to reflect his changed social position. If he had done so, he would not have been the first philosopher to sacrifice principle for honor or worldly goods. It is well known that aware of this danger, Spinoza resisted employment precisely to avoid compromising his intellectual independence. The recognition that others have succumbed to temptation is perhaps one of the reasons that this charge is so often raised against Hegel, particularly by Marxist commentators.

We have already cited passages from Hegel's early writings that support a generally activist reading of his views of political change and of the link of philosophical theory to society. There are other passages in his later writings that support a more quietist, passive view, consistent with his supposed change in opinion about philosophy due to a change in worldly fortunes. Some observers detect a basic difference between Hegel's earlier activist and later, supposedly quietist

---

45. Hegel, *Sämtliche Werke*, VIII, p. 36.

conceptions of philosophy in a justly famous passage in his last book suggesting a merely hermeneutical view of philosophy.

Like other writers of the period, including Kant and Fichte, Hegel takes a hermeneutical view of philosophy. He only rarely comments directly on the problem of interpretation.[46] But his writings are filled with interpretations of other theories. In the present passage, Hegel clearly sees the philosophical task to lie in interpreting what is the case, what exists. The same point can be put in Humean language as the claim that philosophy is properly and necessarily concerned not with the ought but with the is. Philosophy neither should nor can tell us what should be. It has no business in portraying the world as we would have it become, no business in giving advice to others. Its proper task is to show how the state that in fact exists should be understood. Hegel supports his view of the philosophical task as confined to the hermeneutics of past forms of culture in a passage that deserves to be cited at length. He writes:

> One more word about giving instruction as to what the world ought to be. Philosophy in any case always comes on the scene too late to give it. As the thought of the world, it appears only when actuality is already there cut and dried after its process of formation has been completed. The teaching of the concept, which is also history's inescapable lesson, is that it is only when actuality is mature that the ideal first appears over against the real and that the ideal apprehends this same real world in its substance and builds it up for itself into the shape of an intellectual realm. When philosophy paints its gray in gray, then has a shape of life grown old. By philosophy's gray in gray it cannot be rejuvenated but only understood. The owl of Minerva spreads its wings only with the falling of dusk.[47]

This passage, which is often cited by both Hegel's critics and his defenders alike, is generally understood as signaling a retreat from his earlier conviction about the role of philosophy in bringing about social change. Hegel has been read as saying that in virtue of the fact that philosophy is limited to a retrospective analysis of what is the case, it cannot have any social payoff. Read in this way Hegel's theory sounds vaguely like the anti-Platonism of Wittgenstein's early, Tractarian view.

---

46. For a rare passage, see a remark on Philo of Alexandria, where Hegel differentiates between reading in and reading out the truth lodged in the historical, in *G. W. F. Hegel-Werke*, ed. Eva Moldenhauer and Karl Markus Michel (Frankfurt a. M.: Suhrkamp, 1969), XIX, p. 420.

47. Hegel, *Philosophy of Right*, pp. 12–13.

When philosophy has finished, it leaves everything in place; for the deepest existential problems are not amenable to philosophical treatment at all.

The supposed contrast between this reading of his later position and his earlier position could hardly be starker or more troubling for anyone concerned with the social relevance of theory. It consists in abandoning his early, enthusiastic version of the Platonic claim that philosophy is socially indispensable for the converse claim that philosophy is socially irrelevant. If there is any problem, it is that philosophy is itself the problem. If this is so, then the earlier optimism about the times as propitious for basic social change later gives way to a realism about social possibilities; and the conviction that philosophy could be an agent of social change has been given up for a view that philosophy cannot change but can only understand what has occurred. The discouragement provoked by this idea among younger thinkers is well formulated in Marx's famous remark, in the eleventh of his "Theses on Feuerbach," that philosophers have so far only interpreted a world that must be changed.[48]

Continuity in Hegel's View

This way of reading Hegel's later view supposes a clear, deep transformation of his understanding of the relation of philosophical theory to social practice. The supposed difference between the earlier and later views of philosophy's social role lies in a supposed shift in emphasis from the prospective early vision, in Hegel's earlier insistence that theory is socially useful in providing conceptual form to possibilities that are later realized, a vision that has been seen as incompatible with his later assertion that philosophy that only arises after the fact cannot influence what has already come to pass. If philosophy only develops after a form of social life has already grown old, then it necessarily comes on the scene too late to influence what has already occurred and is in the process of becoming history only when it can finally be grasped.

The later Hegelian idea of philosophy as retrospective rather than prospective, often construed as representing a change from social activism to social quietism, has led to a series of objections to his view that can be grouped around four main points. They include an initial

---

48. Karl Marx and Friedrich Engels, *The German Ideology, Part One,* trans. C. J. Arthur (New York: International Publishers, 1970), p. 123.

criticism directed against Hegel's supposed political affiliation as well as three further criticisms following from generally Kantian motives. We can start with an objection motivated less by the nature of Hegel's analysis than by a suspected change in his political allegiance. It has been held that the youthful liberal, attracted by the French Revolution, later came to identify with the Prussian state of his time.

This political objection amounts to saying that Hegel, who was initially attracted toward revolutionary change and the French Revolution in particular, later aligned himself with the state of his time and against social change. If this type of criticism is not based on ignorance, it at least reflects an insufficient acquaintance with Hegel's writings. Suffice it to say that Hegel's identification with the ideals of the French Revolution, from which he never wavered, and that he defends against the political events to which it lead, was always tempered by a critical attitude towards the practical excesses that, in Hegel's view, prevented its ideals from being realized in practice. In an early letter, he criticizes the excesses of Robes Pierre and his followers.[49] Slightly later, in a discussion of Christianity, he remarks that great revolutions are necessarily preceded by the tranquil and secret revolution in the spirit of the times.[50] In the famous passage in the *Phenomenology* on "Absolute Freedom and Terror," he criticizes the negative results of reason run amok, whose action is merely negative, whose work is destructive, and which results in death.[51] It is hence overstating the case to say that Hegel ever identified in an uncritical way with the results of the French Revolution. But he consistently accepted its ideals that, he believed, were the latest and highest interpretation of the concept of freedom. The ideals of equality, fraternity, and liberty were still before his mind when in his last phase he sought to understand their possible realization in the *Philosophy of Right*.[52]

Further, it is perhaps not sufficiently known that his concern with social justice is a continuous motive in his work, throughout his career. Hegel's concern with social justice continues unabated in his writings both early and late and is evident in different ways. Early on, it can be seen in his translation of the letters of the Swiss lawyer J.-J. Cart on the oppression of the people in the Canton of Vaud by the aristocracy in Bern, a situation that he knew because of his service in that city as

---

49. Hegel's letter to Schelling, Christmas Eve, 1794, in *Hegel: The Letters*, p. 29.
50. Hegel, *Hegels-Werke*, I, p. 203.
51. Hegel, *Phenomenology of Spirit*, pp. 355–363.
52. On the interpretation of this work, see H. Ottmann, *Individuum und Gemeinschaft bei Hegel* (New York: de Gruyter, 1977), 2 vols, I: *Hegel im Spiegel der Interpretationen*.

a tutor to the von Staiger family, in what became his initial publication. It is still evident toward the end of his career in his remarks on social justice, anti-Semitism, the persistence of poverty in modern society, and so on in his last book. Hegel's sensitivity to economic issues is particularly interesting since, with the notable exception of Lukács, who focuses on the role of Hegel's awareness of political economy for the formulation of his theory,[53] Marxists consistently argue that the German idealists were unaware of this sector of reality.

The resistance to anti-Semitism is particularly important in view of its persistence throughout German philosophy and culture, for instance in the writings of Martin Luther, a notorious anti-Semite.[54] Kant, the great apostle of the Enlightenment, insists in his later writings on the need to convert the Jews to the true religion.[55] Fries, Hegel's colleague in Berlin, was a notorious anti-Semite, whom Hegel opposed more than once.[56] In the *Philosophy of Right,* Hegel not only attacks Fries several times by name; he also attacks the anti-Semitism that Fries represented, something he would not have done had he held the reactionary political opinions often attributed to him.

Such politically-motivated criticism is more than incidentally *ad hominem.* Even were the public liberal later to have become a closet conservative, it would not count against his theory. Obviously, his theory is independent of his personal political motivations even if they may require consideration to understand his position. The remaining objections are not motivated by political considerations but rather by scepticism about the practical significance of philosophical theory, particularly Hegel's theory. In German Idealism, prior to Marx, Kant, and above all Fichte, were the thinkers most concerned with the link between theory and practice. Kant straightforwardly holds that pure theory is practically relevant. Fichte even claimed that theory only arises out of and serves to resolve the questions that arise in practice.[57] Accordingly, it is appropriate that the more serious objections to Hegel's view of the social relevance of theory arise from a Kantian angle of

---

53. Georg Lukács, *The Young Hegel: Studies in the Relations between Dialectics and Economics,* trans. Rodney Livingstone (Cambridge: MIT Press, 1976).

54. Martin Luther, *Von den Juden und ihren Lügen* (Munich: Ludendorffs Volkswart-Verlag, 1932).

55. "Der Streit der Fakultäten," in Kant, *Kant-Werke,* IX, pp. 305–306.

56. Shlomo Avineri, *Hegel's Theory of the Modern State* (London: Cambridge University Press, 1972), pp. 119–121.

57. This idea is central to his early view. See the "Second Introduction to the Science of Knowledge," in *Fichte: Science of Knowledge (Wissenschaftslehre) with the First and Second Introductions,* trans. Peter Heath and John Lachs (New York: Appleton-Century-Crofts, 1970), pp. 29–88.

vision. In essence, they maintain in different ways that Hegel is unsuccessful in overcoming the difficulties of the critical philosophy.

The first, and, to my mind, weakest criticism is only rarely formulated directly; but it appears to lie behind the conviction that theory is indifferent to practice. An objection of this kind seems to follow directly from consideration of Kant's appropriation of practice through theory that, as we have seen, cannot justify its social impact. Unlike Fichte, Kant is not concerned with practice in the formulation of theory. In fact, from the Kantian angle of vision, practice is theoretically irrelevant, or irrelevant to theory. For morality as for mathematics, natural science and metaphysics, Kant insists on objectivity that can only be secured by an a priori status. Yet since we have also seen that Hegel specifically rejects as inadequate the Kantian effort to provide a theoretical analysis of the moral ought in independence of the practical situation, this criticism, in all its variants, can be dismissed out of hand. Unlike Kant, Hegel is concerned with the details of practical life as well as with the general interpretation of the state as it was known to exist in his time. His *Philosophy of Right* can be considered as an up-dated, more contemporary version of Aristotle's *Politics*, in a word, as a general theory of the modern social context.

A second type of objection, also influenced by Kant, concerns Hegel's supposedly false tendency to equate 'is' and 'ought' that Hume did so much to sunder. Since the publication of the *Philosophy of Right*, this idea has been formulated by various commentators in the most diverse ways.[58] Suffice it to say that in all its many forms, this objection presupposes that Hegel's link to the Prussian state is an unbearable, but necessary result of his standpoint. This criticism is based on a form of *modus tollens*, roughly a refutation of Hegel's theory through its obviously unacceptable consequences. An analogy might be the refutation of Heidegger's theory by demonstrating that it necessarily leads to Nazism to which he in fact turned. If it could be shown that Heidegger's Nazi turning were not contingent but in some undetermined sense followed seamlessly from his theory of being, this would obviously count heavily against his theory.

It is easier to formulate this kind of objection than to make it stick. To do so, at least the following seems to be required. On the one hand, Hegel's relation to the Prussian state would need to be studied

---

58. Among writers who have formulated a version of this objection, we can include Feuerbach, Marx, Haym, Carritt, Hook, Ritter, Fulda, Habermas, Theunissen, Riedel, and Rosen. Concerning the contemporary discussion, see Robert Pippin, "The Rose and the Owl: Some Remarks on the Theory-Practice Problem in Hegel," in *The Independent Journal of Philosophy* 3 (1979), pp. 7–16.

in detail. The mere fact that Hegel was a professor of philosophy in Berlin during a certain period is obviously inadequate to yield a conclusion that he supported or identified with the Prussian state of his time, whatever that means. On the other hand, the facts of the matter must be linked to Hegel's theory, for instance by establishing a relation of practical necessity, or a practical but necessary connection, between what Hegel thought and what he did.

It would be foolish, certainly foolish from the Hegelian angle of vision that specifically insists on the link between the thinker and the historical moment, to try to separate Hegel the great philosopher from Hegel the citizen of the Prussian state of his time. But to concede that Hegel the philosopher and Hegel the man are one and the same does not enable us to establish anything like a seamlesss web between his thought and his actions. For we do not know how theory relates to practice. Even if in practice his relation to contemporary Prussia were consistent with his philosophical theory, it would not follow that one derived from the other. Since it has, however, never been demonstrated and is only asserted that Hegel's relation to the Prussian state is the result of his standpoint, this type of criticism cannot itself remain uncriticized.

A third, more skillful objection arises by denying that philosophical theory, particularly Hegel's theory, is able to grasp the social practice. This objection manifests skepticism about the cognitive ability of philosophy or at least a form of philosophy, as in Kierkegaard's well known claim that Hegelian reason is inadequate to grasp existence. Marxism, which shares Kierkegaard's doubts about Hegelian theory, features another form of the general Kantian argument. Marxists of all stripes tend to argue that the problems of philosophy cannot be resolved on a philosophical basis since philosophy is unable to know its object, more precisely unable to grasp the social context. If this claim were correct, then Hegel's theory could not know the social world. For instance, in writings from his Marxist period, Lukács maintains that philosophy generally ignores the economic matrix that forms the basis of modern society that it cannot understand.[59]

It is easy to see that the Marxist criticism of Hegel's theory for an alleged incapacity to grasp the economic dimension of social reality is doubly defective. Lukács does not show, but rather assumes, as part of his argument, the truth of the Marxist theory of political economy. Further, his criticism is inconsistent since he himself has shown in detail

---

59. Lukács states this argument in a number of places, including *History and Class Consciousness, The Young Hegel,* and *Zur Ontologie des gesellschaftlichen Seins.*

that Hegel's theory is based on a sound knowledge of political economy. Hegel's grasp of economics is on display in a number of places in his work, including a lost book on Steuart and in various places in his texts, above all in the brilliant discussion of the "System of Needs" in the *Philosophy of Right*.[60] It is fair to say that this text serves as the proximate source of the political and economic analysis that Marx, whose view Lukács favors, later develops.

Conclusion: Hegel and the Utility of Philosophy

Consideration of some of the more interesting objections to Hegel's idea of the social relevance of philosophy shows that they are often more or less loosely based on the critical philosophy that constitutes the starting point of his own theory. These criticisms reopen his analysis of Kant. In different ways, they reproach Hegel in effect for being unable to surmount in his own theory deficiencies that he diagnoses in the critical philosophy, in a word for failing to provide an adequate analysis of the relation of theory and practice in place of Kant's inconsistent reading of this issue. In response, it has been argued that Hegel's critics do not pay enough attention to his theory that, when scrutinized, resists the objections raised against it. Yet to refute the criticisms brought against the theory falls short of providing a persuasive interpretation of it.

To go beyond fending off objections to the view, to begin to make sense of it, it is necessary to pick out its essential ideas in order to reconstruct it as a conceptual whole. Now it is hopeless, or at least much harder to do so if there is no central core, if, as Hegel's critics of his supposed later conservative turn seem to suggest, there are two very different analyses of the relation of philosophy to society in Hegel's theory. A first step in this direction is to show a basic continuity in Hegel's theory over time, for instance between the views expressed early on in the letter to Niethammer and later in the *Philosophy of Right*. In practice, this means to bring together Hegel's earlier, prospective, forward-leaning activism and his later, retrospective, backward-leaning, supposed quietism within an overall interpretation. It must further be possible to discern why, from the angle of vision of Hegel's later position, philosophy is relevant to society.

To reconstruct Hegel's analysis of the social relevance of philosophy, it is sufficient to bring together the main aspects of the view

---

60. Hegel, *Philosophy of Right*, §§189–208, pp. 126–134.

previously discussed. The premise of this reconstruction is that the apparently contradictory aspects of the view, such as Hegel's earlier activism and later quietism, are compatible on a higher level, as different aspects of a single conception that remains essentially unchanged. Here are the main aspects of Hegel's understanding of philosophy's relation to society:

1. Philosophy differs from other forms of thought in determining concepts, as distinguished, say, from the physical or pictorial representations of art and religion;
2. Philosophy arises retrospectively, when a form of society is already in place;
3. Concepts tend to realize themselves;
4. Philosophical concepts are intrinsically related to society.

In part, the argument necessary to make out the claim for the social utility of philosophy has already been made, in part it still needs to be made. Hegel's view of philosophy as conceptual but not representational is laid out in the *Phenomenology*, especially in the last chapter, where he analyzes "Absolute Knowing," a near synonym for philosophy in that work. The view that philosophy arises retrospectively is stated in the passage cited from the *Philosophy of Right*, and the claim that concepts tend to realize themselves is present in many places in Hegel's writings, including the letter to Niethammer, cited above, and the discussion of the idea of freedom in modern times in the little book on *Reason in History* quarried from Hegel's lecture notes.

We have already noted that for Hegel modern times are shaped by the self-actualization of the idea of freedom. We may disagree with his example—for the evidence to support his claim is at best equivocal—and yet agree that ideas function as causes since they have an influence all their own.[61] It is hard to deny that the ideas of Hegel and his followers, including a certain Karl Marx, have directly and indirectly influenced the world in a manner that even the most ardent enthusiast of the power of the concept could not have foreseen. It has even been argued that his right wing and left wing descendants confronted each other at the Battle of Stalingrad.[62]

---

61. This is a response to the dilemma posed in Kant's third antinomy concerning the relation of freedom and determinism. See *Freedom and Determinism,* ed. Keith Lehrer (New York: Random House, 1966).

62. Herbert Marcuse, *Reason and Revolution: Hegel and the Rise of Social Theory* (Boston: Beacon, 1969).

For philosophy to be socially relevant, two requirements must be met. First, philosophy, or a certain kind of philosophy, must be rooted in the social context, in order to justify the link of theory to practice, or the social utility of theory that is so troublesome to Kant. Otherwise, the link between theory and social practice is at most contingent. Second, if the role of philosophy is to understand what has already happened, and if such analysis can only be provided retrospectively, then a retrospective form of social hermeneutics must have a prospective dimension as well.

Obviously, a retrospective form of social hermeneutics is useful for society if and only if philosophy can grasp its object, or comprehend what it analyzes—Lukács's closely Kantian point—and if theory relates to practice. Hegel's theory contains an argument for its relation to practice that can be understood as a distant form of Kant's Copernican turn. As Hegel and a virtually endless list of later commentators have pointed out, Kant has no way of arguing for the relevance of his view of morality. Hegel's solution to this difficulty follows Fichte in building the link of theory to practice into the theory that emerges directly from and returns to practice.

This point depends on Hegel's view of spirit in opposition to Kant's view of pure reason. Kant follows philosophy's traditional self-understanding as independent of but essential for the social context. The philosophical instrument in this anticontextualist view is unconstrained by its surroundings. For Hegel, on the contrary, philosophy is no more than the highest form of culture. Its instrument, or spirit, is a contextualized form of reason inseparable from, and, accordingly, limited by, its own historical moment. Philosophical theory is relevant since it arises out of and returns to the social context. The link between theory and practice does not need to be justified since it is always and already there.

Other philosophers going all the way back to Socrates have been concerned with the social relevance of their craft. In the German idealist tradition, Hegel's turn to real practice, as opposed to the theoretically edulcorated form available within the Kantian transcendental analysis, is anticipated in Fichte's awareness that real human freedom is not infinite, as Kant thought, but exists meaningfully only within the interstices of the interactions between finite human beings with each other and their surroundings. Hegel's view of the practical relevance of philosophical reason draws on Fichte's understanding of philosophy as a theoretical response to practical concerns, what Dewey, the erstwhile Hegelian, later calls the stresses and strains of existence.[63] But Hegel surpasses Fichte's rather sketchy understanding of history[64] in order to relate types of theory to types of social being. For Hegel, philosophy is not practically relevant because it is pure, but rather because it is impure, in virtue of its constitutive relation to the world in which we live.

Hegel's dual insistence on philosophy as self-realizing but as following upon the events it analyzes derives from his underlying view of reason in context, or spirit. His hermeneutical analysis of the historical moment, what Husserl later called the life world, is specifically relevant to understanding what should be, not in the sense of an empty ideal—as this term is some-times applied to Plato's *Republic*, but which Hegel understood as an expression of Greek life[65]—but in order to comprehend, and through that comprehension to surpass, what in fact is. For Hegel, reason is always and already operative in historical development. Philosophy does not initiate but rather increases the force of reason in the historical context. The relevance of philosophy lies in helping us to understand our world and ourselves in a way that contributes to social change. In sum, Hegel sees philosophy as socially relevant not because it stands over against the social context, but rather because it is rooted in the context that it initially comprehends at the level of thought and then later helps to transform through the realization of its concepts.

The appeal of Hegel's view lies in its supposed ability to navigate between the dual problems arising if reason is pure and hence practically uninteresting or impure in a way that fails to preserve its very rationality. When Kant isolates philosophy from the social context, it becomes impossible to understand its supposed link to the intrinsic ends of all mankind. Marx's distrust of speculative philosophy has led to the Marxist distrust of theory, in practice to an instrumentalization of reason that destroys it.[66] Hegel neither denies practice with Kant by resorbing it into theory nor denies theory with the Marxists by instrumentalizing it in a way that reduces it to practice.

In conclusion, Hegel neither denies nor minimizes but rather helps us to understand the interest of philosophical reason for society. In comparison with those, such as Kant, who hold that theory is

---

63. John Dewey, *Reconstruction in Philosophy* (Boston: Beacon, 1960), p. v.

64. Johann Gottlieb Fichte, *Die Grundzüge des gegenwärtigen Zeitalters*, ed. Alwin Diemer (Hamburg: Felix Meiner, 1956). See also Tom Rockmore, "Fichte, la connaissance et l'histoire," in *Revue de métaphysique et de morale*—forthcoming.

65. Hegel, *Philosophy of Right*, p. 10.

66. Max Horkheimer, *Eclipse of Reason* (New York: Seabury Press, 1974).

relevant because it is isolated from practice, Hegel's contribution is two-fold. He understands that a theory that is isolated from practice is only incidentally relevant to it; and he further understands that a philosophical theory that is rooted in its own historical moment and strives to achieve a rational comprehension of the present contributes in this way to another, more rational form of social life.

8 Hegel, Foucault, and Critical Hermeneutics

Shaun Gallagher

To the extent that modern utopianism would deny certain hermeneutical principles, one can contrast a critical theory that is utopian to one that is hermeneutical. Utopian thought seeks to free itself from the force of the past and from circumstances of the present, to move in the direction of a perfected future. Hermeneutics, in contrast, while allowing for the possible transformation of past traditions and present conditions recognizes that this possibility is inescapably constrained by the historical effects of the past and the resistances of the present. We might say that hermeneutics "modestly sets up house within necessity," whereas utopianism seeks to design a new edifice outside the requirements of reality.[1] On the basis of this distinction I want to explore conflicting conceptions of critical theory found in Hegel, Habermas, and Foucault.

Jürgen Habermas interprets Hegel as moving away from an early appreciation and practice of political critique toward a later acquiescence in the face of political reality. One aspect of this move concerns Hegel's privileging of particularity over universality. Indeed, Habermas

---

1. Herbert Marcuse once characterized Hegel's concept of freedom in this way: "it modestly sets up house within necessity." Marcuse probably meant a particular necessity. With respect to hermeneutics we mean the necessity of particularity. See Herbert Marcuse, "Philosophy and Critical Theory," in *Critical Theory: The Essential Readings*, eds. David Ingram and Julia Simon-Ingram (New York: Paragon House, 1992), p. 7.

blames Hegel's own "particularism" on his inability "to transcend his time and his circumstances."[2] This interpretation of Hegel motivates a question about the role played by universalism in critical theory. If we distinguish two parts of critical theory, the critique of what is and the critical reconstruction of what ought to be, then the issue I want to address concerns to what extent some form of universalism is required for either part. To what extent is it actually possible to reach a universal perspective from within a situation that calls for critique, and to what extent is it still possible to conduct a critical reconstruction, if a universal perspective is impossible?

For Habermas these questions are related to other issues concerning modern time consciousness, the role played by utopianism in critical theory, and the requirement that critique must be conducted on the basis of a rationality that itself is not susceptible to critique. Especially with respect to the latter issue, Habermas places Foucault, in relation to Hegel, on the opposite extreme of the critical scale. If Hegel, in his later work, gives up critique in favor of speculative observation from the heights of a transmodern absolute rationality, Foucault pushes critique to its bottom-most foundations by engaging in a self-defeating, postmodern critique, that is, a critique so radical that it undermines the very grounds of rationality required for critique. Hegel and Foucault are also condemned by Habermas for what they have in common: an orientation toward the historical past that excludes the possibility of a critical utopian prospectus for the future.

I want to argue that precisely where Habermas finds a lack of critique, that is, in the later Hegel, one can find the basis for a conception of critique different from Habermas' own. In contrast to Habermas' reading, not only is critique possible for the later Hegel, but Hegel develops, in principle, even if not in practice, a hermeneutical conception of critique that reorders the relation of particular to universal. I will not claim that Hegel actually carries out a critique of this sort. Hegel was unable to free himself from the demands of his systematization to employ the appropriate elements of his system as critical instruments. To put such a concept of critique into practice one would need, as Foucault suggests with respect to Marxism and psychoanalysis, to put the theoretical or systematic unity of Hegel's thought into abeyance.[3] Still, Hegel's particularism, if viewed under this qualification, could be in fact the basis for what Foucault calls a "discontinuous,

---

2. Jürgen Habermas, *Theory and Practice*, trans. John Viertel (Boston: Beacon, 1973), p. 194; hereafter cited as TP.

3. See Michel Foucault, *Power/Knowledge: Selected Interviews and Other Writings*, ed. Colin Gordon (New York: Pantheon Books, 1980), p. 81; hereafter cited as P/K.

particular and local criticism," and thus could be a less utopian and more appropriate basis for critique than the Kantian universalism taken up by Habermas.

Of course, my intent is not to claim that Hegel and Foucault fully agree on the nature of critique. Indeed, I would expect some resistance to the very idea that Foucault could be considered in a favorable comparison to Hegel. Furthermore, if we are seeking a critical theory informed by hermeneutics, Foucault is no friend to hermeneutics and often characterizes his own enterprise as something other than hermeneutics. Nonetheless, in opposition to Habermas's readings of both Hegel and Foucault, and in some respects, in opposition to more general interpretations of Hegel and Foucault, I will argue, in a limited and qualified fashion, that one can use Hegel and Foucault to define a certain conception of critical theory that is opposed to the one Habermas traces on a straight line from Kant through the Frankfurt School.[4]

Critique: From Hegel to Habermas

Habermas has always understood his own concept of critique in the light of his reading of Hegel. According to Habermas, "Hegel inaugurated the discourse of modernity," and recognized the essential dimension of critique involved in the self-understanding of modernity.[5] Modern rationality has a built-in capacity for self-critique which Hegel attempted to activate in both his early theological and political studies. According to his theological writings, both orthodox and modern Enlightenment forms of religion fail to integrate themselves in the social and political dimensions of life, and thus fail to attain their true universality. True universality, in this sense, is dependent upon religious spirit becoming embedded within the particulars of *Sittlichkeit*. In his early political-journalistic writings, critique plays the role of a "preventive reflection" that unmasks "merely pretended universality" and reveals, as Habermas puts it, "the decadence of the particular by confronting it with the mirror of the universal interests to which it still

---

4. My use of Hegel and Foucault in this context, while hopefully falling short of abuse, is done in the spirit of Foucault's own practice with regard to Nietzsche: "For myself, I prefer to utilize the writers I like. The only valid tribute to thought such as Nietzsche's is precisely to use it, to deform it, to make it groan and protest" (P/K 53–54). The protest should not be too great, however, if Romand Coles is right in his claim that Foucault belongs to a tradition that includes Kant and Hegel. See "Communicative Action and Dialogical Ethics: Habermas and Foucault," *Polity* 25 (1992), p. 89.

5. Habermas, *The Philosophical Discourse of Modernity*, trans. Frederick G. Lawrence (Cambridge, MA: MIT Press, 1987), p. 51; hereafter cited as PDM.

presumes" (TP 181–182). Habermas prefers this young Hegel who would grant philosophy a critical role, "almost in the sense of the Young Hegelians' . . . claim for critique as preparation for a revolutionary praxis" (TP 180). Like Hegel's early journalism or Habermas's own participation in the debate known as the *Historikerstreit*, critique, in the spirit of the Enlightenment, can be embodied in a "historical-critical discussion" or publicly conducted debate.[6]

According to Habermas, and he is not alone in this interpretation, when the mature Hegel discovers the objective power of *Geist*, he gives up the notion of critique and concludes that philosophy cannot instruct the state on "what it ought to be; it can only show how the state, the ethical universe, is to be understood."[7] For the Hegel of the *Philosophy of Right*, Habermas contends, political critique, made possible in the freedom granted to public communication is not really effective. Faced with the rationality of the constitution and the constancy of national sentiment, critique is rendered innocuous, made harmless by the maturity of the nationalist spirit in its constitutional expression (PR 319). Thus theory should not direct itself critically against the state, but should simply describe what the state is.

Habermas' reading of Hegel is informed by his own conception of a critical reflective practice that detaches itself from particularistic and nationalistic prejudices. If this is what critique must be, then it seems that the later Hegel abandons critique and makes it impossible. In contrast to Habermas, I want to suggest that Hegel is working with a different model of critique, one informed by a more hermeneutical conception of the relation between the particular and the universal.

Hegel's principle in this regard, one that I consider to be a hermeneutical principle, is clearly expressed in *The Philosophy of Right*: "the universal does not prevail or achieve completion except along with particular interests and through the co-operation of particular [instances of] knowing and willing. . . ." (PR 260). This principle is exemplified throughout his analysis of the political individual, civil society, and the state. The individual, embedded within the particularites of familial life and multiple movements of production and exchange, conforms to universal law only by following his or her particular interests (e.g., PR 200ff). In a similar fashion, the administration of universal rights within civil society continues to be limited by particularistic

---

6. For a discussion of Habermas' participation in the historians' debate, see Shaun Gallagher, "The *Historikerstreit* and the Critique of Nationalism," *History of European Ideas* 16 (1993), 921–926.

7. Hegel, *The Philosophy of Right*, trans. T. M. Knox (Oxford: Oxford University Press, 1967), §11; hereafter cited as PR. Also see Habermas, TP 178–179.

requirements and wills (PR 230, 231). Even in the most universal expression of the state, i.e., in war, state rights "are actualized only in their particular wills and not in a universal will with constitutional powers over them" (PR 333). Thus, the force of the idea of universal law is limited by the reality of particular histories and conditions of nations.

National self-consciousness, according to Hegel, is the internal reflection of the particularistic external institutions that constitute a nation. This reflective understanding is not necessarily acquiescence, however; it can be "a vehicle for the contemporary development of the collective spirit in its actual existence. . . ."[8] At the same time, taking its start from is own particular situation, this reflective understanding, even if it becomes philosophical as defined in Hegel's "Preface," lacks any hint of a utopian tenor. To the extent that theory "goes beyond the world as it is and builds an ideal one as it ought to be, that world exists indeed, but only in [the theorist's] opinions, an unsubstantial element where anything you please may, in fancy be built" (PR 11). Hegel cites the Greek proverb: *Hic Rhodus, hic saltus*, and suggests what today one might call a postmodern translation: "Here is the rose, dance thou here" (PR 11). But for Hegel, the rose is not without why, and his advise comes closer to the Derridian conception of "you must start where you are," than to a Nietzschean prescriptive for dancing at the abyss. Clearly, Hegel rejects the philosophical starting point of first seeking out the universal (or the future utopia) and then applying it to the particular situation. The starting point must be with the particular situation, because there is no way for a philosopher to go beyond it. In this respect, Habermas is right to insist that Hegel was not able to transcend his time or circumstances. Indeed, Hegel acknowledges this as a sound hermeneutical principle: "Whatever happens, every individual is a child of his time; so philosophy too is its own time apprehended in thoughts. It is just as absurd to fancy that a philosophy can transcend its contemporary world as it is to fancy that an individual can overleap his own age, jump over Rhodes" (PR 11).

This does not mean that there is no access to the universal. Rather his hermeneutical principle defines that access. The universal can be found only within the particular. The particularistic aspects of the individual nation embodies a universality that is expressed in the political constitution and reflected in the sense of national identity experienced

---

8. Hegel, *The Philosophy of Mind* (Encyclopaedia, Part Three), trans. William Wallace (Oxford: Clarendon Press, 1971), §550; hereafter cited as PM. Also see PR §265; and *The Philosophy of History*, trans. J. Sibree (New York: Dover, 1956), pp. 43–46; hereafter cited as PH.

by the citizen (PR §269). Universality is never independent of the particularistic nature of national identity. Thus, the constitution of any particular nation, as the expression of universal principles, "depends in general on the character and development of [that nation's] self-consciousness" (PR 274).

Although critique is still possible, the concept of a critical reflection that would somehow escape the limitations of finite and less than ideal situations is ruled out. Critique, which is dialectical, cannot be carried out from a position, hypothetical or real, external to the particular time and place of the philosopher, citizen, or would-be ideal legislator.

> The proposal to give a constitution—even one more or less rational in content—to a nation *a priori* would be a happy thought overlooking precisely that factor in a constitution which makes it more than an *ens rationis*. Hence every nation has the constitution appropriate to it and suitable for it. (PR 274, Remark).

A real constitution is a historical entity. A historically determined national consciousness, which rules over the formation of the constitution, limits the universality possible in any national identity.

All of this clearly contrasts to Habermas' view of critique and his conception of postconventional universality. Habermas attempts to work out the possibility of postconventional (universal) identity in explicit contrast to Hegel's concept of national identity and its dependency on a self-conscious appreciation of national history.[9] On his view, only a critical reflective practice that takes its bearing from universal rather than particular laws can lead us toward a postconventional identity based on "constitutional patriotism."[10] To have a postconventional identity is to embrace values, not because they are held as authoritative by some particular person, group, or nation, but because they are based on a rational universality and consistency. Constitutional patriotism is directed away from particularistic national qualities of citizenship toward universal constitutional principles consistent with the Enlightenment concept of world citizenship. Enlightenment determinations of

---

9. See my "Some Particular Limitations of Postconventional Universality: Hegel and Habermas," in *Phenomenology, Interpretation, and Community*, ed. Lenore Langsdorf and Stephen Watson (Albany: SUNY Press, 1996), pp. 115–126.

10. See Habermas, *The New Conservatism: Cultural Criticism and the Historian's Debate*, trans. Shierry Weber Nicholsen (Cambridge: MIT Press, 1989), pp. 193, 227, 256; hereafter cited as NC; and *Communication and the Evolution of Society*, trans. Thomas McCarthy (Boston: Beacon Press, 1979), pp. 79ff., 95–129; hereafter cited as CES.

legality, morality, and sovereignty "are best suited to the identity of world citizens, not to that of citizens of a particular state that has to maintain itself against other states" (CES 114). Habermas, in contrast to Hegel (PR 333), thus embraces a Kantian internationalism.

Habermas would reverse Hegel's principle, that the universal can be sought out only from a position embedded in the particularities of national life. The principle of constitutional patriotism demands that the universality embodied in a nation's constitution rule over and define the limits of the particularity of any nation's self-identity. For Habermas, "the imperatives of the self-assertion of national forms of life through power politics no longer simply dominate the mode of action of the constitutional state but find their limits in postulates of the universalization of democracy and human rights" (NC 256). This involves moving from a pretended universality embodied in conservative sociocentric regimes and limited by a particular national consciousness, to universal principles consistent with internationalism and gained through unforced, enlightened consensus. In this move "identifications with one's own [national] forms of life and traditions are overtaken by a patriotism that has become more abstract, that now relates not to the concrete totality of a nation but rather to abstract procedures and principles."[11]

Brief Excursus on Time Consciousness and Utopian Energies

Habermas puts into question the possibility of a critique taking its start from the Hegelian *saltus*, which is essentially tied to the *hic*, to the *topos* of the particular situation. Indeed, if Habermas' critical theory does not take its start "beyond the world as it is" in order to build "an ideal one as it ought to be," it does seem to depend on what Hegel refers to as an "unsubstantial" procedure by which "anything you please may, in fancy be built" (PR 11). While Habermas does not fashion an abstract utopia, he is not shy about championing utopian energies. On this score Habermas insists on the value of a modern time consciousness that Hegel himself once recognized. This is an awareness of our own position in time that "expresses the conviction that the future has already begun: It is the epoch that lives for the future, that opens itself up to the novelty of the future." (PDM 5) In every case, modern historical consciousness is ordered to the future; and this means that in every case particularity is ordered to universality. Habermas quotes Hegel's *Phenomenology*: "It is surely not difficult to see that our time

---

11. NC 261; translation revised. Also see PDM 40.

is a birth and transition to a new period. The Spirit has broken with what was hitherto the world of its experience and imagination and is about to submerge all this in the past; it is at work giving itself a new form. . . ." (PDM 6).[12] For Habermas, modernity involves an orientation to the future that allows consciousness of the past to be overlaid by conceptions of progress and utopia.

Habermas laments the present-day loss of clarity afforded by the concept of a utopia as "a legitimate medium for depicting alternative life possibilities that are seen as inherent in the historical process itself. A utopian perspective is inscribed within politically active historical consciousness itself" (NC 50). For Habermas there is a strong connection between the universalism necessary for critique, modern time consciousness, and utopian energies—connections that have been severed and obscured: "Today it seems as though utopian energies have been used up, as if they have retreated from historical thought. The horizon of the future has contracted. . . . The future is negatively cathected; we see outlined on the threshold of the twenty-first century the horrifying panorama of a worldwide threat to universal life interests. . . ." (NC 50). In Habermas' view, theorists like Foucault, pursuing a Nietzschean nihilism, only help to "extinguish the last spark of utopia and destroy the last traces of Western culture's self-confidence" (NC 52).

Habermas, of course, is interested in the rejuvenation of utopian energies in connection with his project of communicative action. Seyla Benhabib has pointed out that Habermas' project has the potential to go beyond his utopian proceduralism. She finds "an unmistakable utopian content" associated with the very concept of postconventional identity.[13] For Habermas, however, this utopian perspective can be attained only through a universalization of the realm of particular needs. In this way "internal nature," the particularity associated with the realm of needs, "is thereby moved in a utopian perspective; that is, at this stage internal nature may no longer be merely examined within an

---

12. Concerning utopian energies in the early Hegel, see David M. Rasmussen, "Reflections on the 'End of History': Politics, Identity, and Civil Society," *Philosophy and Social Criticism* 18 (1992), 235–250.

13. Seyla Benhabib, "The Utopian Dimension in Communicative Ethics," in *Critical Theory: The Essential Readings*, eds. David Ingram and Julia Simon-Ingram (New York: Paragon, 1992), p. 390. Also see, "In the Shadow of Aristotle and Hegel: Communicative Ethics and Current Controversies in Practical Philosophy," *The Philosophical Forum* 21 (1989–90), 1–31. Benhabib states: "Universalizability is not only a *formal procedure* but involves the utopian projection of a way of life as well" (13). The utopian here is a society designed to include everyone in the ongoing moral conversation. "Discourse ethics projects such moral conversations in which reciprocal recognition is exercised, onto a utopian community of human kind" (23).

interpretive framework fixed by the cultural tradition in a nature-like way. . . . Inner nature is rendered communicatively fluid and transparent to the extent that needs can, through aesthetic forms of expression, be kept articulable or be released from their paleosymbolic prelinguisticality" (CES 93). This way of dealing with the substantiality and particularity of needs is possible only if this realm is ordered as secondary to and controlled by the universalized discourse of rights.[14] Precisely on this point it is important to raise a question essentially connected to the issues of universality and utopianism—the question of terrorism.

With respect to utopianism and time consciousness, George L. Kline defines the issue of terrorism in terms that pose a difficulty for conceptions of critique based on universalism. For Kline the problem involves an obsessive orientation toward the world-historical future, often found in utopian theories. This orientation is not confined to any one ideological program; it is clearly found in the theories of both Marx and Nietzsche, and quite often is defined in contrast to Hegel's "idolatry of the factual."[15] The concept of a historical utopia, as defined by Habermas, is characterized by the same feature of a future-directed orientation (NC 50–51). The most pernicious aspect of this future orientation is the assumption that for the sake of achieving the perfection of a universal utopian future, particular cultures, communities, and individuals existing in the present "could justifiably be reduced to the function of *means* for the realization of that historical *end*."[16] Kline finds evidence of this terroristic willingness to sacrifice present generations in both the theory and practice of regimes dedicated to the realization

---

14. Benhabib notes that Habermas follows Mead in this regard ("Utopian Dimension," p. 395). Benhabib supports a concept of *universalizable* need-interpretations: "a certain anticipatory utopia, a projection of the future as it could be, becomes necessary. Since the lines of development leading from present to future are fundamentally underdetermined, the theorist can no longer speak the language of evolution and necessity, but must conceive of herself as a participant in the formation of the future" (p. 398).

15. Nietzsche, *On the Uses and Disadvantages of History for Life*, cited by George L. Kline, "The Use and Abuse of Hegel by Nietzsche and Marx," in *Hegel and his Critics*, ed. William Desmond (Albany: State University of New York Press, 1989), p. 5.

16. George L. Kline, "The Potential Contribution of Classical Russian Philosophy to the Building of a Humane Society," paper read at the Colloquium on "The Problem of the Unity of Mankind in Russian Philosophy," *World Congress of Philosophy*, (Moscow, August 1993). This is the latest formulation of a problem that Kline defines in a number of papers, including "'Present', 'Past', and 'Future', as Categoreal Terms, and the 'Fallacy of the Actual Future'," *Review of Metaphysics* 40 (1986), 215–235; "Form, Concrescence, and Concretum," *Explorations in Whitehead's Philosophy*, eds. Lewis S. Ford and George L. Kline (Bronx, NY: Fordham University Press, 1983), pp. 104–146; and "The Past: Agency or Efficacy?" in *Akten des XIV. Internationalen Kongresses für Philosophie* (Vienna: Herder Verlag, 1969), IV, 580–584.

of some future utopian world. Quite commonly, this kind of terror is associated with a nationalism that is imperialistic and chauvinistic, that is, with the type of nationalism that is falsely universalized and exported across political and ethnic borders. This is a type of nationalism that is quite distant from Hegel's concept, expressed in his view "that every nation has the constitution appropriate to it and suitable for it."

The mature Hegel, as Kline points out, scrupulously avoids the rhetoric of future orientation and provides a much more adequate model of time consciousness in his metaphor of organic growth.[17] According to this model, the present circumstance is both the ontological and axiological point of departure toward the future. That the real is rational means that the only access we have to a universal rationality is to be found precisely in the reality of the present as it has been shaped by the past. One does not step outside of the particularities of the present (the real) in order to find an externally (rationally) defined universality that is then used as a standard for condemning and terrorizing the present for the sake of constructing a future utopia.

The question that must be raised is whether the utopian energy of universalism championed by Habermas, even as it moves away from chauvinistic nationalism, implies a similar potential terrorism. Does a critique that appeals to the standard of universality necessarily devalue and instrumentalize the present; does it deny the intrinsic value of the present, existing generations? Jean-François Lyotard, for one, reads Habermas in precisely this way. Lyotard interprets Habermas' quest for universality as a quest for a totalizing unity of which Lyotard remains suspicious. Habermas' project can find its legitimacy only "in a future to be accomplished," in a preference for "the universality, self-determination, and transparency of the future promised by emancipation" over "the particularity, randomness, and opacity of the present."[18] Although Lyotard usually associates Hegel with the same kind of quest for universalism, and indeed considers Habermas' project to be in some respects Hegelian (PE 3, 18), he also sees in Hegel an awareness of the danger of terrorism. In Hegel's view a critical hermeneutics of suspicion which takes the universal, in the sense of absolute emancipation, as its guide, always ends in a terror that puts every particular reality under suspicion. "So it judges any particular act, even when it is prescribed

---

17. See Kline, "The Use and Abuse of Hegel," p. 12; Hegel, PhG, Preface §2.

18. Jean-François Lyotard, *The Postmodern Explained*, trans., Don Barry et al. (Minneapolis: University of Minnesota Press, 1992), pp. 18, 26, 50. Hereafter cited as PE.

by law and executed according to the rules, as failing to match up to the ideal. Terror acts on the suspicion that nothing is emancipated enough—and makes it into a politics. Every particular reality is a plot against the pure, universal will."[19]

Whether or not the terroristic arrangement of the universal in opposition to the particular is a necessary result of Habermas' project, at the very least it threatens as a possibility. But is it necessary that critique be based on a universalism that seems associated with the terrorism implied by a utopian future orientation? Is there another basis for critique that reads the dialectic of the particular and the universal in a different way?

Foucault and the Hegel of Particulars

Foucault, not unlike Hegel, offers a model of critique that takes its point of departure from historical contents rather than from utopian schemas or the metanarratives of totalitarian theories. Critique, according to Foucault, needs to reveal the historical knowledge that is displaced or hidden by functionalist or systematizing thought. His genealogies are contrasted with "the tyranny of globalizing discourses with their hierarchy and all their privileges of a theoretical *avant-garde....*" (P/K 83). Genealogy provides the opportunity to use a historical knowledge of power struggles; in contrast, globalizing discourse, what Lyotard calls 'metanarrative', attempts to create a utopian future. A metanarrative has two necessary characteristics: first, it claims a universal scope. Its range is meant to cover all other narratives. Second, it is normative in the specific sense that it claims to supply the criteria to adjudicate conflicts among all other discourses. Foucault's genealogies, in contrast, remain on a local or regional level; they remain rooted in the particular and they refrain from universalizing their results. Foucault distinguishes two steps: "If we were to characterize it in two terms, then 'archaeology' would be the appropriate methodology of this analysis of local discursivities, and 'genealogy' would be the tactics whereby, on the basis of the descriptions of these local discursivities, the subjected knowledges which were thus released would be brought into play" (P/K 85). Genealogies, as they are put into play, however, do not offer adjudicative procedures that attempt to resolve the struggles they discover through historical description. Not unlike Hegel's characterization of

---

19. *Postmodern Explained*, p. 54.

philosophy as the gray in gray of theory, Foucault notes, in an essay in honor of Jean Hyppolite, "genealogy is gray."[20]

The critical theorist might object that if the genealogical procedure refuses to adjudicate, refuses, as Hegel would say, to reconstruct reality as it ought to be, then genealogy loses its critical bite. Yet Foucault pictures genealogy as waging a struggle, and it is in this struggle that it finds its critical edge. By focusing on the particular it struggles against the pretense of universality made by sciences, metanarratives, and universalizing procedures (P/K 126). It struggles against the theoretical *avant-garde* that claims to have privileged access to the future. It does so precisely by exposing the pretense of universality to "all the discontinuous forms of knowledge that circulate about it" (P/K 85). Genealogies, then, are critical, not in spite of the fact, but because they lay no claim to universality. Indeed, their criticality is to be found precisely in their disruption of claims to universality.

Not unlike Hegel? It is true that Foucault, like Lyotard, would list Hegel's discourse as one of the 'globalizing discourses' that he attempts to struggle against. Foucault, after all, is author of a famous philosophical apprehension: "our age, whether through logic or epistemology, whether through Marx or through Nietzsche, is attempting to flee Hegel. . . ."[21] Foucault, more specifically, struggles against Hegelian politics, "the kind of politics which, since the beginning of the 19th century obstinately insists on seeing in the immense domain of practice only an epiphany of triumphant reason. . . ."[22] Yet, it is clear that Foucault's engagement with Hegel (how else to struggle against Hegel) is one from which he learns. On this score I want to note three things.

First, the Hegel that Foucault was fleeing, or struggling against, was the one provided for him by his teacher, Jean Hyppolite. Two things are clear from Foucault's remarks about Hyppolite: (1) there is no question of a clean break with Hegel. "But truly to escape Hegel

---

20. Foucault, "Nietzsche, Genealogy, History," trans. Donald F. Bouchard and Sherry Simon, in *The Foucault Reader*, p. 76. On the notion that genealogy can be critical, see Rudi Visker, "Can Genealogy be Critical? A Somewhat Unromantic Look at Nietzsche and Foucault," *Man and World* 23 (1990), 441–452. For a more Habermasian view, see Larry Ray, "Foucault, Critical Theory and the Decomposition of the Historical Subject," *Philosophy and Social Criticism* 14 (1988), 69–110.

21. Foucault, "The Discourse on Language," trans. Rupert Swyer, in *The Archaeology of Knowledge* , tran. A. M. Sheridan Smith (New York: Pantheon Books, 1972), p. 235. Hereafter cited as AK.

22. Foucault, "Politics and the Study of Discourse," trans. Colin Gordon in *The Foucault Effect: Studies in Governmentality*, ed. Graham Burchell, Colin Gordon and Peter Miller (Chicago: University of Chicago Press, 1991), p. 69.

involves an exact appreciation of the price we have to pay to detach ourselves from him. It assumes that we are aware of the extent to which Hegel, insidiously perhaps, is close to us; it implies a knowledge in that which permits us to think against Hegel, of that which remains Hegelian" (AK 235). (2) Hyppolite provides Foucault with a transformed Hegel. Hyppolite works an alteration on Hegel by which he transforms "the Hegelian theme of the end of self-consciousness into one of repeated interrogation" (AK 236). Hyppolite's Hegel provides a philosophy that is capable of contact with non-philosophy. Specifically we could say that Hyppolite provided a Hegel of particulars rather than a Hegel of universals, and thus, a philosophy that has as its task, not to abstract, but rather "to maintain a certain reticence, to break with acquired generalizations and continually to reestablish contact with the non-philosophical. . . . to examine the singularity of history, the regional rationalities of science, the depths of memory in consciousness. . . . [the] singular individual, within a society and a social class, and in the midst of struggle" (AK 236).

Second, Foucault's struggle against Hegel in some respects found its way into his struggle to define the concept of power. Foucault struggles with a notion of power that involves the concept of repression, a concept that he himself employed in his early work. "Though one finds this definition of power as repression endlessly repeated in present day discourse, it is not that discourse which invented it— Hegel first spoke of it, then Freud and later Reich" (P/K 90). Foucault works out his own notion of power by combining the concept of power as repression with a concept of power as struggle, which he associates with Nietzsche. He contrasts this struggle-repression model with an older view he terms the 'monarchical-juridical' or 'contract-oppression' model. But in the mid-70s we find Foucault questioning the notion of repression as inadequate for explaining contemporary mechanisms of power (P/K 92). Specifically, he suspects that, in the end, the notion of repression remains tied to the traditional monarchical-juridical view.

It is quite easy to read Hegel as holding to a monarchical-juridical model of power. According to this view the "essential role of the theory of right, from medieval times onwards, was to fix the legitimacy of power; that is the major problem around which the whole theory of right and sovereignty is organized" (P/K 95). Foucault indeed does read Hegel in this way. "As always with relations of power, one is faced with complex phenomena which don't obey the Hegelian form of the dialectic. . . . 'Dialectic' is a way of evading the always open and hazardous reality of conflict by reducing it to a Hegelian skeleton. . . ." (P/K 56, 114–115). Thus, Foucault's struggle to define power is also a struggle to free himself from, or perhaps, to transform Hegel and the hypothesis of repression.[23]

Third, it's possible that Foucault found something more positive in Hegel. In his analysis of *Sittlichkeit*, Hegel suggests that power is embedded in every human and institutional relation in a way that cannot be reduced to the simple hegemonic, monarchical model. This idea is connected to Hegel's view that economic relations are not disembedded from other dimensions of *Sittlichkeit*. An embedded economic system is one in which the economic factors of a society are so integrated into the substance of society that, in practice, they are not distinguishable or detachable from other factors of the moral and social infrastructure such as kinship, marriage, generational differences, the variety of private associations, or public solemnities. The life Hegel describes as *Sittliche* involves relations that are at once familial, economic, political, and moral, with no actual priority awarded to any one of these dimensions.[24]

Foucault, in attempting to work out a theory of power that is not reducible to either a monarchical-juridical model or to an economism that views power as subordinate to economic relations, seeks a theory that would provide an alternative to the concept of functional subordination, yet recognize "that the relations of power do indeed remain profoundly enmeshed in and with economic relations and participate with them in a common circuit" (P/K 89). It is possible to read Hegel's analysis of civil society as a theory that would recognize the indissoluble interconnections between politics and the economy, without reducing one to the other. In effect, it is possible to read Hegel's analysis, at one level, as focusing on the particularity of power relations within an early modern civil society, in a way that is not unlike the analysis that Foucault was seeking. Foucault's use of the term 'government' suggests what Hegel recognized as the multi-dimensional and comprehensive nature of power relations. The very broad meaning of the word 'government' included reference not only to "political structures or to the management of states; rather it designated the way in which the conduct of individuals or of groups might be directed: the government of children, of souls, of communities, of families, of the sick."[25]

---

23. Visker argues that "Foucault never really succeeded in leaving the hypothesis of repression behind him. . . ." ("Can Genealogy be Critical?" p. 447).

24. I have worked this out in more detail in "Interdependence and Freedom in Hegel's Economics," in *Hegel on Economics and Freedom*, ed. William Maker (Mercer University Press, 1987), 159–181.

25. Foucault, "The Subject and Power," Afterward to *Michel Foucault: Beyond Structuralism and Hermeneutics*, eds. Hubert L. Dreyfus and Paul Rabinow (Chicago: University of Chicago Press, 1982), p. 221. This essay hereafter cited as SP.

The individual embedded in the multiplicity of power relations that constitute civil society, is, as Foucault points out, a subject in two senses: a subject by way of being subjected to such relations; and a subject maintaining an identity in conscience and self-knowledge. It is precisely in this dual sense of the subject that Hegel describes the essence of freedom. Freedom is actualized precisely when the subject self-consciously recognizes and affirms or wills its actual subjectification. Foucault also insists that government, in the broadest sense of the term, requires and implies freedom: "Power is exercised only over free subjects, and only insofar as they are free" (SP 221). But, for Foucault, freedom is not the actual affirmation or willing of subjectification; it is the constant possibility of refusing particular subjectifications. Not the conformity of the will, but the possibility of "the recalcitrance of the will," is the sign of freedom. "Rather than speaking of an essential freedom, it would be better to speak of an 'agonism'—of a relationship which is at the same time reciprocal incitation and struggle; less of a face-to-face confrontation which paralyzes both sides than a permanent provocation" (SP 222).

In the end, of course, Hegel and Foucault differ fundamentally on the question of the nature of power and domination. Hegel works with the conception of a monarchical power that operates as the principle of his state system. This, to some degree, gets in the way of critique, because, as he sees it, the state properly orders and centers all of the multiple relations of the embedded civil society—and he reads this as freedom rather than domination. Thus, Foucault suggests, "the theory of sovereignty, and the organization of a legal code centered around it, have allowed a system of right to be superimposed upon the mechanism of discipline in such a way as to conceal its actual procedures, the element of domination inherent in its techniques, and to guarantee to everyone, by virtue of the sovereignty of the State, the exercise of his proper sovereign right" (P/K 105). It is possible that Foucault, in proposing a new conception of power, remains more faithful to Hegel's conception of multi-dimensional embeddedness—an embeddedness within mutual power relations of domination and "multiple forms of subjugation that have a place and function within the social organism"—a power that is spread out in "more regional and local forms and institutions" (P/K 96)—and thereby a conception that provides the ground for a critique that remains connected to the particular contexts of human relations. It is, then, quite easy to contrast a system of spirit (Hegel) to a system of discourse/power (Foucault): "rather than worry about the problem of the central spirit, I believe that we must attempt to study the myriad of bodies which are constituted as peripheral *subjects* as a result of the effects of power" (P/K 98). Nonetheless, with his conception of embeddedness, Hegel actually comes close to discovering disciplinary power and its effects.[26] Perhaps on this count Habermas' observation is close to right: his own particular time and place prevented him from moving beyond the conception of sovereign power.

Critical Hermeneutics without Universals

Hegel's analysis of *Sittlichkeit*, if it does not precisely reach the level of a critical hermeneutics, provides its basic principle. The fact that Habermas controverts this principle leads him in the direction of a utopian critical theory, and away from a 'depth hermeneutics' anchored in particular *topoi*. The fact that Foucault affirms this principle leads him in the direction of a critical hermeneutics and thereby qualifies his own conception of a post-hermeneutical analysis.[27]

Hegel's Hermeneutical Principle

First, we must note that there is no general agreement among Hegel interpreters concerning the relationship between the universal and the particular. Habermas himself reviews three approaches. Conservative interpretations of Hegel make the abstract concept of universal right conform to the particular character of nationalist spirit [*Volksgeist*]. Liberal interpretations find in Hegel the primacy of universal right over particularistic national identity. Finally, left Hegelians (Habermas here cites Herbert Marcuse) object to the threat that "substantive morality" associated with nationalistic particularities poses to universal principles (TP 134–136).

I interpret the principle explicated by Hegel to be a principle consistent with philosophical hermeneutics. It is not that the universal

---

26. Both Hegel and Foucault would study the concept of right, not as it ought to be, but as it manifests itself in the age. They both ask how things work. Hegel's answer is filtered through his systematic and monarchical schema; Foucault is guided by his new view of power. Is this a difference of ages as well as of concept?

27. Even if Foucault is not concerned with devising commentary on particular discourses, and therefore is not doing hermeneutics in its traditional form, still, is he not concerned with understanding the meaning and effects of particular discourses, and therefore, in some sense, still doing hermeneutics? On this issue, see Richard Palmer, "Beyond Hermeneutics? Some Remarks on the Meaning and Scope of Hermeneutics," *University of Dayton Review* 17 (1984), p. 5; and "On the Transcendentality of Hermeneutics," in *Hermeneutics: Questions and Prospects*, ed. Gary Shapiro and Alan Sica (Amherst: University of Massachusetts Press, 1984), pp. 84–95.

is made to conform to the particular, or that the particular necessarily threatens the universal; rather, it's simply the case that we have no way to understand the universal except from within the particular situation in which we happen to find ourselves. If, as Hegel puts it, "the universal does not prevail or achieve completion except along with particular interests and through the co-operation of particular [instances of] knowing and willing," then our reach for the universal will always be constrained by particular circumstances. In essence, this principle predates the Enlightenment, and expresses an ancient tradition that stretches back to the Greeks. In the contemporary field of hermeneutics, Hans-Georg Gadamer develops it further in his discussions of the hermeneutical situation and the concept of *phronesis*. *Phronesis* does not operate on the basis of universal, context-independent rules, procedures or utopian goals. With *phronesis* we lay out no grand schemes for the future; rather we start from the particular situation and do the best we can. With *phronesis* we occupy no universally justified position from which to judge, although we are always in a position and we always are required to judge. So, we can only judge case by case.[28]

Hegel's principle is hermeneutical precisely insofar as it expresses the concept of *phronesis*, a concept that clarifies the relation between the universal and the particular.[29] For Hegel, we begin to discern the universal only from within our particular circumstances. The concepts of *Sittlichkeit* and *phronesis* are, for Hegel, dialectically connected. Precisely because the citizen and the legislator are embedded within their *ethos*, within the multiple dimensions of *Sittlichkeit*, without the possibility of escape to the unfettered universal, they require *phronesis* as a way of coping. At the same time, to have *phronesis* one requires an *ethos*, a *sittliche* backdrop, the particularity supplied by one's historical situation. Thus, *Sittlichkeit* provides the resources for *phronesis*, and *phronesis* provides the means of dealing with and transforming

---

28. See Hans-Georg Gadamer, *Truth and Method,* 2nd rev. ed., revised translation by Joel Weinsheimer and Donald G. Marshall (New York: Crossroad Press, 1989), pp. 301–302. In Gadamer's terms, knowledge of a situation is always an imperfect knowledge that is embedded within the situation. The model for such knowledge is *phronesis* (see *Ibid.*, pp. 313ff). Gadamer explains the model of *phronesis* in hermeneutical terms: "it does not mean first understanding a given universal in itself and then afterward applying it to a concrete case." Rather, the actual understanding of the universal itself is constituted only through our understanding of the given case (see *Truth and Method*, p. 341). For further discussion see my essay, "The Place of *Phronesis* in Postmodern Hermeneutics," *Philosophy Today* 37 (1993), 298–305.

29. Again, this conflicts with Habermas' reading, according to which Hegel had abandoned *phronesis* even before he abandoned critique (see TP 126–129).

Sittlichkeit. Phronesis, in this regard, can be both suspicious and critical, but it cannot be utopian. On the model of a critical hermeneutics that would employ Hegel's principle, there are no universal prescriptives that can be legitimately formulated in advance of particular situations that call for judgment.

Habermas' Non-hermeneutical (Utopian) Theory

For Habermas, the critical task is not directed at simply understanding the present situation, but at changing it, by limiting the particularity of the circumstance according to a universal norm or normative procedure. This conception of critique clearly depends upon a principle directly opposed to Hegel's. Habermas allows for the possibility of a procedural disconnection from the particular. Thus, in critical reconstruction particular national interests would no longer dominate the universal aspects of the constitutional state, but would "find their limits in postulates of the universalization of democracy and human rights" (NC 256).

In Habermas' conception of the critical enterprise, one attempts to stand outside of particular traditions and institutions in order to develop a rational justification of transnational universal laws. Still, for Habermas, as well as for Hegel, critique always requires a self-conscious reflection on one's particular history. For Hegel, this self-reflection is embedded within the particularity of a nation's traditions and is thus limited. For Habermas, self-reflection is a 'gaze' that critically appropriates its history in the light of an abstract and universal idea that we access as a measure and use to decide "which of our traditions we want to continue and which we do not" (NC 263). With this orientation to the universal, does critique still remain faithful to the demands of the hermeneutical situation, which is always a particular, historical situation?

In Habermas' debate with Gadamer, one of the issues involves precisely this question: To what extent can one detach oneself from the particular circumstances of life? To what degree is it possible to attain the universal? The critical gaze is, as Habermas acknowledges, educated by its history. And he does recognize the force of the particular in the realm of individual identity formation. On the level of an individual life, identity does not depend solely on moral choice, i.e., a choice that requires orientation within a universalistic framework.[30] There are other, particularistic forces involved in deciding 'who one wants to be.'

---

30. Habermas, *The Theory of Communicative Practice*, vol. 2, trans. Thomas McCarthy (Boston: Beacon, 1987), p. 97. Hereafter cited as TCP II.

> There is an indissoluble element of arbitrariness [*Willkur*] in the choice of a life project. This is to be explained by the fact that the individual cannot adopt a hypothetical attitude toward his own origins and background, that he cannot accept or reject his biography in the same way as he can a norm whose claim to validity is under discussion (TCP II 109)

Thus, the individual is embedded within *Sittlichkeit,* within a set of cultural values, within a particularistic collective identity, within a historical tradition. Yet Habermas still insists on the ability to disconnect or to detach oneself from the particular in order to instigate a decision within a universalistic framework (see NC 225, 257, 261). Even if the individual is "the *product* of the tradition in which he stands, of the solidary groups to which he belongs, of socialization and learning processes to which he is exposed" (TCP II 135), he can also adopt a critical attitude in which "only *universal* norms let themselves be distinguished as moral. . . . [At the postconventional stage], the ego can no longer identify with itself through particular roles and existing norms. It has to take into account that the traditional accustomed forms of life prove themselves as merely particular, as irrational; therefore it must retract its identity, so to speak, behind the line of all *particular* roles and norms. . . ."[31] On Hegel's view, in contrast, embeddedness within *Sittlichkeit* means that there is never the possibility of moral disconnection. Freedom, for Hegel, is conformity to the universal as it is embedded within and limited by the arbitrariness and contingency of particularity.

Gadamer's position is similar to Hegel's in this respect: particularistic traditions will always limit universal aspirations, rather than the other way around. The hermeneutical situation is always constrained by the particular traditions that define the life of the interpreter. As Gadamer puts it, "[l]ong before we understand ourselves through the process of self-examination, we understand ourselves in a self-evident way in the

---

31. Habermas, *Die Entwicklung des Ich,* cited and translated in Jerald Wallulis, *The Hermeneutics of Life History: Personal Achievement and History in Gadamer, Habermas, and Erikson* (Evanston, IL: Northwestern University Press, 1990), p. 75. Not unlike Husserl's view of phenomenological reduction, for Habermas, on the postconventional level there is a "shift in focus to a reflectively devalued social world that has been stripped of its naturalness" ("Justice and Solidarity: On the Discussion Concerning 'Stage 6'," trans. Shierry Weber Nicholsen, *Philosophical Forum* 21 (1989–90), p. 50. The methodological disconnection from the lifeworld involves a distinction between the procedure of rational justification of universal principles and rules, and their application to particular situations. On Habermas' view application involves the use of principles and rules already supplied by disembedded justificatory procedures of discursive argumentation. This comes closer to technical application than to a practice of *phronesis.* (see Ibid., 50–51).

family, society, and state in which we live."[32] Critical reflection itself is in every instance an interpretational practice. In the attempt to appeal to transnational, universal rights, the interpreter is already bound up within a particular system of national values, prejudices, and traditions. One can only approach the universal from within the particular, but without ever escaping the particular. Still, this does not make critique impossible.

Foucault and the Possibility of Critical Hermeneutics

Habermas is puzzled about Foucault's evocation of Kant's essay *What is Enlightenment?* He tries to place Foucault within the heritage of critical theory, on a line that runs from Kant to the young Hegel, to Marx and the young Hegelians, and through the Frankfurt School, a path that delineates the project of modernity. But this is the line that runs to Habermas himself, not to Foucault. From Habermas' perspective, it would be difficult to fit Foucault into the tradition of critical theory, precisely because Foucault develops a critique of critical reason, a critique of the Enlightenment, a critique of the very foundations of critique, and is thus embroiled in a disabling contradiction.

What Foucault finds valuable in Kant's essay *"What is Enlightenment?"* is the form of the question:

> What are we? in a very precise moment of history. Kant's question appears as an analysis of both us and our present. I think that this aspect of philosophy took on more and more importance. Hegel. Nietzsche. . . . But the task of philosophy as a critical analysis of our world is something which is more and more important. Maybe the most certain of all philosophical problems is the problem of the present time, and of what we are, in this very moment (SP 216).

Foucault follows Baudelaire, but in this does not escape Hegel, in defining modernity as an attitude of "permanent critique of our historical era."[33] Rather than supplying the answer in terms of its claim to non-ideological politics, the Enlightenment requires that we critically question the Enlightenment answer. The Enlightenment imposes itself in the form of a question. This imposition is what Gadamer would call an instance of historical effect, and according to Foucault, it orients

---

32. *Truth and Method*, p. 276.

33. Foucault, "What is Enlightenment," in *The Foucault Reader*, ed. Paul Rabinow (New York: Pantheon Books, 1984), p. 42; hereafter cited as WE.

critical analysis to the present time: "We must try to proceed with the analysis of ourselves as beings who are historically determined, to a certain extent, by the Enlightenment. Such an analysis implies a series of historical inquiries. . . . oriented toward the 'contemporary limits of the necessary', that is, toward what is not or is no longer indispensable for the constitution of ourselves as autonomous subjects" (WE 43).

This is a line of critical theory that, in opposition to all of Habermas' readings, I want to trace, perhaps only as a possibility, through the later Hegel, Gadamer, and Foucault. Its starting point is not a universal conception of power or an overarching conception of rationalism, as one might find in the Frankfurt School, but a local analysis of different processes in different fields.[34] Critical hermeneutics puts claims to universality into question: it asks, "in what is given to us as universal, necessary, obligatory, what place is occupied by whatever is singular, contingent, and the product of arbitrary constraints?" (WE 45). In opposition to Habermas, Foucault conceives of critique not as "the search for formal structures with universal value, but rather as a historical investigation into the events that have led us to constitute ourselves and to recognize ourselves as subjects of what we are doing, thinking, saying" (WE 46).

As a starting point, the present does not lead to consensus or to a perfect future, but to the possibility of critical refusal. "Maybe the target nowadays is not to discover what we are, but to refuse what we are. . . ." (SP 216). Thus, Foucault suggests, critique takes the form of "a possible transgression." As such, it does not promise universal consensus, but local agonism, provocation, the possibility of struggle, the possibility of refusal. Critical thought needs to be a 'constant checking,' and the first order of business for this checking is the Hegelian moment: "We have to know the historical conditions which motivate our conceptualization. We need a historical awareness of our present circumstance" (SP 209).

Critical hermeneutics involves struggle which is immediate in two ways: it is struggle at a local level, and it is not oriented toward a

---

34. "I think the word rationalization is dangerous. What we have to do is analyze specific rationalities rather than always invoking the progress of rationalization in general. Even if the *Aufklärung* has been a very important phase in our history and in the development of political technology, I think we have to refer to much more remote processes if we want to understand how we have been trapped in our own history. I would like to suggest another way to go further towards a new economy of power relations, a way which is more empirical, more directly related to our present situation, and which implies more relations between theory and practice. It consists of taking the forms of resistance against different forms of power as a starting point." (Foucault, SP 210–211).

future. "In such struggles people criticize instances of power which are the closest to them. . . . They do not look for the 'chief [remote] enemy', but for the immediate enemy. Nor do they expect to find a solution to their problem at a future date (that is, liberations, revolutions, end of class struggle)" (SP 211). Thus, critical hermeneutics is motivated by other than utopian energies: critique "must turn away from all projects that claim to be global or radical. In fact we know from experience that the claim to escape from the system of contemporary reality so as to produce the overall programs of another society, of another way of thinking, another culture, another vision of the world, has led only to the return of the most dangerous traditions" (WE 46-47).[35]

To give up the power of an ought that derives from an already known universal, from the future already dreamed, is not to give up the responsibility to act in response to existing conditions. We can act with genuine responsibility only in the full knowledge that we do not have an already-known universal or a complete right to or claim on the future. In this context, individual judgments and the practices of constitutional democracy are more ambiguous and unsure. In critical reflection informed by *phronesis*, the situation is not made clear-cut, or black and white, but is interpreted in shades of Hegel's and Foucault's favorite color: *grau, gris,* gray.

---

35. This is clearly the motivation for Foucault's reservations about Habermas' project and his worry about its utopian tenor. See *The Final Foucault,* eds. James Bernauer and David Rasmussen (Cambridge: MIT Press, 1987), p. 18.

Part III
Alterity and Communality

9 The Speculative Concrete: I. A. Il'in's Interpretation Of Hegel

Philip T. Grier

For most philosophers in the modern period the contrast between the concrete and the abstract has not been regarded as problematic, nor has it attracted much attention. Especially in the English-speaking world, the distinction has most often been employed in the manner bequeathed by the seventeenth and eighteenth century Empiricists, without being subjected to much critical scrutiny. This could be taken as evidence of a certain carelessness, since a little investigation into the philosophical history of the distinction reveals a considerable variety of usages, depending upon whether abstract and concrete were understood to qualify terms, names, ideas, concepts, or something else, and also upon the author and the philosophical period in question.[1] The authors of some more careful recent attempts to examine the distinction as it occurs in contemporary philosophical parlance have been dismayed to discover that there is no single, settled usage, or common core of meaning, to be discerned.[2] The modern tradition does

---

*Research for this paper was supported by Grant No. RI-20675-93 from the National Endowment for the Humanities.

1. For example, the article on *Abstrakt/konkret* in the *Historisches Wörterbuch der Philosophie*, Hrsg. von Joachim Ritter, Band 1, 33–42, is very informative on this point.

2. The use of this distinction in the empiricist/analytic tradition has recently come to seem troublesome to several philosophers working in that tradition. See, for example, David Lewis, *On the Plurality of Worlds* (Oxford: Blackwell, 1986) pp. 81–86; and Susan C. Hale, "Spacetime and the Abstract/Concrete Distinction," *Philosophical Studies*, LIII

not appear to have settled on any single doctrine of the abstract and the concrete, despite a tendency in much of the literature to treat the terms as though they were unproblematic.

Two important philosophers in the modern tradition, Hegel and Whitehead, represent exceptions to this general tendency. Both of them departed from the more usual practice of casually employing the term concrete without developing an explicit doctrine of concretion (or abstraction), and made such a doctrine central to their respective philosophical positions. Hegel developed an elaborate doctrine of speculative concreteness as an ultimate criterion of reality for his system; Whitehead in his account of reality developed a complex set of contrasts between concrescences and concreta which were central to his system.

One of the contemporary philosophers who has directed the most careful attention to the doctrines of concreteness (to use the looser term for the moment) employed by Hegel and by Whitehead is George Kline. In a series of works produced over a number of years, Kline has made a significant contribution to our understanding of both philosophers' treatments of what for each of them is a crucially important doctrine.[3] He has devoted special attention to the doctrine of speculative concreteness in Hegel, overlooked by a significant number of commentators. He is also the author of an important critical study of Whitehead's distinctive philosophical vocabulary, focusing especially upon his usages of forms, concresences, concreta, and concrete. In a nice coincidence, it was also George Kline who first told me of the existence of I. A. Il'in's two-volume Russian language commentary on Hegel, and as it happens, that work offers exceptional insight into Hegel's doctrine of the speculative concrete.

(1985), 85–102. Similar difficulties were voiced by Laverne Shelton in a paper read at the 1980 Eastern Division APA Meeting: "The Abstract and the Concrete: How Much Difference Does This Distinction Mark?" See also the work *Concretum* by August Seiffert (Meisenheim am Glan: A. Hain, 1961), pp. 356. Seiffert, examining contemporary usage of the term 'concrete' concludes that ". . . this little word has become a philosophical panacea, simply a stamp of approval." (p. 124, quoted in the *Historisches Wörterbuch Der Philosophie*, Band 1, 41–42).

3. Kline's works on this topic include "Some Recent Reinterpretations of Hegel's Philosophy," *The Monist*, XLVIII (1964), pp. 34–75; "Form, Concrescence and Concretum: A Neo-Whiteheadian Analysis," in *The Southern Journal of Philosophy* 7 (1969–70), pp. 351–60; "Form, Concrescence and Concretum," in *Explorations in Whitehead's Philosophy*, Ed. Lewis S. Ford and George L. Kline, (New York: Fordham University Press, 1983); "Concept and Concrescence: An Essay in Hegelian-Whiteheadian Ontology," in *Hegel and Whitehead: Contemporary Perspectives on Systematic Philosophy*, Ed. George R. Lucas, Jr. (Albany: State University of New York Press, 1985).

Historical Introduction

Historically speaking, the first major, systematic commentary on Hegel organized explicitly around his doctrine of the speculative concrete was published in 1918 by the Russian philosopher Ivan Aleksandrovich Il'in.[4] Il'in was born in Moscow in 1883, educated in the Faculty of Law at Moscow University (1901–06), and made a *privat-dozent* there in 1909.[5] After returning from a two-year period of philosophical study abroad in 1912,[6] he taught at Moscow University until 1922. He was exiled by the Bolsheviks from Soviet Russia in that year, at age 39, and settled in Berlin. He then escaped from Nazi Germany in 1938, and lived in Switzerland until his death in 1954.

His commentary, *Filosofiia Gegelia kak uchenie o konkretnosti Boga i cheloveka [The Philosophy of Hegel as a Doctrine of the Concreteness of God and Man],*[7] was published in two volumes totalling 670 pages. Many years later, at the urging of friends, Il'in undertook to translate his own commentary into German, a language in which he possessed native fluency. However, owing to ill health, and his desire to spend the time remaining to him on other still-uncompleted major projects, he was unwilling to take the time necessary for a translation of the complete Russian text. He translated into German all of Volume One, plus the last two chapters only of Volume Two, omitting eight chapters (257 pages) of the original, and published this

---

4. For a discussion of Il'in's own documentation of this claim, see below p. 20.

5. There are two good published sources of bibliographical information concerning Il'in: N. Poltoratsky, *Ivan Aleksandrovich* Il'in: *Zhizn', trudy, mirovozzrenie (Sbornik Statei)* (Tenafly, NJ: Hermitage Press, 1989); and Yu.T. Lisitsa, "Ivan Aleksandrovich Il'in: Istoriko-biograficheskii ocherk," in *I.A. Il'in, Sobranie sochinenii* (Moskva: Russkaia Kniga, 1993), Tom pervyi, str. 5–36.

6. In the period 1910–12 Il'in visited the Universities of Heidelberg (presenting a paper in Prof. Jellinek's seminar), Freiburg (a paper for Prof. Rickert), Berlin (preparation of a master's thesis on Hegel), Göttingen (papers for Prof. Husserl and Prof. Nelson), and the Sorbonne, and returned once again to Berlin (Prof. Simmel). Source: Poltoratsky, *Ivan Aleksandrovich Il'in,* pp. 11–12.

7. I. A. Il'in, *Filosofiia Gegelia kak uchenie o konkretnosti Boga i cheloveka,* v dvykh tomax (Moskva: Izd. G.A. Lemana i S.I. Sakharova, 1918) Tom pervyi, *Uchenie o Boge,* xi + 301 str.— hereafter cited as FG I; Tom vtoroi, *Uchenie o cheloveke,* 356 str.— hereafter cited as FG II. Volume One of this work was submitted by Il'in as his master's dissertation, and Volume Two as his doctoral dissertation. The defense of both volumes was held in a single session under dramatic circumstances in 1918, following which the Faculty of Law unanimously awarded him both degrees. (See Poltoratsky, *I.A. Il'in,* p. 12). Access to these two volumes outside of Russia has been difficult; until very recently, only one set was known to be held in the U.S., and that unavailable for circulation or copying.

work in Switzerland as a single volume in 1946, under the title *Die Philosophie Hegels als Kontemplative Gotteslehre.*[8]

In terms of its depth, subtlety, and sophistication, Il'in's commentary should be widely recognized as one of the more significant ones published in this century. In actuality the original Russian edition has remained essentially unknown to Western Hegel scholars up to the present; those acquainted with Il'in's interpretation of Hegel have worked only from the truncated German text. That text has never become very widely known, but it has attracted the admiration of a number of scholars who have studied it with care.

Unfortunately, due to singularly unlucky historical timing, neither of these attempts by Il'in to bring his commentary to the attention of a wider circle of philosophers succeeded in the measure deserved. The original work was published on the eve of the Civil War in Russia, and though it did not go completely unnoticed, the task of sorting out the subtleties of German metaphysics could not command much attention in the midst of the Russian Civil War. By the time peace was restored, the Bolsheviks were firmly in control, the intellectual climate had been sharply altered, Hegel was declared a "bourgeois idealist philosopher," and Il'in forced into exile. So ended his first attempt to communicate his interpretation of Hegel to the wider world.

His second attempt was initially not much more successful, as the timing of this second publication was not much more historically fortunate than the first. The Swiss edition appeared immediately after the close of WWII, in 1946, at a time when most of Europe was preoccupied with sorting out the devastation of the war, with the resettlement of refugees, and with the task of rebuilding war-shattered economies.

The intended audience for the work again had little time for, or interest in, the subtleties of German metaphysics. The prevailing mood among many Western intellectuals was determinedly empiricist, antimetaphysical, and specifically antagonistic to German metaphysicians, who in various obscure ways were being held responsible for the rise of Nazism. A few months earlier, in 1945, Karl Popper had published his notoriously anti-Hegelian work *The Open Society and its Enemies.* The popular success of Popper's work confirmed and exacerbated, as it was apparently designed to do, the general antipathy to German Idealism, especially in the English-speaking world. Thus the world into

---

8. Professor Dr. Iwan Iljin, *Die Philosophie Hegels als kontemplative Gotteslehre* (Bern: A. Francke AG Verlag, 1946), 432 Seiten. For Il'in's own account of his doubts about the philosophical validity of the drastically foreshortened German text, and his reluctance to spend the time to translate even that portion of the original, see the "Vorwort" to the Swiss edition, pp. 12–13.

which Il'in launched the second, Swiss edition of his commentary was little better prepared to consider it seriously than was the world of the first, Russian edition.

Despite the unpropitious historical circumstances in which both editions made their appearances, Il'in's commentary has made a significant impact upon a number of Hegel scholars such as Gustav Müller, Wilhelm Seeberger, Hans Küng, and Cyril O'Regan, to name a few.[9] For example Hans Küng, whose massive study of the theological implications of Hegel's philosophy was very strongly influenced by Il'in, describes it as "far and away the most thorough Introduction to Hegel's thought process and theology" published since the end of World War II.[10] Cyril O'Regan's recent work *The Heterodox Hegel* also treat's Il'in's commentary as an important source for his interpretation of Hegel.[11] Wilhelm Seeberger also relied upon it substantially in his *Hegel, oder die Entwicklung des Geistes zur Freiheit.*[12]

All of these scholars made use only of the shortened German translation, however, which is missing most of the original Volume Two. The Russian edition has been effectively lost to Western scholars for many decades, and had little explicit impact upon Russian scholars throughout the Soviet period. Fortunately, the full text of the original Russian edition has just been re-published in Russia, and it is also scheduled to appear in Il'in's *Collected Works.*[13] At the same time, Russian scholars are beginning to study Il'in's work, and new studies of Hegel there are beginning to show the influence of Il'in.[14] Perhaps

---

9. Gustav Müller refers to it in his *Hegel: the Man, his Vision and Work* (New York: Pageant Press, Inc., 1968), pp. 7 and 392.

10. See p. 22, n. 35 of the English edition: *The Incarnation of God: An Introduction to Hegel's Theological Thought as a Prolegomena to a Future Christology*, Trans. J.R. Stephenson (New York: Crossroad, 1987). The original edition is *Menschwerdung Gottes* (Freiburg: Herder KG, 1970).

11. Cyril O'Regan, *The Heterodox Hegel* (Albany, NY: SUNY Press, 1994).

12. Wilhelm Seeberger, *Hegel, oder die Entwicklung des Geistes zur Freiheit* (Stuttgart: Ernst Klett, 1961).

13. The complete text of the commentary was re-published in 1994 by the publisher *Nauka* in St. Petersburg, with an introductory essay by I. I. Evlampiev. The *Sobranie sochinenii* [Collected Works], edited by Yurii T. Lisitsa, is being published by the *Russkaia Kniga* publishing house in Moscow. Volumes 1, 2 (Books 1 and 2), 3 and 4 had all appeared by early 1995.

14. Of particular interest are the works of I. I. Evlampiev and A. V. Krichevskii. For an account of the contemporary revival of interest in Il'in in Russia, see my article "The Complex Legacy of I. A. Il'in" in *Russian Thought After Communism: the Recovery of a Philosophical Heritage*, ed. James Scanlan (Armonk, NY and London, England: M.E. Sharpe, 1994), pp. 165–86.

the comparative neglect of his commentary will be remedied by its third appearance.

Il'in's commentary takes the whole of Hegel's mature philosophy as its subject matter. In the attempt to understand that system, he makes use of every available text from the earliest to the last, stressing only the crucial distinction between those for which Hegel himself was the direct author, and those compiled from the notes of his auditors.[15] Unlike certain commentators, he makes no invidious distinctions between the *Phenomenology* and the later system; rather, he treats the *Phenomenology*, the *Science of Logic,* and the *Encyclopedia* as a continuously unfolding philosophical project.[16] That said, it should also be acknowledged that Il'in's interpretation focuses above all upon *The Science of Logic* as the crux of Hegel's thought, and therefore, his most important philosophical achievement. Correspondingly, I believe that Il'in's greatest achievement as an interpreter of Hegel lies in the subtlety and depth of his commentary on the central themes of the *Science of Logic.*

Il'in's work is not so much a commentary upon Hegel's texts in the more usual sense, but an attempted reconstruction of Hegel's philosophy as a whole. The work is not organized as a part-by-part discussion of distinct texts in the same sequence employed by Hegel. The organizing principle of Il'in's commentary is thematic: each chapter constitutes an essay on a central theme, something which Il'in regards as a distinctive insight in Hegel's thought. The sequence of chapters in turn constitutes Il'in's logical reconstruction of the whole of Hegel's mature philosophy.

His technique depends in part upon excavating numerous references throughout Hegel's texts on some particular point, and then treating that point somewhat independently of the details of any particular textual passage. While the content of some chapters can be identified specifically with some portion of a single text, others are drawn from very widely-scattered aspects of Hegel's work. In both cases though Il'in's concern is to reconstruct a theme, not to provide a passage-by-passage *explication de texte.*

Il'in on Translating Hegel

Before turning to examine some of the highlights of Il'in's interpretation, a few observations concerning language are in order. Il'in's

---

15. See the "*Vorwort*" to the Swiss (German) edition, p. 9.

16. In a certain sense, Il'in does profess to find a break in the continuity of Hegel's project, from earlier to later, one which forced Hegel to compromise his original insight. Il'in's attribution of this compromise to Hegel's project involves several themes, and will be discussed in more detail below.

work could be viewed as an interesting test of Gadamer's well-known opinion that Hegel's philosophy could not be translated into any of "the major cultural languages" with complete success.[17] In particular he claimed that translations into any of the major European languages strongly influenced by Latin would inevitably distort Hegel's thought, making it appear to be simply an extension of traditional metaphysics, failing to render the supple, speculative core of Hegel's meaning, grounded as it was in the German language.

Il'in reveals no sense of linguistic helplessness or undue strain in rendering Hegel's thought into Russian.[18] He proceeds with every evidence of complete confidence in the resources of the Russian language to render the nuances of speculative reason, seldom finding it necessary to resort to the practice (as is often the custom with non-German Hegel commentators) of inserting Hegel's German terms in parentheses at every turn. Indeed, rather than relying slavishly on Hegel's terminology at every point, he observes on occasion that Hegel falls into terminological inconsistency (e.g., FG I, 246n), or that his use of equivocal terms invites terminological confusion (FG II, 29). One of the very few explicit references he makes to an issue of translation, in fact, is to point out that were there an exact German equivalent of a certain Russian term (*poshlost'*), Hegel would undoubtedly have used it at a particular point in his text.[19] Thus, Il'in believes, Hegel's thought can be rendered more precisely in Russian than in German on at least one point. These

---

17. Hans-Georg Gadamer, *Hegel's Dialectic*, trans. P. Christopher Smith (New Haven and London: Yale University Press, 1976), p. 112.

18. Il'in was apparently recognized by his contemporaries as an uncommonly fine writer. Lisitsa notes that he was "an exceptional stylist and connoisseur of his native tongue whom archimandrite Konstantin compared with 'metropolitan Filaret of Moscow, that—along with Pushkin—greatest master of language.'" Lisitsa, *op.cit.*, str. 6.

19. FG I, p. 17. The dictionary definitions of *poshlost'* are 'vulgarity,' 'commonness,' 'triviality,' 'banality.' However, Il'in was fascinated by this Russian word, writing an entire essay on the term sometime in 1911, which eventually saw the light of day as a separate chapter in Volume One of his *Aksiomy religioznogo opyta*, Paris, 1953. (Cited in Lisitsa, *op. cit.*, p. 11 and p. 366, note 67). He felt that the Russian term *poshlost'* (as elaborated by himself) described better than any German term available to Hegel the condition from which Spirit freed itself in its long travail to come to itself, to achieve knowledge of itself as Spirit. "It can be accepted without doubt that if the German language contained in its resources a term corresponding to the Russian word *'poshlost','* then Hegel would have designated that path as the path of "catharsis of spirit from *poshlost'*." (*ibidem*).

are obviously not the sentiments of a man trembling before the near impossibility of translating Hegel's German into Russian.[20]

Heidegger tried to illustrate the alleged impossibility of an adequate translation of Hegel by pointing to the opening sentence of Vol. 2 of the *Logic*: "Die Wahrheit des Seins ist das Wesen." Neither *Wahrheit*, nor *Seins*, nor *Wesen* is supposedly translatable on the basis of the Latin metaphysical terminology used in Italian, Spanish, French, or English.[21] Gadamer, echoing Heidegger's claim that *Wesen* is exceedingly difficult or impossible to translate here, goes on to claim that, "one immediately becomes aware of the fact that the statement in question is not so much a statement about *Wesen* as it is the language of *Wesen* itself speaking."[22]

Gadamer's claim sounds remarkably similar to one of Il'in's most constantly repeated remarks about Hegel:

> Thus, according to the *method of his philosophizing*, Hegel must be recognized not as a dialectician, but as an intuitivist, or, more precisely, as an intuitive-contemplative clairvoyant. If by 'method' is meant the 'type and means' of cognition subjectively practiced by the philosopher, then one may regard Hegel as a 'dialectician' only in a completely superficial, rationalistic approach. He neither 'searches' for contradictions in concepts nor 'strives' to reconcile them afterward; he doesn't think 'analytically' and then 'synthetically.' He continually and concentratedly contemplates, and intently describes, the changes taking place *in the object itself*: he scrutinizes by means of thought. In this consists his 'subjective' method of cognition. It is *not he* who practices the 'dialectic,' but the *object*. (FG I, 121).

This at first glance surprising claim, that Hegel is not a 'dialectician,' but an 'intuitivist,' is Il'in's way of stressing his view that the course of Hegel's thought is dictated by the object itself, and not by some previously dreamed-up doctrine of dialectical method applied arbitrarily to the ostensible object of inquiry. He credits Hegel with a capacity perhaps exceeding that of any other philosopher, to follow the development of the thought-object itself with scrupulous detachment and exactitude. It is interesting that the feat of conveying this supple, object-

---

20. For further discussion of the issue of translating Hegel's philosophy into Russian, see George Kline, "Shpet as a Translator of Hegel," forthcoming in a volume of the proceedings of a conference on Shpet, Bad Homburg, Germany, June, 1986, edited by Hansen-Löwe.

21. Gadamer, *Hegel's Dialectic*, p. 113.

22. Gadamer, *Hegel's Dialectic*, p. 113.

determined course of Hegel's thinking, held by Heidegger and Gadamer to be inseparable from his German language, should be claimed as one of the crucial achievements of Il'in's Russian commentary. In general, Il'in betrays no special anxiety about translation. Rather, he obviously feels that one should not attempt to write about Hegel's philosophy until one has penetrated to the core of it, until the sense of bafflement has been replaced throughout by the certainty of seeing as Hegel saw. At that point Hegel's German loses its mysteriousness, and, Il'in seems to have felt, the problems of translation become manageable. To speak with confidence of having penetrated the thought of Hegel to the point of such lucidity is of course to make a bold claim. However, it should be noted that Il'in makes such claims more than once, and it must be admitted that the power, the confidence, and the subtlety of his interpretation are such that his claim cannot be immediately dismissed.

On Hegel's Speculative Concrete

Volume One contains twelve chapters, the first seven of which form Part One of the work as a whole. These seven chapters provide Il'in's reconstruction of the central themes of Hegel's *Science of Logic.* Those themes are, in order: the empirical concrete, the abstract formal, the nature of speculative thought, the reality of the Concept, the speculative universal, the dialectic, and the speculative concrete. The whole of Part One turns out to be an extended essay on the speculative concrete in Hegel, gradually introducing that theme in a series of steps commencing with the naive common sense view of reality as constituted of discrete, externally related entities and events, the 'empirical concrete.' Il'in rightly treats Hegel's doctrine of the speculative concrete as the central organizing insight of his *Logic,* and hence of his philosophy as a whole.[23] In his very detailed, extensive, and clearly focused treatment of it, Il'in has illuminated Hegel's concept of the speculative concrete to an extent unmatched by any other commentator of which I am aware.

Hegel's use of the abstract/concrete distinction is strikingly different from the one commonly made in the empiricist tradition. In the empiricist usage, the particular (e.g., whatever could be the object of

---

23. Compare Il'in's claim with, for example, Giacomo Rinaldi's similar assertion in his very fine work *A History and Interpretation of the Logic of Hegel* (Lewiston, NY: The Edwin Mellen Press, 1992), pp. 138–40.

some sense experience, the empirically real) is declared to be the concrete, and the universal (e.g., whatever could be shared in common by many particulars) is viewed as the paradigm of the abstract. Speaking in the language of set theory, the individuals comprising the set might be thought of as concrete particulars, and the set itself, an abstract universal. Thus what is real in the empiricist tradition is thought to be what is particular (and hence also concrete); conversely, what is universal is thought to be abstract and hence not concrete, not real.

On the contrary, when Hegel refers to something as abstract, he means that it is being treated as separate, drawn apart from some unity or whole to which it properly belongs. A universal may be treated abstractly as well as a particular. To treat something in this fashion means to adopt a partial, or one-sided view of the thing. As a further consequence, such a separation would suppress the thing's relation to its other, its negativity; hence, what is abstract is also merely positive. To conceive a thing abstractly is to conceive it as merely immediate, not mediated by its relation to some larger whole. To conceive something in this way, outside the context of its relations to the other, to the whole, arrests the movement of thought, halts the self-development of the concept. As a result, the abstract is for Hegel also the contentless, the empty.[24]

Thus for Hegel neither the abstract particular nor the abstract universal could be real. Only what is concrete in the speculative sense can be real, and the meaning of 'speculatively real' can only be grasped in the context of his more general theory of speculative thought or reason.

Il'in introduces the topic of speculative thought, in general terms, in his third chapter. He suggests that Hegel's idea of speculative thought arose in "the philosophical atmosphere created by the *Critique of Pure Reason*" and derived especially from the conviction that thought turning 'inward' to discover its own categories had far more to do with the objectivity of things than did the 'sensory reality of the external world' (FG I, 39). Similarly he traces the origins of speculative thought to the idea of 'subject-object identity' which arose in the aftermath of Kant's *Critique*. "Speculative thought is not merely abstract thinking, but something more: a thinking which distinctively unfolds itself through contemplation" (FG I, 40). Whereas abstract thinking remains distinct from its object, speculative thinking exhibits a unity of thinking subject and object thought (FG I, 43).

---

24. For a more detailed discussion of these points, see my article "Abstract and Concrete in Hegel's Logic" in *Essays on Hegel's Logic*, Edited by George di Giovanni (Albany: SUNY Press, 1990), pp. 59–75.

In the following chapter (Four) Il'in undertakes to explain more precisely the sense in which speculative thought could be conceived as specifying the nature of the real. He points out that whenever Hegel speaks of being or reality without further qualification, he normally means metaphysical substance or absolute reality. "This sense of absoluteness, of substantiality is so joined with the idea of reality for Hegel that it is often taken by him as something self-evident" (FG I, 70). Tracing the origin of this idea, Il'in finds it in Aristotle's doctrine of substance. "This conception of substance as of something which is both *per se* and *in se* was continuously developed by the scholastics, and then was taken up by one of the most influential inspirers of Hegel—Spinoza" (FG I, 71). Spinoza asserted that by substance he meant something which is in itself and is conceived through itself. According to Il'in, Spinoza's conception of substance as self-contained and unitary, produced by nothing external to itself, receiving no influence from without, unique, self-supporting, acting only by the laws of its own nature, becomes in Hegel's language that which maintains itself "in simple and immediate relation to itself" or "that which is equal to itself." Hence the nature of being for Hegel can be expressed in the single word of *Sichselbstgleichheit*" (FG I, 72).

Il'in observes that, "From this point of view it is not difficult to understand how the convergence and identification of thought and reality are produced" (FG I, 72). But of course Hegel also conceives of thought as inwardly dynamic, self-moving, self-developing—a conception to which he was led by Leibniz and Fichte, on Il'in's account. " 'To be' means to carry within a principle of spontaneous creativity directed to itself; it means to create itself from itself" while remaining self-identical. Il'in concludes, "Here is first revealed the substantial coincidence of thought and reality in its entire significance," and with it the essential meaning of speculative thought: "speculative thought is absolute reality, and absolute reality is speculative thought" (FG I, 73).

In the following chapter, Il'in moves one step closer to the topic of speculative concreteness, introducing the concept of the speculative universal. He points out that Hegel identifies three different concepts of the universal, two of which he rejects as false and unphilosophical (FG I, 93ff.).

In the most elementary concept of universality, the universal refers to that which is 'common to all' in a plurality of individual elements. The universal is something constant, while the individuals are various. The relation between the universal and the individual elements is composed of the many relations obtaining between the one universal and each of the elements, all of which relations are similar to each other. In its most minimal sense, such a conception of universality might involve nothing more than common membership in an otherwise random aggregate of unrelated individuals. Such a conception would be appropriate to a purely empirical/sensory conception of the real.

The second concept of the universal identified by Hegel is the abstract rational one; in it the relations of the individual elements to the universal are no longer constituitive of it, internal to it, but rather external. In the abstract formal notion, universality is not thought of as an aggregation of individuals, but is something separated by abstraction from them, conceived apart from the individuals. Hegel likewise rejects this concept as incapable of inclusion in an account of reality from the standpoint of speculative thought.

The concept of universality adequate for speculative thinking exhibits some quite distinctive features:

> Thus, speculative universality is something self-conscious; it is self-knowing reason. It is just as much object, given to consciousness, as it is subject, consciousness: object comprehending subject, and subject comprehending its object;—an identity of subject and object. (FG I, 95).

The crux of this doctrine of the speculative universal lies in posing and resolving the central problem of the nature of the relation connecting the universal with the individual. According to Il'in, "This relation reduces to the fact that the individual enters the universal as its living part, and the universal enters the individual as its living essence." (FG I, 96). Moreover, the doctrine of the speculative universal introduces a third element, the particular (*Besonder*) which mediates between the universal and the individual (FG I, 98).

Il'in discusses the development of the speculative universal in especially great detail, focusing on the relations among the universal, particular, and individual, as well as the acts of negation through which the particular and the individual emerge from the speculative universal. Faintly echoing Plotinus' notions of the procession and return, Il'in asserts that in order to grasp the connections among the elements of the speculative universal, it is necessary first to think one's way with Hegel from the universal to the individual, and then to think through the reverse movement.

> The path from the universal to the individual is the path from the less determinate to the more determinate; from the less substantial to the more substantial; from the more simple to the more complex; from the more plain to the more diverse; from an implicit, potential unity to an explicit, actual unity in multiplicity. (FG I, 99).

However, thought arrested at the stage of abstract rationalism scorns to descend to the individual, turns away from this depth in which the concept could acquire itself, and remains incapable of speculative development. In Il'in's words, the first act by which speculative thought asserts and reveals itself is by negating itself in the barren and dead form of the merely abstract universal. This first self-assertion/self-negation of speculative thought marks the termination of purely formal, abstractly rational thought (FG I, 99–100).

The (now speculative) universal which results from this first act of self-negation is self-supporting objectivity, "a creative power in the form of absolute negativity which relates itself to itself" (FG I, 100). The speculative universal has split itself (Hegel's *Ur-theil*) into two independent moments, both of which nevertheless remain united in the universal. The speculative universal, now a unity of differences, has set out on the path of self-determination, differentiating itself, developing content, 'deepening' itself (FG I, 100–101).

This first act of self-negation brings to the speculative universal a certain determinateness: the universal becomes a 'determinate universal,' in other words, particular. " 'Particularity' (*die Besonderheit*) is nothing other than 'determinate universality' " (FG I, 101). The particular is the self-differentiated content of the universal, and the content of the universal is the content of all the particular concepts created by the universal in itself. In this inter-penetration of contents between the generic, whole universal and the specific, partial particular, the individual is discovered.

The second act, the second negation, of speculative thought generates this individual. "The particular, containing in itself the universal or what is the same thing, the universal in the form of particularity again turns upon itself and carries out a new splitting-apart and determination, the outcome of which is the individual" (FG I, 105). Or in Hegel's words, ". . . as the second negation, that is as negation of the negation, it [the universal] is *absolute determinateness* or *individuality* and *concreteness*."[25] Thus Il'in accounts for the connection between speculative universality and substance in Hegel.

Turning to the dialectic, the topic of Chapter Six, Il'in observes that many commentators have made entirely too much of this topic. First, the dialectic is not the method of Hegelian philosophy, nor the form of his thought, as though that could be separated from the

---

25. Hegel, *Science of Logic*, Miller translation, p. 603; see p. 113: "Universality filled with content is itself all possible content; it is living, concrete Universality, or living, all-embracing substance."

content of the Concept.[26] He denies that Hegel should be thought of primarily as a dialectical thinker; he is rather an intuitionist who 'sees' and describes the actual movement of the Concept, the objective rhythm of its self-development.

That pattern of development can be simply described as one by which the Concept, uncovering its hidden, latent determinateness, begins with an act of self-negation, self-splitting, and concludes with the negation of that negation, with a rejoining of what was split apart (FG I, 126). This dialectical process is described by Hegel as the actualization, or realization of the Concept.

> The speculative Concept is of course always real, as such; it is reality itself, the very substance of being. But its reality consists in the distinctive, objective circumstance of speculative thought-determination; and these thought determinations in the Concept can be more or less [numerous]. For that reason, the more thought determinations that are uncovered and asserted in it, the more reality the Concept will have; or, what is the same thing, the farther it has moved in the dialectical process of self-actualization. (FG I, 139).

The rhythm of speculative thought is characterized by this movement of splitting-apart (the self-negation, self-determination of the Concept, which considered in itself is a movement of abstracting) and the growing together or con-cretion of these distinct, newly uncovered determinations as moments of (members of) the now more concrete whole. Il'in restricts the meaning of the dialectic to this action of splitting apart—dialectical negation is the self-splitting, self-differentiation of speculative thought; the counter-movement is that of con-cretion, of growing together. These two movements are inter-related, and each requires the other in the self-development of the Concept. Indeed, it is the interwoven movements of dialectical splitting and speculative concretion which exhibit the true connection between the abstract and the concrete in speculative thought:

> The 'abstract' and the 'concrete' from one side are continually combined and *coincide*: because the rhythm of speculative concreteness is the rhythm of *thought* itself, of the *objective concept* itself, i.e., of 'speculative abstraction' itself. Where there is no 'abstract speculative,' i.e., no objective concept, there is of course no possibility of its distinctive rhythm, its immanent law, i.e., *concreteness* is impossible. From the other side, the 'abstract' and the

---

26. To distinguish 'form' and 'content' in the dialectic is possible only from a rationalistic point of view (FG I, 123).

'concrete' to a certain degree *exclude* one another: the greater the 'abstraction' in the objective concept, the less 'concreteness' there is; and, conversely, concretion of the concept fills up its emptiness, satiates its indefiniteness, and at the same time frees it from 'abstract' dissatisfaction. In the process of development and definition of the Concept, the abstract *itself* blossoms into new definitions, enriches itself with content, and 'concretizes' itself. (FG I, 145).

In Il'in's view, the heart of Hegel's philosophy lies in his doctrine of speculative concreteness, or more precisely, in this process of speculative con-cretion. His treatment of this topic takes place in Chapter Seven which is simultaneously the culmination of Part One, the exegesis of the major themes of the *Logic*, and also in several ways the pivotal chapter for Il'in's interpretation of Hegel's philosophy as a whole.

According to Il'in, Hegel's distinctive use of the term 'concrete' emerged when he noticed, behind the standard meanings of this ancient and outworn term, its original sense of a *growing together* [concresence] of what was separated or distinct. Hegel's allusion to this original, ordinary sense of the term in the context of his account of speculative thinking produced a new, philosophical sense which was of extremely great importance for Hegel's philosophy as a whole.

Speculative concreteness serves as the ultimate criterion of actuality for Hegel. This, according to Il'in, is the "cardinal experience," the "fundamental idea" to which the entire philosophy of Hegel is dedicated (FG I, 141). Concreteness not only constitutes the outcome of every dialectical splitting-apart, and the highest result of the entire dialectical movement, but is also the main moving force and at the same time the ultimate goal of all being and becoming.

He claims that it is "recognition of this criterion of reality and value, as fundamental and universal" that makes any philosopher a follower of Hegel (FG I, 142). Conversely, putting it still more strongly, Il'in asserts that

> however much a thinker may have borrowed from the philosophical riches of this great intuitivist, however much he may have imitated his style, indifference to the *fundamental idea* makes him alien to the basic doctrine of the "teacher." Only one who consciously acknowledges that *the dialectical realization of speculative concreteness in the element of real thought is the substance of all being and all perfection* can be recognized as an Hegelian.[27]

---

27. FG I, 142. The translation given here of the italicized passage is based on the German. The same passage in the Russian edition is slightly obscure, and Il'in clarified it in the German translation.

Despite this, Il'in was well aware that very few nineteenth or early twentieth century commentators on Hegel had focused upon the idea of speculative concreteness as central to his philosophy, and he regarded this as a significant puzzle to be explained. As part of his explanation, Il'in points to the fact that Hegel himself seemingly provided no special place for a discussion of speculative concreteness in his system, neither in the *Logic* nor in any of the 'subordinate' branches of his philosophical science (FG I 142). This can be explained, according to Il'in, precisely by the central, universal significance of speculative concreteness for the system as a whole.

> In its capacity as the category of categories, it could not find a place for itself within the ordinary sequence of 'determinations.' It is *everywhere*, and in part, *nowhere*. It is not, as it were, itself a 'content,' but the very deepest character of all contents. One could say that it is not the 'what,' but rather the 'how' [of the system]; with the significant qualification, however, that this mode of being always *changes* the very content of the categories subordinated to it and itself serves as the measure of the degree of their reality and perfection. Perhaps this deep-seated and hidden 'secondariness' of the idea of the 'concrete' prevented commentators and critics of Hegel to this day from realizing and revealing it. (FG I, 143).

Confirmation of the truth of Il'in's insight can be found in recent work of Errol Harris, who has also considered this problem of the status of the 'concrete' and the 'abstract' in relation to the categories of the *Logic*. He points out there that the abstract and the concrete . . .

> are rather terms indicating the degree of completeness and integrity of the category under consideration (whichever it may be). It is because they do this that they figure repeatedly in the exposition of the dialectical progression, and not as "official" categories in the logical series. They belong, as it were, to the metalanguage of logic.[28]

In his 1918 Russian edition, Il'in carefully reviewed the history of Hegel commentary from the point of view of the speculative concrete, and concluded that it remained almost unexplicated in the literature (see FG I, 143, 287–88, 294–95). He found that scarcely any of the major commentators grasped the significance of Hegel's distinction between the empirically concrete and the speculatively concrete. Most

---

28. Errol Harris, "Abstract and Concrete in Hegel's Logic," in his *The Spirit of Hegel* (Atlantic Highlands, NJ: Humanities Press, 1993), pp. 77–78.

of them employed the term 'concrete' in a very loose way, as something like 'ordinary reality,' or simply treated the meaning as obvious and in need of no special explanation. Such well-known philosophers as Wundt, Windelband, Eduard von Hartmann, Trendelenburg, Dilthey, Lasson, and Glockner are all cited by Il'in as having failed to grasp Hegel's use of the term, or failed to deal with the issue at all.[29] Only a very small number of now relatively-obscure commentators seemed to grasp Hegel's idea of the speculative concrete as the criterion of reality. On this honor roll Il'in includes only Christian Weisse[30] (1829), Franz Exner[31] (1842), the Frenchman A. Lèbre[32] (1843), and Anton Springer[33] (1848). While each of these seemed to have correctly grasped Hegel's concept of the speculative concrete, according to Il'in, none of them produced a detailed explication of Hegel's texts in the light of that concept.

The situation has of course significantly improved at present; however, failure to grasp the distinctiveness of Hegel's doctrine is not unknown among twentieth-century interpreters. For example, in the mid-1960s, George Kline examined eight recently published commentaries on Hegel's work as a whole, and found only two which did not confound Hegel's notion of the speculative concrete with the ordinary empiricist meaning of the term occasionally or constantly.[34] The only work which seemed almost completely reliable on this score, in Kline's opinion, was Wilhelm Seeberger.[35] Interestingly, Seeberger "gives full credit" *to Il'in*, whom he had read in the German, for explicating and clarifying Hegel's concept of the speculative concrete.[36] Il'in's treatment of the speculative concrete remains one of the most lucid and systematic in the literature.

---

29. For a more complete account of Il'in's opinion on this problem, in addition to the pages cited in the Russian edition, one must also consult the German edition, pp. 389–90 and pp. 400–401.

30. In *Über den gegenwärtigen Standpunkt der philosophischen Wissenschaft in besonderere erziehung auf das System Hegels*, 1829, S. 116. Cited in Il'in, German edition, p. 390 (citation incomplete).

31. *Die Psychologie der Hegelschen Schule*, 1842, S. 112. Cited in Il'in, German edition, S. 390.

32. *Crise actuelle de la philosophie allemande. Revue des deux Mondes* (1843). Il'in, German edition, S. 390.

33. *Die Hegelsche Geschichtsanschauung*, 1848, S. 9. Cited in Il'in, German edition, S. 390.

34. George L. Kline, "Some Recent Reinterpretations," pp. 34–75. See esp. pp. 40–45.

35. Wilhelm Seeberger, *Hegel: Oder die Entwicklung des Geistes zur Freiheit* (Stuttgart: Ernst Klett Verlag, 1961), pp. 639.

36. As quoted by Kline, "Some Recent Reinterpretations, p. 42.

Hegel on Tragedy and the Other

Turning now to one other significant aspect of Il'in's interpretation, perhaps the single most tortured problem in contemporary debates concerning Hegel would be the reality or the unreality of the other, or other-being (*Anderssein*), in his philosophy. Indeed, some contemporary philosophers see the problem of the reality of the other as one of the most fundamental topics of first philosophy.[37] It is often alleged that for Hegel the other turns out to be a kind of illusion, since the subject involved in mediation is ultimately *Geist*, or the absolute subject, and the other is not genuinely other, but a result of the self-othering of the subject, an other which is not finally distinct from the self. Or to put the problem in slightly different terms, it is often alleged that Hegel's system cannot finally treat difference as real, since "self-mediation seems to encompass the self and the other, and all differences are caught up within this self-contained circle."[38]

A further dimension of this problem arises in connection with Hegel's conception of God. As Robert Williams has recently reminded us, Hegel was the first philosopher to formulate the death of God motif, and to develop the theological implications of that claim consistently.[39] In the metaphysics of standard Christian theology, it is held that Christ's human nature suffered and died on the cross, but the divine nature is immutable and impassible, i.e., incapable of change and therefore untouched by the tragedy of suffering or death. But Hegel, citing the Lutheran hymn in which the phrase "God himself lies dead," argued that God incarnate must also be capable of change and suffering, i.e., that tragedy is real.

In his early essay on *Natural Law* Hegel argued that tragedy is superior to the ancient form of comedy because it exhibits the reality of conflict and suffering: ". . . the true and absolute relation is that the one [nature] really does illumine the other; each [nature] has a living bearing on the other, and each is the other's serious fate. The absolute relation, then, is set forth in tragedy."[40] By contrast he viewed classical

---

37. See for example, Michael Theunissen, *The Other: Studies in the Social Ontology of Husserl, Heidegger, Sartre and Buber,* trans. Christopher Macann (Cambridge: MIT Press, 1984), and Robert R. Williams, *Recognition: Fichte and Hegel on the Other* (Albany, N.Y.: SUNY Press, 1992).

38. See William Desmond, *Desire, Dialectic and Otherness* (New Haven: Yale University Press, 1987), p. 120. Desmond's conclusion is discussed in Williams, pp. 256ff. and p. 274, notes 17 and 20.

39. Williams, pp. 232ff.

40. Hegel, *Natural Law,* trans. T. M. Knox (Philadelphia: University of Pennsylvania Press, 1975), pp. 105–06, quoted in Williams, p. 234.

Christian theism, as in Dante's *Divine Comedy*, as an inferior form in which the reality and triumph of God is taken to be secure beyond all possibility of conflict, opposition, or struggle.

In the *Phenomenology*, however, the reality of tragedy and conflict in the Absolute seems to come into question. There, in the religion of revelation, the mutual forgiveness of sins, and reconciliation through and with the Divine are treated as the ultimate outcome of human history as well as of the self-development of the Absolute.[41] This has led Otto Pöggeler to conclude that Hegel's early assertion of the reality of tragedy, suffering, and death eventually gives way to a teleological conception of reality in which the seriousness of tragedy is displaced, rendered merely apparent, by a final all-embracing reconciliation in the Absolute.[42] In a similar vein, Werner Marx has argued that Hegel's conception of the Absolute ultimately reverts to an abstract identity of self-sameness, and hence to the traditional Christian metaphysics of impassibility, in which the darkness of tragedy retreats before the inevitable victory of the divine light.[43]

Both of these lines of criticism lead to the conclusion that Hegel's system ultimately disappoints in some quite significant respect. Either it fails to provide for the reality of tragedy, abandoning his earlier conception of the seriousness of conflict and suffering in the Divine in favor of an all-embracing teleology; or it fails to provide for genuine difference, ultimately absorbing all difference in an abstractly self-identical absolute, thus reverting to a traditional form of Christian metaphysics.

Both of these themes, currently the object of much discussion among Hegel scholars, received extended treatment by Il'in. He too regarded the interlinked questions of the reality of tragedy and suffering in the Divine, and the reality of other-being, as decisive for the success or failure of Hegel's grandest ambitions. Most fascinatingly however, he concluded that Hegel's system was ultimately a failure—more precisely, that Hegel's original intentions had to be abandoned in a whole series of significant compromises—just because Hegel was

---

41. Williams, pp. 234–35.

42. Otto Pöggeler, *Hegels Idee einer Phänomenologie des Geistes* (Freiburg: Alber Verlag, 1973), pp. 90ff. Pöggeler's thesis is discussed critically by Williams in *Recognition*, Chs. Ten and Eleven. [Also see the essays by P. Christopher Smith and Susan Armstrong in this volume].

43. Werner Marx, *Heidegger and the Tradition*, trans. Theodore Kisiel (Evanston, Ill.: Northwestern University Press, 1971) pp. 55–57. Critically discussed in Williams, *Recognition*, Chapters Ten and Eleven. Williams cites several other recent commentators who have come to very similar conclusions concerning the subordination of difference to absolute self-identity in Hegel; see p. 284 note 93.

forced to admit the ultimate reality of suffering, tragedy, and death in the Divine, and was also forced to acknowledge the ultimate impotence of the Absolute to mediate the whole of reality, the inability of the Absolute to finally overcome the independent reality of the Other. It is Il'in's conviction that Hegel's recognition of the ultimate reality of tragedy, and his recognition of the reality of an Other which would not completely yield to mediation by the Absolute, together shaped the outcome of the system as a whole, and entailed that it fell significantly short of Hegel's original ambitions.

Il'in attributes to Hegel's system as a whole the ultimate intent of a theodicy, which was to be realized by establishing the truth of pantheism.[44] That Hegel intended, among other things, to produce a theodicy is not deniable; whether pantheism is the best description of it is another matter.[45] A more subtle question concerns the extent to which producing a theodicy should be seen as the master intention behind the entire project, the intention to which all others are subordinate.[46] Il'in supposes throughout (although this does not become the central problem until Volume Two) that the ultimate issue for Hegel was the relation of God to the world. The extremely detailed and illuminating explication of speculative concreteness in Volume One was for Il'in above all an examination of the nature of God as the absolutely Real. The speculative universal, the Concept, develops, perfects, itself to the point of containing within itself every determinate category belonging to the Real. This doctrine of speculative concreteness represented in Il'in's mind, the possibility that the whole of Reality could be

---

44. "Hegel wollte eine Theodizee schreiben, und zwar in der Form des Pantheismus." Il'in, German edition, S. 381.

45. Il'in repeatedly asserts that Hegel's ruling intention was to produce a theodicy, and to do so by establishing the truth of a 'pantheism' which was also an 'a-cosmism.' The 'pantheism' he attributes to Hegel means "to recognize the reality of the world only to the degree that God is present in it" (FG I, 185) or "apart from the Divinity nothing is real" ("Tezisy k" dissertatsii" [Unpublished dissertation summary, c. 1918], no. 14). By 'akosmism' he means that "the world as something self-realized [*samobytnoe*], independent, doesn't exist" ("Tezisy k" dissertatsii," no. 14; see also FG I, 186). Il'in's insistence upon this way of characterizing Hegel's original intentions may seem a bit odd when one takes into account that Hegel himself devoted quite a few pages at the end of the *Encylopedia* to repudiating all of these merely "exoteric," "popular" ways of characterizing philosophy (all of §573). He specifically repudiates the "acosmical" version of pantheism. See Hegel, *Philosophy of Mind*, trans. William Wallace and A. V. Miller (Oxford: Clarendon Press, 1971), p. 310. The reasons for Il'in's insistence on these characterizations of Hegel's original intent remain something of a puzzle.

46. I would argue that Il'in's interpretation goes subtly astray in its broadest contours by insisting on the primacy of the original motive of theodicy to the exclusion of other equally determining, but distinct motives for the Hegelian project.

grasped as divine, thus achieving a complete theodicy, and he attributes to Hegel the original intention of demonstrating just that.[47]

Having attributed this original intention to Hegel, Il'in argues that Hegel himself was disappointed to discover at a certain point that the project of pantheism could not be completed in a way which achieved the intended theodicy. Rather, he faced the necessity of compromising his original intention. He was forced to admit that not all of reality would yield to the speculative Concept, and hence not all the cosmos could be dissolved in the Divine.

The recalcitrant aspect of Being allegedly encountered by Hegel was the Other, the contingent, the irrational particular, the self-willed finite ego, evil. Il'in gives Hegel much credit for acknowledging the failure of his original vision, for explicitly recognizing the necessity of compromising it, and for working out some of the implications of this compromise in detail. All of the original second volume of Il'in's commentary deals in one way or another with the details of these compromises, with Hegel's confrontation with the Other.

Il'in locates the critical impasse in Hegel's philosophy several ways: in the largest sense it is a failure of the transition from the *Logic* to the *Realphilosophie*; in a more specific sense, Il'in argues that the crisis of the system surfaces in its most acute form in the political philosophy, in the failure of Hegel's account of the rational idea of the state; in another form it consists of the impossibility of a philosophy of history which could serve as a completed theodicy; in still another form, it consists of the impossibility for Absolute Spirit to reconcile what proved to be irreconcilable at the level of Objective Spirit.

Il'in elaborates on each of these themes at a length which makes it impossible to summarize even briefly here; however, the form of this critical impasse which Il'in presents most vividly concerns civil society as a moment of the rational state, or—a term which Il'in uses perhaps more frequently than Hegel—the Absolute State. Il'in argues that Hegel was ultimately unable to depict the reality of civil society as a genuine moment of concrete ethical substance, and that this led to the failure of his political philosophy as a whole, and consequently

---

47. See for example, the German edition, p. 381: "Hegel wollte eine Theodizee schreiben, und zwar in der Form des Pantheismus. Aber der Pantheismus ist dazu nicht geeignet. Denn, wenn alles Seiende in Gott ist, und wenn es auser Gott nichts gibt, so bleibt noch die Möglichkeit, das in Gott selber keine Einheit, keine totale logische Vernünftigkeit, keine erschöpfende Zweckmäsigkeit und keine Freiheit von chaotischen Trieben vorhanden ist. Ist Gott wirklich die allumfassende Substanz, so leidet dies Substanz ungeachtet ihrer Grösse und ihrer herrlichen Energie, an *innerem Zwiespalt*, und ihr Weltgang zeugt vom *Mangel an wahrer Göttlichkeit.*

to a significant transformation and diminution of his philosophical position.[48]

> The philosophy of Hegel, despite its original intention, discovers the limits of God and humanity in the doctrine of the 'state' and in the doctrine of 'the historical process,' recognizing that it is not given to the power of Spirit to overcome to the end the distinctive order of the empirical element. (FG II, 259).

In brief, it was the historical reality of the bourgeoisie which, or so Il'in was convinced, could not be absorbed into Hegel's idea of the rational state without seriously undermining his philosophy as a whole.

> Already in early researches he considered it essential to assign the entire sphere of life of the second estate [i.e., of civil society] to the 'inorganic', or what is the same thing, to the 'real' element (the concrete-empirical), so that that concentration and isolation [of the second estate] could render the evil element harmless for the life of the remaining parts of the state. In accordance with that intent, the second estate, dedicating its energies to commercial activity, to 'particular' interests, to trade and enrichment, was left in separation, led a private life and, sunk in the particularity and chance of empirical life, proved to be incapable of virtue, or of freedom, or, accordingly, of political life. It was, to be sure, capable of elementary honesty or 'respectability' in observing contracts and cultivating formal right. However genuine ethical life remained for it merely an abstract and unrealized idea: 'the bourgeoisie' is capable neither of 'absolute [ethical] indifference,' nor of political courage, nor of public life. (FG II 263).

Il'in argues that in order for Hegel to make it appear that this indigestible element, the commercial class, could nevertheless be mediated by the concrete universal, by God in the form of the Absolute State, he was forced to introduce a tacit duality in the Absolute itself, thereby admitting the tragedy of suffering and death as a reality in the divine nature. Quoting Il'in again,

> And therefore, this presence of an entire estate living by no means in the 'absolute and eternal,' and viewing ethical life only in an alien manifestation, inevitably draws the entire state into a process

---

48. See, for example, his remark at FG II, 241: "The fundamental characteristics of the state outlined by Hegel in his latest and most mature treatise on the philosophy of right admit a whole series of compromises which were realized, noted, and sometimes more deeply illuminated in his early works."

of tragic character. The Divine Spirit, creating its world 'forms,' has a dual nature and its life consists of a unity of these two elements. But in order to create this unity, it is necessary for it to give over part of itself to the empirical element, and consequently, to 'suffering and death.' (FG II, 264).

It is interesting to speculate whether Il'in's attitude to what he viewed as the scandal of Hegel's attempting to exhibit the mediation of the bourgeoisie, the commercial class, within the self-development of the Absolute State, should be explained as the reaction of a devoutly orthodox Russian intellectual with aristocratic proclivities to the world view of a devoutly Lutheran German intellectual who seemed contentedly middle-class—but that would lead me astray.

In any event, Il'in develops this theme of the tragic reality of suffering and death for God at considerable length, drawing on numerous elements of Hegel's work. Although he introduces the theme particularly in the context of Hegel's doctrine of the state, he clearly believes that the necessity of accomodating the evil (*durnaia*) element of the empirical-concrete in the self-development of the Absolute forced a whole series of compromises in the structure of the mature system, some of which Hegel acknowledged openly, others of which he passed over in silence. By pointing out and underscoring this theme of the reality of tragedy, the reality of divine suffering and death, Il'in felt he was confirming the validity of his own interpretation of Hegel's system as one which was radically compromised by its author.[49]

The very centrality of this theme of the reality of tragedy in the life of Divine Spirit in Il'in's interpretation, could be taken as significant support for the similar interpretation recently offered by Robert Williams in his book on *Recognition.* The ultimate conclusions of Il'in and Williams concerning the success or failure of Hegel's system are somewhat divergent, but there are numerous points of intersection in the two interpretations, and Il'in's support for Williams' theses tends to be clearest just in those areas where Williams undertakes to overthrow the reigning critical consensus.[50]

---

49. The last two chapters of Volume Two explore these implications for the system in ways too numerous even to list here. Talk about compromises in the structure of the system as a whole occurs through both volumes of Il'in's commentary, beginning (so far as I am aware) at FG I, 204 and 210.

50. It is also worth pointing out that although Il'in does not develop the theme of recognition (*Anerkennung*) himself as a prominent one, there is one passage where he appears to endorse one of Williams' most crucial claims, that Geist is socially constituted through the mutual recognitions of a community of self-conscious rational beings:

However, unlike Williams, Il'in treats the fact of suffering and death in the Divine not as a point in favor of Hegel's philosophy, but as one of its failures. According to Il'in, "a suffering Absolute is not absolute; and a struggling Divinity is not God" (FG II, 334). He rejects what he regards as Hegel's conception of the Absolute, involving the reality of tragedy and death, in favor of the traditional Christian metaphysics of the Divine as impassible. Il'in's personal response to Hegel's Absolute is left as simply that: a personal judgment which he articulates only on the last page of his commentary; he chooses not to engage in theological debate with Hegel, restricting himself to the task of providing the most meticulous commentary of which he is capable. I believe that commentary still deserves close attention from contemporary Hegel scholars.

Hegel and Il'in as "Enlighteners"

One more point concerning Il'in's relation to Hegel seems too striking to pass over: as a serious young man coming of age during the Enlightenment, Hegel had framed for himself the vocation of a *Volkserzieher*. To quote H. S. Harris, "he knew that he was going to be, like Socrates, a teacher, an enlightener of his own people in his own time, and ultimately of mankind."[51] It was only after a number of years of industrious preparation for this role that Hegel was gradually driven to the recognition that philosophy had a prior claim on him. By comparison, Il'in seems to have responded to the lure of philosophy quite early on, devoting at least eight years to a continuous and intense study of

---

The *Volksgeist [narodnyi dukh]* is a universal self-consciousness, as an organic con-creteness of a plurality of individual consciousnesses and self-consciousnesses. The essence of 'all spirituality', 'substantiality,' is precisely 'universal self-consciousness,' i.e., not only the integral self-consciousness of the individual (subjective spirit), but also "the positive awareness of oneself in the self of the other," "a non-distinction of self from other," and an awareness of one's self recognizing the "recognition" of the free soul of another human being (objective spirit). In a word, developed universal self-consciousness consists in the fact that each is aware that both he himself, and others, recognize both himself and others—free through identity and identical through freedom, and moreover, through identity and freedom, real both in himself and in others. (FG II, 216–17).

51. H. S. Harris, *Hegel's Development: Toward the Sunlight, 1770–1801* (Oxford: Clarendon Press, 1972), p. xix.

Hegel, culminating in his two-volume commentary.[52] Having come to terms with Hegel, however, Il'in then spent the rest of his life in a pattern of activity which bears a striking resemblance to the career Hegel had originally planned for himself, that of *Volkserzieher*, devoting himself to the cause of an eventual renewal of Russian religious, moral, legal, and political life. Whatever their philosophical or religious differences, Hegel would surely have understood and approved of Il'in's special sense of vocation.

---

52. See the "*Vorwort*" to the German edition of his commentary, pp. 8–9.

10 *The* Korporation *in Hegel's Interpretation of Civil Society*

Michael Prosch

I n this chapter, I seek to elucidate an often overlooked part of Hegel's analysis of civil society in the *Philosophy of Right*. This part concerns the final dialectical phase (*Moment*) of civil society, namely what Hegel terms the '*Korporation.*' Along with the *Polizei*, i.e., the public authority or regulatory powers, the *Korporation* is a mediating institution within civil society, one which provides an ethical context superseding the merely economic relations of a market economy. The chapter is organized around three questions, namely, what does Hegel mean by '*Korporation,*' which groups and individuals are members of a *Korporation*, and what is its economic and ethical role within the context of civil society?

Hegel's Concept of the *Korporation*

A *Korporation* is, first, a kind of *Genossenschaft*, the general term Hegel uses for 'association' (PR, §251; PR [1819], 202).[1] Besides the *Korporation*, another type of association noted by Hegel is the *Gemeinde*, i.e., the

---

1. References to works by Hegel are incorporated in the text using the following abbreviations:

PR: *Grundlinien der Philosophie des Rechts*, ed. by Eva Moldenhauer and Karl Michel as Band 7 of *Werke in zwanzig Bänden* (Frankfort a/M:

community. Although he occasionally seems to imply that a *Gemeinde* is itself a type of *Korporation* (e.g., PR, §288), in his lectures of 1824–1825 he makes a definite distinction between the two. There he notes that a community is an "abstract whole, which contains many particular interests within itself" and is analogous to a "small state" (VRP IV, 621). A community, then, is like a modern municipality (or rural county), i.e., an association of individuals based simply on territorial connection or physical proximity.

Still, although every citizen is a "member of a community, his particular interest is his trade [*Gewerbe*]" (VRP IV, 621). This "particular interest" is the unifying force behind the *Korporation* (cf. PR, §251). Hegel brings out the contrast between the *Korporation* and the Community by comparing the former to a *Zunft*, i.e., a *guild* (VRP IV, 621). As a first approximation, then, a *Korporation* is a socioeconomic association somewhat like a (late medieval, European) guild.[2] However, Hegel does not identify his notion of the *Korporation* with that of the guild. He is well aware of the many negative aspects of European guilds, such as their tendency toward "ossification" (VRP IV, 623, 628), their "provinciality" and "petty guild-spirit" (VRP IV, 628), and their special privileges (PR, §252R). The need to draw a line between his

---

Suhrkamp, 1970). Unless otherwise noted by 'tr. Rvsd.', translations are those of T. M. Knox in *Hegel's Philosophy of Right* (Oxford: Clarendon Press, 1957). References to both the German and English texts are to *section* (§) numbers; R signifies a remark added by Hegel.

PR [1819]: *Philosophie des Rechts: die Vorlesung von 1819/20 in einer Nachschrift*, ed. By Dieter Henrich (Frankfort a/M: Shurkamp, 1983).

VRP: *Vorlesungen über Rechtsphilosophie 1818–1831*, 4 volumes, ed. By Karl-Heinz Ilting (Stuttgart: Frommann-Holzboog, 1973–74). References are to volume number and page.

2. The analogy is to late medieval, European guilds, because the reader is likely to have some familiarity with these and because these were the types to which Hegel referred. An interesting overview of diverse treatments of the relationship between European guilds and civil society, beginning with the medieval period, may be found in Antony Black, *Guilds and Civil Society in European Political Thought from the Twelfth Century to the Present* (Ithaca: Cornell University Press, 1984). For the philosophical and historical roots of Hegel's theory in particular, see G. Heiman, "The Sources and Significance of Hegel's Corporate Doctrine," in *Hegel's Political Philosophy: Problems and Perspectives*, ed. Z. A. Pelczynski (Cambridge: Cambridge University Press, 1971), pp. 111–35.

It is worth noting, however, that guildlike associations are much more common and widespread than the usual emphasis on medieval European guilds would lead one to believe. For example, such associations existed in ancient Babylonia at least from the Achaemenid (Persion) period, in ancient India from before 300 BC, in the Hellenistic Near East (as in the Seleucid *koinā*), in Sasanian Iran, in most Islamic nations from at least the fourteenth century up to the present, and, of course, in the Roman/Byzantine Empire (the *collegia*).

own conception and that connected to the old guilds is one reason why he uses the new term *'Korporation'* (borrowed from French *corporation*) in his published work, rather than the common German term for guild, i.e., *Zunft*.

With this in mind, it becomes impossible to translate *Korporation* into English as guild, admittedly the closest cognate term. The look-alike English term corporation (used by Knox in his translation of the *Philosophy of Right*) also will not do, for it has not been used in *Hegel's* sense since the era of Adam Smith.[3] In contemporary usage, corporation means primarily a limited liability, joint-stock business enterprise, which, as will become apparent, fails to capture what Hegel means. The remaining option, then, is simply to use *Korporation* as a specific term in its own right; henceforth, I shall drop the italics and also use an English plural, i.e., Korporations.

To Whom Does the *Korporation* Pertain?

For the present essay, a Korporation may be defined as a socioeconomic association of individuals united by the fact that they share the same trade or line of work within the context of crafts, industry, or commerce. It is true that Hegel also classifies religious congregations or communities as Korporations (PR, §270R), but this type of Korporation is not what he has in mind in the context of his discussion of the Korporation in the context of civil society. This type is thus ignored here.[4]

As remarked above, Korporations pertain to members of what Hegel calls the *Stand des Gewerbes*, i.e., the class of commerce and industry, and in his view they pertain only to members of this social class (PR, §250). The other two social classes in Hegel's interpretation of class-division are the agricultural class and the "universal" class, neither of which require Korporations in his view (PR, §250). This is not

---

3. See the treatment of corporations in Adam Smith, *An Inquiry into the Nature and Causes of the Wealth of Nations*, 2 volumes (London: J. M. Dent & Sons, 1977), I, pp. 107–130.

4. Religious communities may, of course, perform some of the same functions as the socioeconomic Korporations, such as caring for the poor, providing education and training, etc. Although examples here are legion, perhaps the best example of such welfare work by a religious community is still the foundations for numerous social needs formed and operated by Zoroastrians in India (the Parsis) and, to a lesser degree, in Iran. See, e.g., John R. Hinnells, "The Flowering of Zoroastrian Benevolence: Parsi Charities in the 19th and 20th Centuries," in *Papers in Honour of Professor Mary Boyce*, ed. By H. W. Bailey *et al.* (Leiden: E. J. Brill, 1985), pp. 261–326.

the place to enter into a full discussion of Hegel's view of the formation of social classes in civil society and his reasons for excluding certain classes from membership in Korporations.[5] Suffice it to say that he believes the agricultural class remains bound up in family ties (think of the family farm) and so already has a kind of natural association. On the other hand, the universal class, consisting of civil servants, soldiers, doctors, lawyers, scholars, clerics, and the like (VRP IV, 521), does not need Korporations, since their professions are directly concerned with universal purposes (cf. PR, §§205, 250). With the exception of those in the service of the state, however, it is difficult to understand why Hegel excludes the rest of the members of the universal class from Korporations. After all, there are certainly differences between the work, e.g., of doctors and college professors, and each of these groups does currently have its own professional association, i.e., Korporation. Whatever one makes of this—and in regard to the universal class, Hegel's arguments are definitely strained—it remains true that Korportations are relevant for members of the commercial and industrial class.

Within this broad social class, Hegel distinguishes three distinct groups, namely, those engaged in (1) artisan or craft work, (2) manufacturing (or industry), and (3) trade and commerce (e.g., merchants, bankers) (PR, §204). Furthermore, within each of these groups, work is "split . . . into different branches" (PR, §251), and, of course, there are many such branches. Now, the very fact that one is able to speak meaningfully about distinct branches of commerce and industry shows that there exists some way of distinguishing these branches from each other. In short, within each branch there is something shared among, and common to, those active in that branch. This shared 'commonality' (*Gemeinsames*) sets this branch apart from others and is manifested by an 'implicit likeness' to each other of participants in a given branch, i.e., a likeness in their particular way of life and, especially, in the kind of work they perform (PR, §251).

Korporations are simply an institutional expression of this already present commonality. Each Korporation unites within one association all individuals engaged in a specific type of work. It is important that such institutional embodiments of shared commonalities exist, because the conscious articulation of seemingly haphazard groupings provides an ethical context, an ethical whole, for individuals who otherwise remain mired in self-interest and the abstract relations present in a market economy (what Hegel calls the "system of needs"). In Hegelian

5. On Hegel's account of social classes see Michael Prosch, "Hegel's Conception of the *Aufhebung* of the Merely Economic Realm" (Ph.D. dissertation, Bryn Mawr College, 1991), pp. 79–106.

phraseology, the Korporation lifts individuals up out of their isolated self-interests, which come to be recognized as actual shared interests, to the level of a (relatively) universal interest, that of a whole branch of work in civil society.

By calling such an interest "universal" (PR, §251), Hegel means to emphasize only its relative universality. He speaks of each Korporation as having a "universal purpose," but quickly notes that this is "no wider in scope than the purpose involves in commerce and industry, its proper business [*eigentümlich Geschäft*] and interest" (PR, §251; tr. rvsd.). Still, it is universal in relation to the particularity it supersedes, i.e., the self-interested, limited purposes of individual members of civil society subject only to relations of a market economy.

Now, does it follow from Hegel's discussion that all members of this social class are members of a Korporation? This question has proved to be problematic, particularly for those under the influence of Bernard Cullen's arguments on this subject.[6] The problem is twofold and concerns whether all participants in industry, commerce, and crafts are members of a Korporation and whether every branch within these groups has a Korporation. Cullen and other commentators[7] deny the universality of the Korporation in each of these instances. It is important to meet this challenge, for if all participants in every branch of industry, commerce, and crafts are not members of Korporations, then the large mediating role which Hegel claims the Korporations play in civil society is significantly diminished.

Hegel does at least seem to think that all participants in a particular branch of industry or commerce, whether workers, managers, or owners ("employers" or "capitalists"), should be members of an appropriate Korporation, since he never specifically excludes any particular group (cf. PR, §§204, 250–254). Cullen agrees that this is probably how Hegel wanted to be read,[8] yet he claims that he really cannot be so read, for workers cannot be members of Korporations.[9] His argument turns on Hegel's characterization of the member of a Korporation.

---

6. Bernard Cullen, *Hegel's Social and Political Thought* (New York: St. Martin's Press, 1979); also, "The Mediating Role of Estates and Corporations in Hegel's Theory of Political Representation," in *Hegel Today*, ed. By Bernard Cullen (Aldershot: Avebury/Gower, 1988), pp. 22–41.

7. E.g., Shlomo Avineri, *Hegel's Theory of the Modern State* (Cambridge: Cambridge University Press, 1972), p. 109; Thomas E. Wartenberg, "Poverty and Class Structure in Hegel's Theory of Civil Society," *Philosophy and Social Criticism*, 8 (1981), pp. 168–82 (cf. p. 180).

8. Cullen, *Hegel's Social and Political Thought*, p. 111.

9. *Ibid.*, p. 106; Cullen, "The Mediating Role," p. 32.

Hegel states that for a *Gewerbsmann*, i.e., a man engaged in some sphere of commerce, industry, or crafts, to be a member of a Korporation he must have the "requisite skill and rectitude" that the particular line of work demands (PR, §252). Further, his job must be his "vocation," i.e., he must have an enduring commitment to a certain mode of earning his living. Thus, a "day-laborer [*Tagelöhner*]" or a "man who is prepared to undertake casual employment on a single occasion" (PR, §252R) is not engaged in the kind of work that Hegel thinks pertains to a Korporation member. Rather the member of such an association must be a "master" (*Meister*), by which Hegel means someone who is a member "not for casual gain or single occasions but for the *whole* range, the universality, of his particular subsistence" (PR, §252R; tr. rvsd.).

From these rather innocuous statements Cullen derives the astonishing conclusion that the working class as a whole, or at least those engaged in industrial pursuits, is eliminated from belonging to Korporations. He reasons thus:

> The factory worker is living from day to day: he can be—and is— periodically dismissed. . . . And this is why he is excluded from memberships of a Korporation, which is only open to a *Gewerbsmann*, who is "master" and secure in his employment (sec. 252R).[10]

This conclusion, however, is based on a profound misinterpretation of the meaning of Hegel's statements.

First, a *Gewerbsmann* is not simply a businessman, as Cullen seems to think.[11] 'Businessman', with all its connotations, is too modern a translation of this term. What Hegel means is simply someone "engaged in commerce, industry, or crafts." Second, as I have noted, Hegel states with sufficient clarity what he means by calling the *Gewerbsmann* master. Clearly, Hegel does not think that 'master' is coterminous with 'employer,' as Cullen assumes.[12]

Furthermore, the "day-to-day" life of the factory worker is not the same as the way of life of a day-laborer. The latter hires himself out for the day, working at whatever job happens to be available. Accordingly, a day-laborer works at various jobs and has no particular occupation. But this description does not apply to the case of the factory worker, since the latter has a constant job and a specific occupation,

---

10. Cullen, *Hegel's Social and Political Thought*, p. 106.
11. *Ibid.*, p. 102.
12. *Ibid.*, p. 123n3.

involving determinate work in a particular factory. His liability to dismissal no more makes him a day-laborer than a non-tenured professor's liability to non-reappointment makes her a day-laborer.

Therefore, there is no reason to suppose that Hegel means to exclude workers engaged in commerce, industry, or crafts from membership in Korporations. The only occupations of workers that Hegel specifically excludes are those of the general handyman and the casual laborer, and it is clear that these occupations lack certain characteristics which Hegel thought necessary for Korporation membership.

Even if Hegel means to include workers, does this mean that every branch of industry, commerce, and crafts is organized in Korporations? Cullen's complete view is that a Korporation represents only the "interests of employers in a particular industry, or of self-employed members of a given industry of profession."[13] The first part of this assertion, *viz.*, that only employers (and not workers) are members of Korporations, has already been disallowed, but the second part also needs to be refuted.

At issue here is whether Korporations pertain only to craft-based production and certain professions, or whether they pertain to every branch of crafts and industry and commerce. By 'self-employed' Cullen appears to mean artisans, such as shoemakers, and professionals, such as doctors and lawyers.[14] The notion that a Korporation is best understood as an association of artisans is shared by other commentators. For instance, Erdös thinks the Korporation definitely pertains to craftsmen but is dubious about whether industry and commerce have Korporations;[15] while Denis thinks that Hegel only "wants to denote a craft society conforming to the medieval tradition."[16]

If these commentators are correct, Korporations are really only associations of artisans and, perhaps, professionals. They would then cover the same craft and professional occupations as the medieval guilds (as Denis plainly states), but they would be irrelevant for all occupations within the modern spheres of manufacturing and commerce. This would imply that Korporations, as understood by Hegel, are rather trivial aspects of a modern economy based to a great extent

---

13. Cullen, "The Mediating Role," p. 26.

14. These are his examples: see Cullen, *Hegel's Social and Political Thought*, p. 93.

15. Ernst Erdös, "Hegels politische Oekonomie im Verhältnis zu Sismondi," in *Hegel-Jahrbuch 1986*, ed. By Heinz Kimmerle *et al.* (Bochum: Germinal, 1988), pp. 75–86 (cf. p. 81).

16. Henri Denis, *Logique hégélienne et systèmes économiques* (Paris: Presses universitaires de France, 1984), p. 33. Like Cullen, both Erdös and Denis appear to have misconstrued Hegel's use of the term '*Meister.*'

on manufacturing. Yet, this reading cannot be correct, for a number of reasons.

First, although the German states were relatively backward in developing large-scale manufacturing enterprises, Hegel was well aware of the British situation and the development of industrial enterprises there, as well as in Holland and France. Hegel did not write from a parochial German standpoint, and he knew that such manufacturing enterprises were one of the important foundations of the new civil society for which he was attempting to provide the philosophical grounds.[17] Thus, there is no reason to suppose that he would consider an organization by Korporations to be inappropriate for the manufacturing (and commercial) trades.

Second, Hegel argued that the dismantling of the (few) Korporations that existed in England had contributed to England's problems with poverty and unemployment and was partly responsible for the increasing moral degradation of its citizens (PR, §245R; cf. PR [1819], 206; VRP III, 711). It would be strange for him to fault the English for doing away with an institution which had no relevance for the new form of the organization of work, namely, factory-based manufacturing. Surely, if Korporations were truly associations appropriate only for those involved in craft-based production, i.e., for artisans, then the English acted correctly in dismantling them when the industrial organization of work supplanted craft production. Furthermore, in his argument against completely *laissez-faire* freedom of trade, Hegel takes as his chief negative example the conditions in industry in Britain, while opposing these conditions with those prevalent where Korporations exist (cf. VRP IV, 624–27). He apparently thought that there was no inherent conflict between Korporations and industry.

Therefore, duly-constituted Korporations may be formed by individuals engaged in quite varied occupations in crafts, industry, and commerce, and they include all individuals—workers as well as managers and employers—engaged in the various branches within this sphere of the economic system. We are now in a position to discuss what functions the Korporations play in the context of civil society.

---

17. Although he recognizes Hegel's acquaintance with manufacturing in Britain, Denis still presumes that Hegel did write from the limited viewpoint of conditions in Germany alone; thus, he misses the integrative nature of the Korporation (see Denis, pp. 32–34). Kersting provides a needed reminder that Hegel's theory of the Korporation was especially meant to aid in overcoming the "deficiency in harmonization which was increasing on account of the growing industrialization" of Europe. See Wolfgang Kersting, "Polizei und Korporation in Hegels Darstellung der bürgerlichen Gesellschaft," in *Hegel-Jahrbuch 1986*, ed. By Heinz Kimmerle *et al.* (Bochum: Germinal, 1988), pp. 373–82 (quotation from p. 380).

The Specific Function of the *Korporation* in Ethical Life

The overarching task of a Korporation is to unify the 'atomic' individuals of civil society (or, specifically, those who are members of the social class of commerce and industry) into an ethical whole, while providing them with a degree of economic security. For Hegel, these two aspects (the ethical and the economic) are intimately connected; in fact, the ethical nature of a Korporation is part and parcel of its social and economic functions. Hegel terms these functions the 'right' of a Korporation and describes them as follows:

> The Korporation has the right, under the oversight of the public authority, (a) to look after its own interests within its own sphere, (b) to accept members, according to the objective quality of their skill and rectitude, in a number determined by the general context, (c) to protect its members against particular contingencies, (d) to provide the education to enable others to become members. (PR, §252; tr. rvsd.)

Though this is a relatively clear delineation (especially for Hegel!) of a Korporation's functions, it does require some unpacking.

First, what Hegel means by the "oversight of the public authority" is simply a general proviso to the effect that Korporations cannot be allowed to engage in activities, or make rules for their members, which conflict with the welfare of the public in general. Since it is the function of the public authority to provide for public safety and welfare (cf. PR, §§232–241), it is reasonable that oversight of Korporations is one of its duties.

Second, the fact that a Korporation has the right to "look after its own interests within its own¯sphere" follows directly from what has already been said above. It has this right primarily because those who are engaged in occupations within a particular sphere—and thus constitute the membership of a specific Korporation—are obviously most familiar with this sphere. Neither the state (as a whole) nor the public authority (as the regulator of the general operation of civil society) has the competency to work out the details of intra-industry goals and regulations.[18] Hegel clearly expects that each branch of commerce and industry will engage in a good deal of self-control through its Korporation,

---

18. Cf. Emile Durkheim, *Professional Ethics and Civic Morals*, trans. by Cornelia Brookfield (London: Routledge, 1957), p. 40. The first part of this work (the first three chapters) provides an account of the Korporation similar to Hegel's in many respects.

without "meddling" by the public authority (PR, §§252R and 288). In a sense, the Korporation thus plays the role of an educational institution for its members, educating them concerning the general interests of their professions. While this self-regulatory right of Korporations preserves the independence of economic endeavors, and so the subjective freedom of individuals to choose their occupations and modes of living, it aids in creating among its no-longer isolated members a conscious, mediated concern for the well-being of the entire membership of a particular branch of the economy (cf. PR, §254).

It follows, then, that Korporations have a right to "accept members, according to the objective quality of their skill and rectitude, in a number determined by the general context." If Korporations are to be self-regulating bodies with respect to the affairs of their distinct sectors of the manufacturing and commercial branches of the economy, then it surely falls within their purview to accept new members. Further, since the skills and capacities required for individuals to become full-fledged participants in a specific branch of industry are already recognized by those working in this branch, the Korporation has the right to require that new members possess these skills.

In order to ascertain whether specific individuals possess the appropriate degree of skill or education, a Korporation may test applicants for membership credentials (PR[1819], 203), and, if necessary, "provide the education requisite to fit individuals to become new members." Besides instituting its own training programs (including apprenticeships), a Korporation could help support independent vocational schools, in order to ensure properly educated members. As an aid in understanding how this aspect of the right of the Korporation is put into effect, one need look no further than to apprenticeship programs in certain trades in contemporary civil societies, for example, in carpentry and plumbing. While anyone may occasionally saw a board or replace a faucet washer, this does not, *ipso facto*, make that person a carpenter or a plumber. To achieve the status of a respected (or recognized) carpenter or plumber requires a period of training in the craft, accomplished in these instances by an apprenticeship program.

It is Hegel's contention that such respect (*Anerkennung*) accorded one as a skilled practitioner of a trade, organized as a Korporation, is of primary significance in the achievement of mediation within civil society. It is by becoming a member of an association representing a respected branch of industry of commerce (i.e., one recognized as 'socially necessary') that allows one to belong to a civic whole, instead of living only for oneself, a point to which I shall return below.

The remaining aspects of the right of a Korporation refer especially to the welfare functions of the Korporation. The right of the

Korporation to "protect its members against particular contingencies" must be treated in conjunction with its right to "accept members . . . in a number determined by the general context." It should be evident that a Korporation is the only institution in a position to determine approximately how many individuals are required in the types of occupations it represents. In order for a branch of industry to thrive there cannot be a shortage of workers in this branch; consequently, the Korporation of this branch will accept and train new members. Nevertheless, no branch of industry or commerce is completely independent of other branches, so that the prosperity of one branch is conditioned by the prosperity of the economy as a whole (a simple point from economics, recognized by Hegel, e.g., in his discussion of the interrelations of work and needs; cf. PR, §187). This notion of the economy as a whole is what Hegel calls here the "general context." It is this context that places the ultimate limit on the number of members that any particular Korporation can accept, since exceeding this limit might have detrimental effects on the welfare of its membership as a whole. This would be contrary to another aspect of the right of the Korporation, namely, the right to "protect its members from particular contingencies."

Other than limiting the number of persons accepted as new members (thus protecting the situation of those who are already members), by what other means does a Korporation protect its members against particular contingencies? First, it gives them a voice in the affairs of the organization of their particular branches of industry and commerce. Instead of being left to their own devices of private self-protection and fruitless attempts to "fight the system" as individuals, the members of a Korporation can speak in one voice. In this way, they can ensure that measures serving to protect those engaged in certain occupations become the policy of every enterprise within the competency of their Korporation. The implementation of general regulations, such as those pertaining to occupational safety and the hiring and dismissal of employees in the various enterprises throughout a branch of industry or commerce, would belong to this protective function of a Korporation (cf. PR, §254).

In addition, a Korporation has the function of safe-guarding (and enhancing) the economic welfare of its members (cf. VRP IV, 629). Thus it would fall within its purview to set a schedule of wages (or salaries) for the different congeries of skills needed within a branch of industry or commerce, wages which would allow each member to subsist at a comfortable standard of living. In general, an important means whereby a Korporation protects its members is by serving as the guarantor of their economic security (cf. PR[1819], 203; VRP III, 712).

At the same time, since the Korporation is an institution which unites its members by these (and other) means into an ethical whole, these members may be expected to relate to each other as 'associates' and not as mere competitors or as individuals interested in their personal well-being alone. This ethical quality of the Korporation establishes a kind of equality among the members (not, of course, a strict equality) and a readiness to provide assistance to those members who have become poor through contingent circumstances. Thus, as Hegel remarks, in the Korporation the "help which poverty receives loses its contingent character and the humiliation wrongfully associated with it. The wealthy perform their duty to their association," by contributing to the relief of their poorer associates (PR, §253R; tr. rvsd.). Or, stated in a somewhat more modern way, the members of a Korporation are "united in a solidary manner [*solidarisch*] for those who fall into poverty" (PR [1819]. 203).

In general, the Korporation provides a 'stable basis' for individual members and their families, since their "security of subsistence" is assured by Korporation membership (PR, §253; tr. rvsd.; cf. VRP IV, 626). Because a Korporation accepts as members only those who possess the capacities (e.g., skills) required for an occupation and is actively engaged in guaranteeing their economic security, becoming a Korporation member provides an individual with a sense of personal achievement. At the same time, it lifts him or her out of the selfish concerns found within the sphere of the system of needs by itself (the market economy) and elevates his or her needs and work to the level of a "conscious effort for a common end" (PR, §254).

As a member of a Korporation, each person is respected as a "somebody." Thus, the Korporation member

> needs no *external marks* beyond his own membership as evidence of his ability and his regular income and success, i.e., evidence that he *is somebody*. It is also recognized that he belongs to a whole which is itself a member of the general [civil] society, and that he actively promotes and has an interest in the comparatively unselfish end of this whole. (PR, §253; tr. rvsd.)

In this manner, a member of a Korporation attains a status recognized both by his or her associates and by those who are members of other Korporations: he or she has a determinate position within civil society, having achieved the dignity or respect accorded a Korporation member.

The merely 'private' individual of the system of needs (the bare market economy) finds a "second family" as a Korporation member (PR, §252). Such an individual does not need to prove in any further manner that he or she is a success (cf. VRP III, 710). He or she accepts the kind of needs, the type of work, and the way of life appropriate to his or her station in civil society. This is the kind of closure that Hegel thinks the

Korporation achieves in regard to the system of needs. If, however, an individual is not a member of a Korporation—or if a given civil society does not have a developed system of Korporations—he or she remains bound to the never-ending cycle of needs, including the most fundamental social need (in Hegel's view), the need for respect as "a somebody." This merely private person, who is a member of no Korporation, remains

> without the *dignity of a social class*, is reduced through his isolation to the self-seeking side of his trade [*Gewerbe*], and his subsistence and satisfaction become *insecure*. Consequently, he will seek to attain *respect for himself* by means of external proofs of success in his trade—proofs which are subject to no limit. He cannot live in the manner of his social class, because [for him] the social class does not exist. . . . (PR, §253 tr. rvsd.)

In short, the individual stuck in the cycle of the system of needs has neither a secure occupation nor the respect due to the dignity associated with the attainment of a determinate position in the socioeconomic sphere. He or she is "reduced to his [or her] private goal[s]" (VRP III, 709) and the never-ending attempt to prove to others that he or she really is somebody successful. This proof often takes the form of taking pride in one's (relatively) high monetary income, contrasting oneself with others merely "through the accumulation of ever-increasing amounts of wealth,"[19] or of collecting "external marks" of success, such as tangible goods not possessed by (most) others, e.g., a large house, expensive jewelry, clothing, or automobile. Such individuals engage in what we would now call 'conspicuous consumption,' and the reader will no doubt be able to think of many additional examples of this phenomenon.

In conclusion, membership in a Korporation leads an individual to the recognition of ethically-based goals which are more permanent and meaningful than private, ephemeral economic preferences. The goal becomes the "attainment of recognition by others and by oneself of one's own importance and contribution to universal purposes."[20] Further, it is Hegel's contention that only societies organized through Korporations may be described as true civil societies having an ethical grounding. What this might say about many of our contemporary societies is, however, a tale for another day.

---

19. Carl J. Nederman, "Sovereignty, War and the Corporation: Hegel on the Medieval Foundations of the Modern State," *Journal of Politics*, 49 (1987), pp. 500–520 (quotation from p. 516).

20. Peter G. Stillman, "Hegel's Civil Society: A Locus of Freedom," *Polity*, 12 (1979–80), pp. 622–46 (quotation from p. 635).

11 Hegel, Kierkegaard, and the Problem of Finitude

P. Christopher Smith

I n his exposition of the experience (*Erfahrung*) of historically ef-
fected and effective consciousness (*Wirkungsgeschichtliches
Bewusstsein*), Hans-George Gadamer raises what must be the crucial question for postmodern thought in regard to Kierkegaard: Does
he, or for that matter, does Feuerbach or Marx or any of the "young
Hegelians," succeed in breaking through Hegel's claim that ultimately
thinking reflection comprehends within itself all reality?[1] To put this

---

1. See H.-G. Gadamer, *Wahrheit und Methode* (*Truth and Method*; henceforth,
WM) (Tuebingen, 1965), pp. 324–32; also pp. 332–44. Gadamer here works out the idea
of experience as *Erfahrung*—in contrast to subjective aesthetic experience as *Erlebnis*
(see WM 52–66)—using Aeschylus' *pathei mathos*, learned through undergoing or suffering, as a paradigm. His point is that "Any experience (*Erfahrung*) worthy of the name
nullifies an expectation" (WM 338). We set out with a conception in mind of what we
are going to *do* (*agein, prattein*) only then to *undergo* (*paschein*) completely unintended
results. Seen this way, Hegel's "*Science* of the Experience of Consciousness" (G.W.F.
Hegel, *Phänomenologie des Geistes* [*Phenomenology of Mind*] [Hamburg, 1952; henceforth, PhG], p. 61, my emphasis), is a contradiction in terms for, "Here, from the start,
the nature of experience is thought of from a vantage point where one has passed
beyond experience" (WM 338). Building on the *pathos* of Aeschylus' *pathei mathos*, I will
take Gadamer's argument against Hegel's reflection philosophy even further: the crucial
pathos that we undergo is, as Kierkegaard shows, a *pathos* or affective feel to things that
conditions what we think before we think it, namely despair.

Translations from Gadamer and Hegel will be my own. In addition, the following
abbreviations will be used: SD: S. Kierkegaard, *Sickness unto Death* in *Fear and Trembling and The Sickness unto Death*, trans. W. Lowrie (New York, 1954), pp. 141–262; and
PhF: *Philosophical Fragments*, trans. D. Swenson and H. Hong (Princeton, 1962).

another way, does Kierkegaard succeed in deconstructing the modern illusion that systematic, conclusive thought is possible? For, as Gadamer points out, Hegel argues very effectively that any "thing in itself" that we, in reflection, posit as existing beyond the limits of consciousness, is precisely a positing of consciousness and hence not beyond it but in it. Both the 'limit' and the 'thing in itself' are, after all, concepts belonging to consciousness, and hence in any reflection on them, consciousness, even if at first unbeknownst to itself, is only relating itself to itself. Indeed, its reflection will reveal to it that precisely what makes the thought of a limit or border thinkable in the first place is the thought or concept of an other against which the bordered and limited thing borders. Hence if consciousness thinks of itself as a limited thing, it is already thinking of a thing-in-itself beyond that limit, already thinking of the other that it says exceeds its thinking.[2]

Gadamer contends, furthermore, that Kierkegaard's recourse to the thou as the other, whose ineliminable otherness we are said to experience in the encounter with him or her, does not at all suffice to break the grip of Hegel's dialectical reflection. For in fact, he counters, nothing informs the dialectic of the *Phenomenology of Mind* so much as the dialectic of recognition in its chapters on consciousness-of-self (*Selbstbewusstsein*) (see PhG 141–150) and its reprise of this dialectic of the I and thou in the exposition of conscience, confession, and reconciliation (see PhG 445–472). It is striking, however, that in his own exposition of human finitude and the insurmountability of our experience of otherness, Gadamer himself would answer Hegel's argument with just such recourse to the I-thou encounter (see WM 340f.).

I contend here that in fact Kierkegaard is far more successful in breaking the hold of systematic reflective thought than are either Gadamer or Heidegger, on whom Gadamer would base his own recovery of the experience or *Erfaharung* of finite consciousness. For of the three it is Kierkegaard alone who really succeeds in escaping the theoretical perspective for us philosophers merely looking on at existence, and in accomplishing the "*Zurueckschlagen*" or counter-

---

2. Gadamer refers to Hegel's *Enzyklopaedie* (Hamburg, 1959), §60., p. 84:
  Therefore it is only unconsciousness not to see that the very designation of something as something finite or limited (*einem Endlichen oder Beschraehkten*) contains the proof of the active presence of the infinite, unlimited; it is only unconsciousness not to see that knowledge of a limit (*Grenze*) can only exist insofar as the unlimited (*Unbergrenzte*) exists on this side, within consciousness.

stroke out of reflection back into existence.[3] Indeed, I would argue that, try as it might, any optically-based, speculative philosophy such as Heidegger's or Gadamer's could never break the hold of reflection. For to do that it would have to deconstruct and resolve itself, as it does only in Kierkegaard, into the acoustical event of hearing the word spoken by an other to us, in our existence.

In what follows here I intend, by tracing comparatively a Hegelian and a Kierkegaardian exposition of the dialectic of finitude and infinitude, to show how Kierkegaard does indeed break the hold of Hegelian dialectical reflection. It is all too easily argued that Hegel's dialectic of the "unhappy consciousness" at the end of his exposition of consciousness-of-self incorporates within itself, and preempts Kierkegaard's dialectic of despair. In comparing the relevant passages from Hegel's *Phenomenology of Mind* and Kierkegaard's *Sickness unto Death*, I wish to show that this is not at all the case. To this end I will underscore, (a) that unlike Hegel he bases his transitions from one stage in existence to the next, not on any logic internal to the conscious thoughts present to a given shape of consciousness, but on shifts in the preconscious *Stimmung*, the voicing, tonality or *pathos* affecting the will;[4]

---

3. See, for instance M. Heidegger, *Sein und Zeit* (*Being and Time*) (Tübingen, 1960), p. 38:

> Philosophy is universal phenomenological ontology starting from the hermeneutics of being-there (*Dasein*) which has, as the analytic of existence, fastened the end of the thread followed by all philosophical questioning at the point where such questioning originates and back to which it reverts (*wohin es zurueckschlaegt*) (my translation).

Gadamer points out that this idea of a "hermeneutics of facticity" or, better, of "facticity's hermeneutics" rooted in our factual existence, comes from Kierkegaard, who admonishes us to abandon abstract philosophy's "floating in metaphysical indeterminacy" and return to our real existence in existential despair (see Gadamer, *Gesammelte Werke* (*Collected Works*), vol. 3 (Tuebingen: 1987), pp. 419–22, and Heidegger, *Gesammtausgabe* (*Collected Edition*), vol. 63, *Ontologie* (*Die Hermeneutik der Faktizität*) (Frankfurt, 1988), p. 5. For Gadamer's own indebtedness to Kierkegaard, see especially WM 84–96.

4. The typescript of Heidegger's 1924 Marburg lectures, *Grundbergriffe der Aristotelischen Philosophie* (*Basic Concepts of Aristotelian Philosophy*) in the Marcuse-Archiv of the Frankfort a.M. Stadsbibliotek, makes clear that Heidegger draws primarily upon Aristotle's exposition of *pathos* or feeling in the *Rhetoric* for his own idea of *Stimmungen* or moods, frames of mind, etc.. Important in the word *pathos* is its origin in *paschein*, to suffer or undergo. This Heidegger underscores by linking *die Stimmung* to *Geworfenheit*, our having been thrown into a situation, and *Befindlichkeit*, or the mental-physical condition in which we "always already" happen to find ourselves. But *Stimmung* as a translation of *pathos* brings out another dimension of the latter insofar as it contains the work *Stimme* or voice. For the *pathos* in which we find ourselves gives things more an acoustical tonality than an optical look and hence is communicated to listener by the tone of what is said. More than *oran* or seeing *akouein* or hearing is thus fundamental to any change in the basic *pathos*, say from despair to faith.

(b) that these shifts are brought about by hearing affective words spoken to the self by a being and power other than itself; (c) that for Kierkegaard this other is second-person being, a thou who *art*, whose words I am willed or not willed to hear, whereas for Hegel any other turns out to be third-person being, an it that *is*, which I either grasp or do not grasp consciously; and, finally, (d) that whereas Hegel sees the other as a positing of the infinite self, Kierkegaard sees the finite self as a positing of the other, as the creation of God.

In this last point lies the deeper reason why for Hegel the experience of otherness is mere appearance to be dispelled while for Kierkegaard the experience of otherness is ultimate. From the beginning Kierkegaard knows what Hegel overlooks and Heidegger was only to learn after his turn: namely, that the ground of what exists, including human existence, cannot be sought in human existence itself and hence is never a ground or bottom of things that we might get to, but always an other beyond our penetration, an *Abgrund*, an abyss, absurd and para-doxical, that ever confounds our presumptions about it. In this light, Hegel's demonstration of consciousness-of-self's 'certainty' that all otherness is self, that I=I, reveals itself to be only the self's project of defiance, namely to eradicate its dependency on a power outside of itself and, in thus destroying the ground of its created being, destroy itself.

Alterity Eliminated: The Dialect of Hegel's "Unhappy Consciousness"

To being with, then, let us ask specifically: is Kierkegaard's dialectic of despair in *Sickness unto Death* but a transitional shape of consciousness in the inexorable logical progression of Hegel's *Phenomenology of Mind*? Is it just a variation in the "unhappy consciousness" on its way to recovery of itself in the certainty and truth of Reason that the other is self? To answer this question we need first to have situated Hegel's unhappy consciousness in the context of his exposition of consciousness-of-self and to have established thereby just what the presuppositions of this exposition are. To be sure, like the despairing consciousness in Kierkegaard, the unhappy consciousness is driven by its inability to harmonize the concomitant dimensions within itself of the eternal and temporal, changeless and changing, infinite and finite. Like some cumulative mechanical defect in an engine, this discrepancy begins as an imperceptible disorder only to end, in the unhappy consciousness, the breakdown of the self. We need here to get back to the origins of this disruption in the coming of consciousness-of-self onto the scene.

Consciousness-of-self is the result of the dialectic of consciousness of something other than self, consciousness of some Kantian thing-in-itself that is supposed to have a being in itself apart from the consciousness we have of it. In its negative function Hegel's dialectic of the pure empiricist's sense-certainty (PhG 79–89), of Lockean perception (PhG 89–102), and of Kantian understanding (PhG 102–129) is intended to annul the hypothesis of any such being *per se* and, thus, of the consciousness that presupposes this being. Positively, however, it is intended as the demonstration (*Beweis*) of the principle of idealism, namely that I=I. All the while consciousness took itself to be relating itself to another, it was in fact only relating itself to itself; every *Gegenstand* or object "standing over against" it was really consciousness's consciousness of itself. And in the consciousness-of-self at which it has arrived it now "grasps (*grieft*) over and beyond this other which, for it, . . . is only itself" (PhG 143). Still, up to this point the demonstration of I=I has only been seen theoretically. Now the conclusion demonstrated must be realized in concrete practice. It has to be 'done.'

But in its Faustian plunge into life, consciousness-of-self at once runs up against the counter-demonstration: the *Selbständigkeit*, the "standing on its own" of the very thing, life, that it assumed to be no longer "standing over against it" (PhG 135). And now that it is putting the theory of I=I into practice, it seeks to eliminate the "standing on its own" of the other by gratifying its own desire (*Begierde*): it desires to incorporate physically the other into itself, to consume it. We note already, however, that even in this exposition of practice and action the unconscious drives in play here remain subordinate to consciousness's aim to demonstrate consciously to itself that I=I. For Hegel, consciousness is fully conscious of the dialectic here, namely that the objects of desire cease to be objects of desire when the desire is satisfied—"when in satisfaction I thirst for desire" (Goethe). Thus this consciousness-of-self, says Hegel, is driven (consciously) beyond physical desire altogether and now seeks the practical demonstration that the other is itself in recognition by another consciousness-of-self. Significantly, Hegel skips over the erotic desire of another consciousness-of-self, which would have provided the missing link between subconscious desire and the conscious quest for recognition by another consciousness of self, but which would have also displayed to him the inevitable embeddedness of all conscious projects in the unconscious *pathos*. Instead, he fast-forwards to what for him is the sheer mental and wholly a-sexual dialectic of recognition. To be sure, the highly-unstable facade of reciprocal recognition in the greeting, with which Hegel begins his exposition here—"each sees the other doing the same thing it does" (PhG 142)—quickly crumbles displaying to us, after Nietzsche, if not to Hegel, the real game being played beneath it, namely a conflict in subconscious wills to power, from which one consciousness emerges as recognized consciousness-of-self and another consciousness, as recognizing and conscious of itself only as a thing for an other. And with that we have arrived at the dialectic of lord and servant (PhG 146f).

Has the subconscious foundation of what transpires here really eluded Hegel? Crucial in answering this question is the quite extraordinary passage, precisely at this critical juncture, on the *Angst* of the servant consciousness, a passage that indeed reads like something straight out of Kierkegaard or Heidegger:

> This consciousness, namely, has not felt anxiety (*Angst*) about this thing or that, or for this or that moment of time, but rather for its entire being (*Wesen*); for it has felt the fear of death, of the absolute Lord. It has been inwardly dissolved in this fear, has trembled in the foundations of itself, and everything fixed in it has quaked (PhG 148).

And just this visceral "liquification of everything standing" (*idem*) will provide the basis for this self's recovering itself in work; for "if it [this servant consciousness] has not withstood absolute fear but rather only a little anxiety here and there, the negative essential being (*Wesen*) has remained external to it" (PhG 149–50). Must we not say that here, just as in Heidegger or Kierkegaard, the subconscious tonality of *Angst* that this consciousness finds itself having undergone does indeed provide the "condition of the possibility" for all subsequent development of conscious thought? Indeed, we read that for this consciousness "fear pervades the entire reality of existence" (PhG 149).

Striking indeed—but whatever possibilities there might have been for Hegel's pursuing this theme, we now see, cut off by an abrupt transition to an utterly impassive Stoicism, a transition that is not really a transition at all but another fast-forward. And, indeed, upon closer examination we see in retrospect that in Hegel the experience of *Angst*, the experience of being absolutely at the disposal of the other, had already issued in what for him is a characteristic dialectical conversion (*Umschlag*) into the opposite. The awareness of one's absolute not-being for oneself in death, directly converts into consciousness of one's pure being for oneself. "The absolute liquification of everything standing is, however, the simple essential being (*Wesen*) of consciousness-of-self, absolute negativity, pure being-for-oneself" (PhG 148). Hence in Hegel's exposition of *Angst* there was from the start suppression of what happens to us, of any passion undergone, and of our being at the disposal of something prior to, and outside of our conscious control;

there was suppression of any being 'for an other.' From the start the subconscious passion of *Angst* undergone was, in fact, already being displaced by another 'condition of the possibility' of the servant's consciousness-of-self, namely service or conscious action done in work: "Through work, however, it comes to and comes to itself" (PhG 148). And the end result for the servant, who alone underwent *Angst* and had to work his way out of it, is therefore the same for the lord: stoicism's singularly dispassionate pure consciousness of being-for-oneself, unaffected by whatever comes to pass and by whatever feeling one might be undergoing. The end result for both is the Stoic's "freedom of consciousness-of-self," as Hegel calls it (PhG 151f.).

Furthermore, that the dialogical experience of two different consciousnesses, the lord and the servant, is here preemptorily reduced to the monological experience of one consciousness, makes patent that Hegel is forcing the "experience of consciousness" to conform to his pre-conceived formula of I=I, a presumption into which, as a sort of Procrustean bed, he forces all the phenomena in his phenomenology. For Hegel rides rough-shod over the fact that the dialectic of the I and thou, be they equals in power, (neighbors, *plesioi*) or be they unequals (lord and servant, *kyrios kai doulos*), always runs up against the ineliminable alterity of the partner. His postulate of I=I precludes acknowledgment of this, and hence he arbitrarily closes off what for him must be rejected as the *schlechte Unendlichkeit* or "bad unendingness" of any encounter of one human being with an other, different one.[5] So

---

5. As the references to recognition (PhG 459, 461) and to the "unhappy consciousness" (PhG 462) contained in it make clear, Hegel's chapter on "conscience, the beautiful soul, evil and the forgiveness of it" (PhG 445–72) is a reprise, now at the level of Spirit, of the dialectic of consciousness-of-self. And indeed, we see the same set of problems here: How is the immediate certainty of I=I (see PhG 458, 461) to be fleshed out with concrete content? And how is the individual, contingent self to be reconciled with the universal. Here, to be sure, the civic, not religious issue is how consciousness of universal obligation and duty may be adhered to in one's individual actions and these thereby given universal validity. For with the best intentions and good will the self still falls into singularity and caprice and still does evil, self-serving things. Consequently, like the unhappy consciousness it finds itself despicable (PhG 468). And like the unhappy consciousness it must confess its failures to someone who speaks for the universal, which here is the spiritual *Gemeinde*, meaning church parish, to be sure, but also town. The confessor, in recognizing his own particularity in the one confessing and in speaking the word of forgiveness, reconciles the individual consciousness to himself and vice versa, and with this their difference is overcome: the I has finally become We and the We, I (see PhG 140).

That despite appearances to the contrary this is not a genuinely dialogical event between an I and a thou, is made clear by the ultimate collapse here of the dialogical back into the monological, out of which it arose in the first place:

suddenly the dialectic is no longer dialogue between two but once again monologue internal to one: whether "on the throne or in chains," whether lord or servant, there is now no difference (PhG 153).

Precisely in having withdrawn any encounter with otherness and in being now at one with itself, the stoic consciousness can now be conscious of itself as an unchanging thinking self in complete detachment from all the shifting content of its thinking. To its consciousness of the transcendence of self in thinking, skepticism now only adds the consciousness of the utter transience and nullity of all content of thinking (PhG 154f.). And with that, the setting is given for Hegel's full internalization in one consciousness of what formerly was experienced between two different consciousnesses: the dimension of the lord (Lord, i.e., God) becomes this one consciousness's awareness of its transcendent immutability, and the dimension of the servant becomes its simultaneous awareness of its own transience and nullity.

This, then, is the development presupposed by Hegel's unhappy consciousness, in which the encounter of the I with the thou has become a dialectic of the unchangeable and changeable that remains internal to one consciousness. As monological this dialectic will end with the self's "reconciliation with itself" (PhG 159)—not with an other. This result Hegel calls *Geist*, which in this context, surely, means self-contained, self-possessed mind, i.e., the *intellectus* or *nous* that in thinking itself thinking grasps all reality, and not the transformative *spiritus* or *pneuma* that "blows where it wants," grasps the self, and carries it away.[6] Put another way, hearing what the Lord has to say to

---

The reconciling yes, wherein both I's relinquish their opposed existence, is the existence of the I which has expanded to duality and which in this duality stays the same and, in its complete externalization, and opposite has the certainty of itself (PhG 472).

R. Bultmann offers a useful corrective to this gnostic misreading of forgiveness that reduces the other to oneself and oneself to the other thereby eliminating the otherness of the other. See in particular his *Jesus* (Muenchen, 1964), pp. 137–8, where he rightly emphasizes that receiving forgiveness is always an experience of the insurmountable otherness of the other, an encounter with the not-I, insofar as precisely nothing in myself could have caused it to be extended or even earned it. As anyone knows who has received it, forgiveness remains an unmerited gift the origin of which lies entirely in the grace of the other.

6. In this regard contrast Hegel's appropriation at the end of his *Enzyklopaedie* (p. 463) of Aristotle's *Metaphysics*, Lambda, 1072b 19–21—"Now intelligence (*nous*) can think itself insofar as it takes part in what is thought. For it itself becomes what is thought when it touches upon and thinks what is thought, and thus mind and what is thought are the same"—with *John* 3:8: "The spirit-wing (*pneuma*) blows where it will and you hear its voice (*tén phonén autou akoueis*) but do not know whence it comes and where it leads." (Translations from the Greek are my own.)

me, a servant of the Lord, will have been entirely displaced by seeing into myself, by introspection: "It itself is the looking (*Schauen*) of one consciousness-of-self into another and it itself is both" (PhG 159).

But we are not yet at this pre-established goal; the unhappy consciousness has not yet reconciled the two parts of itself, infinite and finite, with each other. And this is why it is said to be unhappy: It is a contradiction in which the one contrary does not come to rest in the other contrary, rather in its contrary it produces itself anew as contrary" (PhG 159). This failure at reconciling itself with itself is its *Schmerz*, its pain and sorrow (PhG 160), not any failure to find reconciliation with anyone other than itself. Thus its remorse and sense of sinfulness is not in regard to any breeches of faith with an other, not, for instance, in regard to an unfaithful servant's willful violation of the will of the Lord—here, God—but only in regard to its own self-contradictoriness and inadequacy.

This battle of the self with itself is said now to be experienced wholly internally within the self—even if by definition experience (*Erfahrung*) is of an other outside oneself. To be sure, in the first of what will be three stages here, the immutable universal appears to consciousness 'for it' as an alien judge of the mutable existing individual. But of course we philosophers know 'for us' that such a God of wrath is merely the unhappy consciousness's projection of itself and not really an other to it. We know, that is, that all along I=I and that this is "the experience which consciousness-of-self, divided in two as it is, has in its unhappy lot" (PhG 160). We know, in other words, that its experience is not really experience at all.

In the second stage, to which Hegel devotes the bulk of his analysis here, it appears to this consciousness-of-self experiencing that which for it seems to be other than itself, that the eternal and supersensible has come to it in historical sensible form—as the Christ, for instance (PhG 161). Characteristically, the second person thou-art being of the Christ is disregarded and dialectic here is construed along the lines of the earlier dialectic of the third person sense-datum, as *Sein* or mere being, which is not yet *Wesen* or essential being (See PhG 79f): like the sense-datum the incarnate deity is no longer 'given' when one gets to wherever it was supposed to have been. The grave is empty; the 'this-here-now' is always already the 'that-there-then,' and thus "instead of having grasped (*ergriffen*) the essential being (*Wesen*) it has grasped only inessentiality" (PhG 164). And instead of gaining a concept (*Begriff*) of what it encounters, says Hegel, it swims in a "musical thinking" (*musikalisches Denken*) that is not thinking at all, but some sort of murky devotional contemplation and prayer (*Andacht*) (PhG 163); it lapses, he says, into pure sentiment (*Gemuet*) (PhG 164). Thus here too Hegel, for the purpose of demonstrating that I=I, has systematically deleted the dialogical dimension of prayer and evaded the fact that prayers are not just the cultivation of a state of mind but prayers to someone other than oneself. He has, in other words, cast the thou-art second-person being to whom one prays—"I pray thee . . . "—as a third person it-is, as an object of cognition, and a faulty one at that insofar as it is not grasped conceptually (*begrifflich ergriffen*).

Having been thrown out of its sentimentality and back on itself, this second state of the unhappy consciousness, consciousness, namely, in relation to the eternal universal in temporal particular form, now becomes for Hegel a composite reprise of the human lord's desire and enjoyment and the servant's work. New, however, is that the object desired and worked on here is afflicted with doubleness insofar as now it is Lord God's but thus also of Satan. And insofar as it is God's, this unhappy consciousness must not enjoy the product of its work but deprive itself of any enjoyment of it and give it back. Thus any thinking, *Denken*, here becomes thanking, *Danken*, which is scarcely an advance beyond the previous *Andacht* in grasping things conceptually. And with that, the unhappy consciousness has, in Hegel's view, fallen furthest into a pathological condition: in its eyes its activity (*Tätigkeit*) and deed (*Tat*) have become not 'mine' but 'Thine;' "Thine is the power. . . . " And "Thus," Hegel argues, "instead of returning into itself out of its doing and having verified itself for itself, it reflects this movement of doing back into the other extreme, which is hereby represented to be purely universal, the absolute might" (PhG 166). But as was the case in the experience of *Angst*, such an absolute negation of self converts instantaneously in Hegel into its opposite. For it must recognize that its thanking was its own doing, as was its self-sacrifice, and in fact "by its willing and accomplishing it has put itself to the test as standing on its own independently (*als selbstaendiges*)" (PhG 167).

Having thus been returned to itself, however, this consciousness only turns on itself. Its animal functions and enjoyment become the figure of an enemy that precisely in being defeated always re-engenders itself. They become the obsession of a consciousness that, again, does not think, does not grasp conceptually, but, in this case, only broods (PhG 168). Even so, in Hegel's view there is an advance here over the previous failures at conceptual thinking in *Andacht* and *Danken*: this consciousness is no longer conscious of what it assumes to be an other outside it but in its very brooding is fixated precisely on itself. And to its feeling of unhappiness and sense of the poverty of its actions there now attaches its consciousness of its unity with that very unchangeable being, measured against which it had found itself so inadequate. It is to be underscored that this dialectical conversion into the opposite is entirely monological and that there is nothing like mercy, forgiveness, and redemption by an other here (see note 5). Rather, as in the experience of *Angst*, here too this consciousness's not-being and negation convert in themselves and by themselves into being and self-affirmation. In other words, this consciousness 'stands on its own' and saves itself.

Hence, when it now seeks a 'middle term' and mediator outside of itself (Christ/the priest) to mediate in the logical syllogism that would conceptually link the universal and eternal with the particular and transient in itself (PhG 169), that mediator, like the God of wrath, is really only a projection and externalization of elements in the syllogism (*Schluss*) of its own thinking and not at all the other person to whom it believes it is surrendering its personal decision (*Entschluss*):

> By giving up its own decision, then its own property and its enjoyment, and finally by going through the motions of a business it does not understand, it deprives itself, in truth and completely, of its consciousness of internal and external freedom, deprives itself of the reality of *being-for-itself*, it has the certainty of having externalized its *I* in truth and of having turned its immediate con-sciousness-of-self into a *thing*, into an objective being standing over against it (*zu einem gegenstaendliches Sein*) (PhG 170).

The interpersonal dialectic of the servant's breaking faith with an other, personal being, the Lord, and thereby incurring a debt (*Schuld*; see PhG 169) which can never be paid back but which can only, by the Lord's mercy, be forgiven, is wholly reconstrued here within the Fichtian optic of demonstrating that the infinite thinking self is 'standing on its own,' freely, with precisely no being 'standing over against' it.

So precisely in the very negation of itself, consciousness in Hegel once again affirms itself by itself and with no intervention from an other. In having given its will over to the mediator, it has in effect made its particular will universal, and thus it already has the presentiment (*Vorstellung*), if not yet the concept (*Begriff*), of Reason. It has, that is to say, the certainty "of being, in its individuality, absolutely *in itself* or being all reality" (PhG 171). And with this we have reached the third and final stage of the unhappy consciousness in which, by itself, it surpasses itself and "finds itself as this individual in the unchangeable" (PhG 160):

> In the thought which it has taken hold of (*erfasst*)—that the *individual* consciousness is *in itself* absolute essential being (*Wesen*)—consciousness goes back into itself. For the unhappy consciousness being-in-itself was *beyond* its self. But . . . its unity

with the universal has become for it what it was for us since the elevated individual is the universal that no longer falls outside of it (PhG 175).

One does not need the phenomenological perspicuity of a Kierkegaard or Heidegger, however, to see that Hegel's presuppositions have distorted his own phenomenological descriptions here and blocked out an inevitable component of the self that he is treating: namely the realization that no human self is ever at a point where the natural, *psychikos* will to eliminate otherness, of which the desire to demonstrate that I=I is only a sublimated form, is not thwarted. All dialogical relationships, all relationships between husband and wife, friend and friend, between the one who has broken faith and the one with whom the faith is broken, between sinner and God, sinner and confessor— all these inevitably show that any will to prove to oneself that the other is oneself will at some point be arrested and the other's otherness abruptly asserted. That, for instance is what the frustrations of the human lord and master, who would subordinate the servant, would have shown had Hegel not all along been forcing the dialogical encounter back into the monologue of thought thinking itself thinking. And indeed, in turning to Kierkegaard's parallel dialectic of the infinite and finite self in *Sickness unto Death* as we will now do, it becomes clear by sheer contrast, how much Hegel's dialectic has in fact concealed because of the structure of a deduction of I=I into which he forces the phenomena in question.

Alterity Recovered: Kierkegaard's Dialectic of Despair

For in Kierkegaard two essential aspects of experience (*Erfahrung*), and hence the insuperability of experience itself, are not blocked but kept in view. In the first place, that part of the self which may be called consciousness does not primarily do things but primarily undergoes them. In other words, consciousness, with its acts and performances (Husserl: *Leistungen*), is not the entire 'condition of the possibility' of what it is conscious of. Rather, everything it knows is conditioned by the voicing and *pathos*, the emotional tonality or feel of things; that it always finds itself already having undergone (*epatheis*) (see note 4). Its dialectic, accordingly, is not a dialectic of consciousness but a dialectic of despair—much as Hegel's dialectic of the servant should have been a dialectic of *Angst*, despair and defiance, and not of consciousness-of-self. Hence consciousness, in Kierkegaard, does not fully grasp what is happening to it, what has come over it and grasps it. Kierkegaard, in other words, remains true to the Pauline account of Christian indeterminate, futural experience in existential "fear and trembling:"

> Not that I have already taken hold of it (*ergriffen habe*) or am perfect; rather I chase after it that I might take hold of it (*ergreifen moechte*) now that I have been taken hold of (*ergriffen bin*) by Christ Jesus. My brothers I do not think that I have yet taken hold of it (*es ergriffen habe*) (*Philippians* 3:12; translated from Luther).

In the second place, and consequently, Kierkegaard recognizes that the shifts experienced by us conditioned, existing individuals—as opposed to the fictive construct of "we" philosophers "for us" beyond experience—do not follow from anything which we ourselves have in view within consciousness. They occur only as the result of subconscious shifts in our underlying *pathos*, and these, in turn, are the result of our ongoing encounters with something or someone other than we. And even if the determinant *pathos* felt is initially "the wrath" of the other (St. Paul: *hé orgê*) and one's own despair in response, and is not yet the release and joy of being forgiven, it too is a gift to us, who are the dative object of what occurs here and not the active subjects doing it.

Let us turn, then, to the phenomenon of a consciousness caught in the dialectic of its eternal and temporal dimensions as Kierkegaard describes it, i.e., not as the unhappy consciousness, that has yet to see that it always was at one with itself throughout all its experience of merely apparent otherness, rather as the despairing self that in its open ended futurity always has yet to be returned to its ground in God. To be sure, just as in Hegel we are concerned in Kierkegaard with a self that relates itself to itself, but with an all-decisive difference: if this relationship were really self-constituting, the self would be able to rid itself of its eternal self, to kill itself, which it wants desperately to do. But the emotional tonality, the *pathos* or feel of despair in which it finds itself announces to the despairing consciousness that precisely this it cannot do. The individual in despair cannot consume himself or herself, cannot become nothing, and despairs of ever being able to do so (SD 147).

Hence the phenomenon of the despairing consciousness displays that not it itself, but an other power over it is constitutive of its being, and the dialectic here, quite in contrast to Hegel's, is that "the self cannot *of itself* attain and remain in equilibrium and rest by itself, but only by relating itself to that power which constituted the whole relation" (SD 147; my emphasis). Hence the relationship here is not at all that of a self that relates itself to itself in canceling otherness but instead a "disrelationship in a relation that relates itself to its own self and is constituted by another" (SD 147). And the end of the dialectic is consequently not when the self has, for itself, internalized the externalized other that has always been only itself all along, but rather when "by relating itself to its own self and by willing to be itself the self is grounded transparently in the power which posited it" (SD 147). We note, then, that here the self does not, as in Hegel, do the positing, rather it is posited by another, an other who in an act of mercy takes the self back out of its self-imposed alienation from the source of its being.

Hence, as opposed to unhappiness, in Hegel, over one's inability to reconcile oneself with oneself, despair, in Kierkegaard, is experienced in one's moving away from the constitutive ground of oneself and in asserting oneself against any ground of oneself outside oneself. What the one who despairingly wills to be himself really wills "is to tear his self away from the power which constituted it" (SD 153). And consequently what looks like an advance towards the goal in Hegel is shown by Kierkegaard to be a movement ever further away from the real goal of grounding oneself transparently in the power that constitutes oneself. To take the unhappiness of Hegel's unhappy consciousness as frustration in uniting the eternal and temporal within itself by self-abnegation and renunciation, is thus a superficial misreading of the phenomenon exposed by Kierkegaard's dialectical deconstruction of it: consciousness's unhappiness is really the self's despair at its inability to destroy itself by tearing itself from the external power constitutive of it.

Unsystematically, perhaps, but not surprisingly, given his specific mission to would-be absolute philosophers, Kierkegaard begins his first phenomenological exposition of despair with an existing individual who speaks as "we" "for us," who pursues universal absolute knowledge precisely in evading his task to exist individually, and whose despair Kierkegaard calls "the despair of infinitude due to a lack of finitude," which is to say that in flights of fantastical thought he fails utterly to touch down in his concrete situation. Here we have someone who loves humanity in the abstract, perhaps, but who knows nothing of the existing individual's responsibility to God and neighbor. But one might equally well—and equally unsystematically—have made the beginning with the converse, "the despair of finitude due to the lack of infinitude: "By seeing the multitude of men about it, by getting engaged in all sorts of worldly affairs, by becoming wise about how things go in this world, such a man forgets himself, forgets what his name is (in the divine understanding of it)" (SD 166). Or one might find oneself in the "despair of possibility due to a lack of necessity" (SD

168f.), wherein "The self becomes an abstract possibility which tries itself out with floundering in the possible" and the individual becomes for himself a "mirage" (SD 169), or equally well in the converse "despair of necessity due to the lack of possibility" (SD 170f.), where things close in, there is no escape, and nothing more is possible and *les jeux sont faits.*

There, is, in short, no logical place to make the beginning and no logical, systematic development to be established in turning from one phenomenological shading (Husserl: *Abschattung*) of despair to the next. Indeed, one could even rearrange the entire exposition and begin again, as Kierkegaard now does, with "despair viewed under the aspect of consciousness" (SD 175f.). And if here we begin to find traces of an apparently Hegelian systematic development in consciousness from aesthetical immediacy to ethical reflection, we should note that there is no logical necessity at all to drive this movement from one "stage of life's way" to the next. Indeed *Sickness unto Death* makes plain that the fundamental dialectical movement is not in conscious thought but in the underlying *pathos* of despair and the opposite feelings of melancholy and euphoria, self-abasement and pride, in which despair—dialectically—both manifests itself and conceals itself.

In this new beginning (SD 175f.) we are now to look at despair under the aspect of consciousness and with an eye to just how unconscious or conscious the despairing consciousness is of the despair which conditions its entire conscious existence. We begin, accordingly, with the immediate and unreflective aesthete who is in no way spiritually determined (St. Paul: *pneumatikos*) but wholly "soulishly-bodily" (St. Paul: *psychikos-somatikos*), and who, accordingly, has no consciousness at all of his spiritual disorder, despair. For such a person lives on in the immediate sensuous categories of the agreeable-disagreeable (SD 176). But even though he is not conscious of it, he is in despair, for,

> Every human existence which is not conscious of itself as spirit, or conscious of itself before God as spirit, every human existence which is not thus grounded transparently in God . . . is after all despair (SD 179).

Kierkegaard's argument here is not just *per definitionem*; every *pathos* and tonality in which the aesthete would lose himself—not only his elation but also his melancholy—only masks momentarily the *Grundstimmung* and *Grundton*, the basic tonality of despair that the aesthete is trying desperately to drown out.

Here Kierkegaard has penetrated to the psychological depths of desire (*Begierde*) that remain inaccessible to Hegel. For Hegel's phenomenology, despite his attempts to incorporate things like *Angst* and even *Verzweifelung* or despair in his dialectic (see PhG 67), is expressly a phenomenology of consciousness and mind and is set up in such a way as to preclude exposition of anything constitutive of consciousness and mind other than, and outside these themselves. Kierkegaard shows, however, that the satisfaction of desire is desired only superficially to prove to consciousness that the other is not other but itself—this is only the aspect of it of which consciousness is conscious. Exposed dialectically (in Kierkegaard's sense of the word) at its subconscious depths, the satisfaction desired is desired precisely in order to hide from consciousness the deep-seated despair that comes from just this systematic denial of one's groundedness in a power outside oneself. And the dialectic of the aesthete's erotic desire—notably omitted in Hegel—lies not in the obvious fact that the other once conquered provides inadequate confirmation that it exists only for the conqueror, but in the disguised and hidden fact that there is in such erotic conquest no sufficient elimination of the ground in God that one was unconsciously trying to get rid of. Thus despair always reannounces itself, even if not consciously, as despair.

So the task for consciousness now is to gain transparency where heretofore there had been obscurity. The task is for it to become conscious of what it had heretofore been blocking from its consciousness, namely its groundedness in a power outside of itself. We begin here, again unsystematically, with the conscious despair of the aesthete, a despair of weakness, as opposed to the opposite pole in this continuum from slight to intense consciousness of despair, the despair of defiance. (The more consciousness, the more defiance.) In the despair of weakness, the self, though conscious that it is in despair, is still unconscious of the real reason for this despair (SD 184). The existing individual is really in despair because he has lost the eternal ground in God, but he thinks that he is in despair because of some person or thing that has failed him. In fact, however, he has no self and fails to relate himself to himself; one recognizes that he is a self only by things external to himself (SD 187). Hence the development, if there is to be one, must be that in reflection "the self becomes aware of itself as something essentially different from the environment, from externalities and their effect upon it" (SD 188). But in this dialectic of existential possibilities and not logical necessities it is possible that one may go in precisely the opposite direction and, seeking to rid oneself of despair about oneself, plunge into the external duties of life. But there is only greater despair at this ethical "stage on life's way" to which one then moves (SD 190).

Equally possible, too, is that one might realize not only that one is in despair but realize what this despair is about, namely the eternal; "But then, instead of veering sharply away from despair to humbling himself before God for his weakness, he is more deeply absorbed in despair" (SD 195). Here the kind of self-laceration we saw in Hegel's unhappy consciousness begins but, in Kierkegaard, dialectically exposed as pride in reverse: "this is in fact pride, thou art proud of thyself" (SD 198). And again, Hegel, in staying on the conscious surface of the phenomenon, cannot penetrate to the unconscious depths of it. For this self-abasement, this unhappiness, is at its depths precisely not frustration at a failed attempt to get rid of its finite particular self so that it might be purely infinite and universal and one with God—that is only what consciousness tells us if we question it as Hegel does. On the contrary, at its depths such unhappiness and self-abasement is precisely the self's unwillingness to abandon its finite self humbly to God's forgiveness: "In its despair it cannot forget this weakness, it hates itself in a way, it will not humble itself in faith" (SD 196).

Precisely as pride in reverse, this despair of self-hatred might even potentiate into "the despairing abuse of the eternal in the self to the point of being despairingly determined to be oneself" (SD 201), and with that we have finally reached the despair of defiance, in which the self "is not willing to begin by losing itself but wills to be itself" (SD 201):

> In order to will in despair to be oneself there must be consciousness of the infinite self. This infinite self, however, is really only the abstractest form, the abstractest possibility of the self, and it is this self the man despairingly wills to be, detaching the self from every relation to the Power which posited it. . . . [T]he self despairingly wills to dispose of itself or to create itself, to make itself the self it wills to be (SD 201).[7]

To be sure, like Hegel, Kierkegaard sees precisely in the extremity the occasion of a dialectical conversion into the opposite: this radicalized despair, the despair of defiance he calls the "passageway to faith" (SD 201). It is to be underscored, however, that, unlike the conversion from unhappiness to Reason in Hegel, the conversion from despair to faith

---

7. Et l'Ange, châtiant autant, ma foi! qu' il aime,
   De ses poings de géant torture l'anathème;
   Mais le damné répond toujours: "Je ne veux pas!"
(Baudelaire, from *Le Rebelle*, in *Selected Verse*, trans. Francis Scarfe [Baltimore: Penguin Books, 1961], p. 237).

is fundamentally not a necessary logical conversion in conscious thought but a possible affective conversion in the *pathos* and tonality lying beneath conscious thought and conditioning it. Hence it cannot follow from anything internal to consciousness and thought, but only from an other's word of grace—should I at last become willing to hear and accept it. As the *Philosophical Fragments* make clear the conversion here is thus not induced by some Socratic gadfly—or Hegelian dialectician—who prods me, the experiencing consciousness, to work out the logical consequences of my thoughts and thereby to remember the truth that I had in mind all along. (Compare PhF, Ch. 1, pp. 10ff.)

For my error here is not on the level of consciousness and cognition, but of will. It is not a matter of my being mistaken in my reasoning about some thing but of my being disobedient to some person. It is not error at all, really, but sin, and "Error is then not only outside the Truth, but polemic in its attitude toward it; which is expressed by saying that the learner has himself forfeited the condition, and is engaged in forfeiting it" (PhF 19). Hence, what was education, *Bildung*, in Hegel, must here become redemption and salvation that can come only from the other, an other who by an act of mercy restores the relationship I had broken and effects a 'gut' change, a change in one's *splanchna* or *viscera*, from defiance to faith.

In the end, then, one must ask just who succeeds in incorporating whom in his dialectic. I would have hoped to have shown here that it is in fact Kierkegaard who incorporates Hegel and that in so doing Kierkegaard has, despite Gadamer's dismissal of this attempt, indeed shattered Hegel's claim to infinite absolute knowledge and broken out of the hold of philosophical reflection.

12 A Feminist Reading of Hegel and Kierkegaard

Susan Armstrong

I t was in 1979 while teaching a seminar in the philosophy of Søren Kierkegaard that I reached the end of my tolerance. Suddenly I found that I could no longer tolerate passages that relegated women to finitude, to domesticity. I found myself shuddering when I read for the *n*th time Judge William's panegyric to marriage. My reaction was intense because I loved Søren Kierkegaard: I had filled my own name in the blanks left for "the reader." I had somehow put up with his views on women for eighteen years or so. But in 1979 I had had enough. I told my students to ignore the offensive sections in *Either/ Or, Vol. II.* I have remained intolerant ever since.

This was not the first time I took offense at Kierkegaard. The first time was when I read Kierkegaard in an ethics course taught by George L. Kline at Bryn Mawr in 1961. What offended me then was, in Kline's words, "Kierkegaard's taking time seriously." I was irritated because in 1961 I was a Christian Scientist, and I believed that as such I should dwell in eternal Truth as much as possible.

My topic here, however, is not temporality but women: how a woman might approach the reading of Kierkegaard, and not just Kierkegaard but Hegel, for Kierkegaard is best discussed in relation to Hegel. What so incenses women readers of Kierkegaard and Hegel? And what might women find of value in such a reading?

A woman cannot simply ignore her gender and read as if she were a man. This is so for several reasons, the most obvious being that a woman does not find herself addressed by the texts; rather she finds herself confidently described as a member of a group, whose members possess a number of predictable qualities, the most central being lack of full humanity! Yet this alienation can be of benefit: the woman reader can see clearly the limitations of the texts while appropriating what is useful.[1]

Hegel's characterization of women has been recently discussed by a number of scholars, and so only a summary will be offered here. First, Hegel's consideration of women is limited to the context of the family: according to Hegel women are constrained by nature to their role in family life because of their biological constitution. Hegel maintains that female sex organs remain undifferentiated and inactive, whereas male sex organs are differentiated and hence become "independent and active cerebrality."[2] These supposed anatomical 'facts' mean for Hegel not only that women are less developed as physical organisms than are men, but also that "the difference in the physical characteristics of the two sexes has a rational basis and consequently acquires an intellectual and ethical significance."[3] The male sex is:

> ...mind in its self-diremption into explicit personal self-subsistence and the knowledge and volition of free universality.... The other sex is mind maintaining itself in unity as knowledge and volition...in the form of concrete individuality and feeling. In relation to externality, the former is powerful and active, the latter passive and subjective. It follows that man has his actual substantive life in the state, in learning, and so forth.... Woman, on the other hand, has her substantive destiny in the family, and to be imbued with family piety is her ethical frame of mind. (PR §166).

In an often-cited addition to the above paragraph, Hegel maintains that women are incapable of thinking, which requires universal concepts or ideals. If we compare men to animals, he tells us, women would correspond to plants because of their greater placidity and vaguely unified feelings. Women breathe in ideas, and act by "arbitrary inclinations and opinions" (PR add. 107 to §166).

Man and woman mutually recognize and surrender to each other in marriage; the relation of husband and wife is the primary form in

---

1. Seyla Benhabib calls this approach a "feminist discourse of empowerment." *Situating the Self: Gender, Community and Postmodernism in Contemporary Ethics* (New York: Routledge, 1992), p. 243.

2. Hegel, *The Philosophy of Nature*, vol. 3, ed. and trans. M. J. Petry (London: George Allen and Unwin, Ltd., 1970), §368.

3. Hegel, *The Philosophy of Right*, trans. T. M. Knox (London: Oxford University Press, 1967), §165; hereafter cited as PR.

which one consciousness recognizes itself in another. Indeed, in opposition to the practices of his time, Hegel affirmed the free choice of the spouse. Yet the self-recognition between the husband and wife is limited because, due to the presence of passion, it is a natural self-recognition, that is, a recognition in which Spirit is not actually present. Hence the relationship must exist in something other than itself: the child, who as an other or alien signals the beginning of the end of the marriage relationship.[4]

The limitation of marital self-recognition is clearly seen in Hegel's doctrine of husband and wife as complementary. Man gains access to nature as unconscious Spirit through woman: the woman is the 'middle term' through whom the unconscious Spirit becomes conscious and actual. As man and woman unite, two opposite movements are united: man brings the downward movement of human law, woman brings the upward movement of the law of the "nether world" (PhG §463). The woman represents the *Penates*, the guardian deities of the household. The nether world of which women are inevitably a part provides men with a connection with natural feeling: "In the family he has a tranquil intuition of [self-subsistent unity with himself], and there he lives a subjective ethical life on the plane of feeling" (PR §166). Hegel's focus on the crucial emotional connection which a wife provides her husband indicates that Hegel is describing not human psychology but male psychology—the functioning of the feminine in the male psyche.[5]

For Hegel the family is the most basic element in human life. The family is the sphere of the universal as the undifferentiated unity of the feeling of love between its members. The family is ethical because it successfully spiritualizes the immediacy of natural feeling: family members define their identity and goals in terms of the family. However, the family members are not conscious that their unity is a unity of differences.

Although Hegel was aware of the variability of family arrangements in different cultures and historical periods, he considers only one set of family relations and one particular division of labor between the sexes as rational and normatively right.[6] As we have seen, Hegel

---

4. *Phenomenology of Spirit*, trans. A.V. Miller (Oxford: Oxford University Press, 1979), §456; hereafter cited as PhG.

5. Carl Jung has written extensively on the contrasexual archetype of the anima. See for example "Anima and Animus," in *Two Essays on Analytical Psychology* (Princeton: Princeton University Press, 1972). Scharfstein suggests that Hegel's use of metaphors of night as fearful, deep, and feminine relate to Hegel's own struggles with depression and anxiety. See Ben-Ami Scharfstein, *The Philosophers: Their Lives and the Nature of Their Thought*, (New York: Oxford University Press, 1980), pp. 230–242.

6. For example, see his discussion of Chinese families in PR add. 133 to §213.

justifies this position by explicitly invoking the superiority of the male to the female while acknowledging their functional complementarity in the modern state. This complementarity is described by Susan Okin as the ideology of the "sentimental family," which emerged during the eighteenth century to justify doctrines of the inequality of women.[7] The ideology of the sentimental family was needed because earlier assumptions of natural hierarchy or a God-given great chain of being had been eliminated by the emergence of liberal individualism. With the aid of the idea of the sentimental domestic family, even liberal individualists could continue to affirm the inferiority of women, in the late eighteenth century form of being confined to the pedestal of "the angel in the house."

Hegel understands the family as constituting a legal person, which has its "real external existence in property" (PR §169). The family as a legal person must be represented by the husband. Women are largely barred from the legal domain, and hence from property ownership.[8] But since Hegel maintains that property ownership is necessary for a person to exist as Idea, in order for a person to be embodied, it is apparent to the reader that there cannot be objectively grounded mutuality between women and men in marriage (PR §§41, 46, 51).

The most a woman can hope for, Hegel tells us, is to have a brother. He discusses this relationship by means of Sophocles' play *Antigone*. In the tragedy Antigone honors family law by symbolically burying her brother in defiance of Creon's edict against doing so.[9] In the struggle between Antigone and Creon, the law of the nether world, the divine law, comes into deadly conflict with the law of the human realm.

Hegel maintains that it is through the brother-sister relationship that women have the most prospect of maintaining the required form of universal consciousness, free from passion or distracting struggles for or against independence.[10] In its integration of a blood relationship with freedom from passion, the brother-sister relationship approaches the

---

7. Susan Moller Okin, "Women and the Making of the Sentimental Family," *Philosophy and Public Affairs* ll (1981), 65–87.

8. Hegel does recognize marriage settlements which safeguard legal and property rights for women in the case of death or divorce. PR §172.

9. Several commentators have noted important lacunae in Hegel's treatment of this play. For example, the opposition between Antigone and her sister Ismene is passed over. See Rosalyn Diprose, "In Excess: The Body and the Habit of Sexual Difference," *Hypatia* 6 (1991), 156–171. A reading of Sophocles' play also makes it clear that Antigone's "side" wins out over Creon, an outcome not evident in Hegel's treatment.

10. It is ironic that Hegel's sister, who resembled him in appearance and behavior, suffered a nervous breakdown after rejecting a suitor and exhibited violent jealousy of Hegel's wife. She drowned herself a few weeks after learning of her brother's death. See Scharfstein, p. 237.

limits of family life. But, as Seyla Benhabib points out, in contrast with his friend Schlegel, who lauded Antigone as androgynous and "Divine," Hegel's Antigone represents only the gods of the family and the nether world.[11] Female ethical consciousness remains "an unreal impotent shadow" compared with what the brother can achieve (PhG §451). The sister can attain an intuitive awareness of what is ethical, but she does not attain to consciousness of it. She never rises above immediacy to know herself as this particular self. After Antigone we hear no more of women. The brother, however, moves out of the family as undifferentiated unity into the next stage, that of civil society (historically the modern world since the Renaissance), in which differences become explicit and subjects pursue their own private ends, gradually coming to recognize themselves as members of society, governed by universal laws. In the third stage, that of the state, the universal and particular are reconciled in conscious unity, as an embodiment of the citizens' freedom. For Hegel women are exempted from this dialectic of self-consciousness, in which the subject becomes actual and substantial. Thus women remain the "internal enemy" of the community, the "everlasting irony," unable to disengage from merely private ends of the family in order to grasp the universal purposes of the government.

This Hegelian view might seem to be corroborated by women's endless mourning of the dead, from ancient times to today's latest slaughter. And many of the dead have been killed due to what Hegel would consider to be the higher, rational struggles between governments. But the persistence of women as peacemakers and mourners can be better interpreted as evidence that political struggles often sacrifice individual and family values which should not be subordinated to abstract ends.[12]

By now it is painfully clear what incenses women readers of Hegel. He provides us with ample examples of all the varieties of male bias enumerated by Ann Garry: overt misogyny, distortion, gender coding of concepts (such as freedom and person), and explicit and implicit exclusion of women and women's traditional activities from discussions of mature human life.[13] Hegel's personal life is consistent with the male bias in his writing: Benhabib notes that while Hegel knew some "brilliant, accomplished and nonconformist women" his reaction was generally one of dislike.[14]

---

11. Benhabib, p. 255.
12. For a helpful terminological analysis, see George L. Kline, "Some Recent Reinterpretations of Hegel's Philosophy," *The Monist* 48 (1964), 34–75.
13. Ann Garry, "Why Care about Gender," *Hypatia* 7 (1992), 155–161.
14. Benhabib, p. 254.

The more difficult question to answer concerns whether or not male bias invalidates Hegel's philosophy. Can Hegel be rewritten as recognizing women's full stature as human beings without destroying the central tenets of his philosophy? Let us attempt a limited answer to this question before we venture into deeper waters to address what has been termed "the maleness of reason."

Some scholars maintain that not only can Hegel's view of women be reworked without invalidating the rest of his philosophy, but that it must be. Joanna Hodge argues that it would be more coherent for Hegel to extend the consciousness of freedom to women.[15] Benjamin Barber points out that Hegel's view of women violates his basic tenet that spirit has pre-eminence over nature. Only in the case of women do biological differences limit ethical and spiritual development: "If nature is the bridge espoused by spirit, in Hegel the bride is stood up, spirit going its own way as a bachelor, unenticed by the female gender."[16] Women's different circumstances or stages of development alone do not mandate this doctrine of radical differences in consciousness, since Hegel refuses to grant even to God a reason or spirit different from that of men! Thus to account for the enslavement of groups of women during different periods of history, Hegel could simply have acknowledged that women and the family were suffering from "self-destructive communalism"[17] at specific moments. Such acknowledgment would not require women's permanent exclusion from "participation in the dialectical logic of liberation that eventually emancipates all conscious beings."[18]

Such a reworking of Hegel would include an analysis of personal development as occurring within the family as well as without. Hegel's conception of family members as sharing a simple, immediate feeling of love is woefully inadequate. As Patricia Mills points out, what a woman needs in order to progress into civil society out of the immediate affective unity of the family is an experience of negativity, of contradiction between herself as an individual capable of rational choice

---

15. Joanna Hodge, "Woman and the Hegelian State," in *Women in Western Political Philosophy: Kant to Nietzsche*, ed. Ellen Kennedy and Susan Mendus (New York: St. Martin's Press, 1987).

16. Benjamin R. Barber, "Spirit's Phoenix and History's Owl or the Incoherence of Dialectics in Hegel's Account of Women," *Political Theory* 16 (1988), 5–28; See also Nancy Tuana, *Woman and the History of Philosophy* (New York: Paragon, 1992), p. 108.

17. Heidi M. Ravven, "Has Hegel Anything to Say to Feminists?" *The Owl of Minerva* 19 (1988), 149–169.

18. Barber, p. 26n 71.

and as a family member.[19] And certainly such conflicts are common for both women and men. In her individual development a woman becomes aware of differences within the family: the roots of consciousness lie deep and tangled in her relation to parents, siblings, children, spouse, friends, and lovers. Indeed Antigone herself experiences conflict, not only with Creon as the representative of human law, but with her sister Ismene, who lives out a submissive, loyal, traditionally feminine way of being, though Hegel does not elaborate on this sisterly conflict.

Other scholars maintain that Hegel's philosophy is fatally flawed, that it cannot be made adequate by correcting his view of women. Barber is one for whom the invalidity of Hegel's philosophy is the source of Hegel's unacceptable view of women as undeveloped human beings.[20] Barber points out that Hegel's ahistorical conception of differences between women and men was a result of his view that the prejudices of an age are rational. At dusk the owl of Minerva flies; history is the final arbiter of what is rational. "The constitution of the state is for Hegel the Prussian constitution of the state, and if the Prussian constitution excludes women from citizenship, it does so not at daybreak, but at dusk."[21] For Barber, Hegel fails at reconciling the most profound antinomy of all: the antinomy of time and the eternal. "Without spirit, the principle of resistance and change, there can be no history; but without a conclusion, absent a terminus, history can have no perceived direction, and spirit can only appear arbitrary and irrational."[22] Hegel throws women away because history has discarded them.

Benhabib too finds that Hegel's view of women cannot be corrected while leaving the rest of Hegel intact, because the problem lies in the inadequacy of the dialectic. Women have traditionally been 'the other,' a marginalized group, and Hegel's dialectic does not reconcile the "irony, tragedy and contingency" with which women, and all other marginalized groups, live. According to Benhabib, "there is no way to disentangle the march of the dialectic in Hegel's system from the bodies

---

19. Patricia J. Mills, "Hegel and 'The Woman Question': Recognition and Intersubjectivity," in *The Sexism of Social and Political Theory: Women and Reproduction from Plato to Nietzsche*, ed. Lorene M. G. Clark and Lynda Lange (Toronto: University of Toronto Press, 1979).

20. However, Barber (p. 8) also describes aspects of Hegel's view of women as "emancipatory."

21. Barber, p. 21.

22. Barber, p. 22.

of the victims on which it treads."[23] Kathy Ferguson agrees, describing the incorporation of the world by Hegel's Subject as "monstrously egotistic and self-absorbed:" "The Hegelian Subject's encounter with alterity always ends up with the triumphant proclamation, 'Everything is me!' "[24] The absorption of the other by the Hegelian *Geist* is made possible by Hegel's reduction of being to thought. Rosalyn Diprose points out that Hegel proceeds as if thought or universal meaning comes before the process of signification. Language for Hegel is fully transparent; it can be penetrated completely by reason. There is no excess or remainder from the process of signification.[25]

Yet despite the deficiencies and difficulties in Hegel's theory, several scholars maintain that Hegel's analysis contains the seeds of a more honest and liberating vision of women and men. Part of Hegel's greatness rests on his profound insight into the dialectical movement of thought, and his uncanny ability to show how various positions or shapes of consciousness harbor internal conflicts which require us to pass beyond them.[26] Hegel's emphasis on conflicting historical moments highlights the alterity and instability inherent in the production of meaning; he anticipates twentieth century philosophy by exhibiting that the meaning of a particular is never simply present in the sign but is produced differentially by the singular's standpoint—its relation to and difference from what it is not.[27]

In fact Sandra Harding has identified Hegel as a primary source of feminist Standpoint theory, a theory which emphasizes that human activity structures human understanding: the credentials of the knowledge claim depend on the situation of the knower. In an hierarchically organized society such as ours, the perspectives of marginalized groups such as women provide an invaluable critique of the language and beliefs of dominant groups.[28] Thus starting from women's activities and women's longings for connections with nature, for interrelatedness with others, and for peace, it can be understood as part of a "feminist hermeneutic of self-reflection," which is Hegelian in that liberation

---

23. Benhabib, p. 256.

24. Kathy E. Ferguson, *The Man Question: Visions of Subjectivity in Feminist Theory* (Berkeley: University of California Press, 1993), p. 56.

25. Diprose, p. 158.

26. See Richard J. Bernstein, "Why Hegel Now?" *The Review of Metaphysics* 31 (1977), 29–60.

27. Diprose, p. 158.

28. Sandra Harding, "Who Knows? Identities and Feminist Epistemology," in *(En)Gendering Knowledge: Feminists In Academe*, ed. Joan E. Hartman and Ellen Messer-Davidow (Knoxville: The University of Tennessee Press, 1991).

resides with the oppressed', or "better yet, with what the oppressed have it in us to become."[29]

Another promising aspect of Hegelian theory is the doctrine of *Geist* as telos immanent in the world. A number of feminists (termed "cosmic feminists" by Ferguson and "spiritual feminists" by others) find this telic emphasis congenial. The assumption of immanent purposiveness allows an openness to aspects of experience which oppose the conscious or dominant standpoint of an individual or group—in other words, an openness to diversity. A metaphysics of immanent purposiveness may lead also to an affirmation of the natural process as sacred.[30] And there is a clear congruence between the Hegelian emphasis on internal relations, with the ecofeminist stress on relationship as primary.[31]

So far it is evident that Hegel's view of women is mixed: it is misogynist and is embedded in a metaphysical theory which may or may not provide a basis for a more adequate view of women. But does Hegel conceive of reason itself as male? The maleness of reason has been addressed by feminists in two major ways, the first being that the problem is with our understanding of the nature of women. According to this view, reason is best understood as a gender-neutral thinking process, in which women are perfectly capable of participating.[32] For reasons which go beyond the scope of this essay, I will use instead the second approach, according to which qualities traditionally associated with males are assumed to be paradigmatic of rational humanity.[33] Male and female are here operating as symbols. Male reason is opposed to female, nonrational, nondifferentiated traits. In this pairing neither element can be defined in isolation: as a result of the cultural definition of reason as male, the notion of femininity has been partly formed in relation to and in differentiation from a male norm. Subtle accomodations have been made, which allow feminine traits and activities to be both

---

29. Ferguson, p. 52.

30. For example, see Charlene Spretnak, *States of Grace: The Recovery of Meaning in the Postmodern Age* (San Francisco: Harper, 1991).

31. Patsy Hallen, "How the Hegelian Notion of Relation Answers the Question 'What's Wrong with Plastic Trees?' " *The Trumpeter* 8 (1991), 20–25.

32. Margaret Atherton, "Cartesian Reason and Gendered Reason," in *A Mind of One's Own: Feminist Essays on Reason and Objectivity,* ed. Louise M. Antony and Charlotte Witt (Boulder: Westview Press, 1993), pp. 31–32.

33. Genevieve Lloyd, *The Man of Reason: "Male" and "Female" in Western Philosophy* (Minneapolis: University of Minnesota Press, 1984), p. 75. See also Sally Haslanger, "On Being Objective and Being Objectified," in *A Mind of One's Own: Feminist Essays on Reason and Objectivity, op cit.,* pp. 92–98. Most thinkers prior to the 18th century saw women not as complementary to men, but simply as defective men.

preserved and downgraded. Superior male consciousness is thus provided with a necessary complementation.[34]

Reason is not male in a monolithic sense, however. Lloyd makes the helpful suggestion that some sexually-charged metaphors of reason are not constitutive of the thought of the thinker in question, whereas other symbolic operations of male and female are more deeply embedded in the conceptualization of reason, for example, that reason is a transcending of the feminine, "a conceptual containment of the feminine nonrational."[35] Given this definition of the maleness of reason, it is clear that for Hegel reason is male, in the sense that it inherently involves traditionally masculine characterisitics of abstraction, impersonality, universality, domination of the natural and immediate, objectivity, and freedom. Yet Hegelian reason partakes of some traditionally feminine characteristics—for example, materiality and particularity. Reason develops by means of differentiation in the material world (though it also overcomes or integrates this differentiation).

Eliminating the maleness of reason (along with assumptions concerning race and class) has recently been described as resulting in increased historical accuracy, rigor, and even objectivity.[36] And it is that, of course, but it is more. And perhaps that more includes an increased self-awareness of the philosopher as writer. Jacques Derrida describes philosophy as "the project of effacing itself in the face of the signified content which it transports and in general teaches."[37] Derrida's point is that there is no transcendental signified, "nothing outside of the text." Philosophic writing presents itself as objective, that is, as exhausted by the message it delivers. But the philosopher, like all writers, is "inscribed in a determined textual system" to which the philosopher has generally been blind. Certainly Hegel did not seem to be aware of his system as a text, as a kind of writing, which as such always requires a supplement.

A feminist reading pushes beyond even this deconstructionist critique to observe that in philosophic writing the author does not appear at all. Instead, impersonal assertions are offered which are meant to characterize reality, similar to assertions in the natural sci-

---

34. Lloyd (*The Man of Reason,* p. 105) cautions that as a consequence the affirmation of female difference (as in some radical feminist theories) is dangerous.

35. Genevieve Lloyd, "Maleness, Metaphor, and the 'Crisis' of Reason," in *A Mind of One's Own, op. cit.,* pp. 76–78, 82.

36. Susan Bordo, "'Maleness' Revisited," *Hypatia* 7 (1992), 197–207.

37. Jacques Derrida, *Of Grammatology,* trans. Gayatri C. Spivak (Baltimore: Johns Hopkins Press, 1976), p. 160.

ences. Addelson and Potter note that objective scholarly work means that the agency of the scholar is suppressed. "The author disappears from the philosophy text," leaving a vision of author and reader as "vehicles for the transmission of impersonal truth." And not only are the philosopher and reader not personally present in any sense in the text, but the people whose positions the philosopher debates are absent as well. What these people might mean in their social contexts is never addressed.[38]

In this respect, feminists have a great deal to gain from paying more attention to Hegel's successor, Søren Kierkegaard.[39] Kierkegaard's writing is explicitly concerned with the issues of existential communication between persons and of writing as a horizon within which the text lives. His use of pseudonyms is designed to avoid any claim to objective scholarship, metaphysical assertion, or direct communication. His authorship is intentionally deceitful.[40] Unfortunately Kierkegaard's extraordinarily inventive style and intensity are used in the service of an interpretation of women which is dismaying.

The view of women presented by the pseudonymous authors, as well as by entries in Kierkegaard's *Journals* (which presumably express his own views and which he did anticipate would be published), may be classified into three main categories. The first category coincides with the aesthetic stage of existence. From the standpoint of A, who is probably the Seducer in *Either/Or*, vol. I, "young girls" (presumably adolescents) at their best are charming, beautiful, innocent, and naive. The infinite is natural for a young girl only in the sense that imaginatively and affectively she can give herself wholly to her beloved. While Cordelia (the main subject of interest to A) can be artfully brought to break off her engagement to A on the grounds that she comes to believe that a secret love is better than a public, external bond, this is the closest she is capable of getting to self-consciousness. After she allows A to have sexual intercourse with her, she has given away

---

38. Kathryn Pyne Addelson and Elizabeth Potter, "Making Knowledge," in *(En)Gendering Knowledge, op. cit.,* p. 269.

39. I have located only one thorough discussion of the relationship of men and women in Kierkegaard, and that not by a feminist: Gregor Malantschuk, *The Controversial Kierkegaard,* trans. Howard V. Hong and Edna H. Hong (Waterloo, Ontario: Wilfred Laurier University Press, 1980). Malantschuk argues for interpreting Kierkegaard's views from 1850 onward as hermetic, written from "an extreme Christian point of view." I have not accepted this interpretation.

40. See his *The Point of View for My work as An Author: A Report to History,* ed. Benjamin Nelson (New York: Harper, 1962), p. 87.

everything of interest to him; she no longer offers resistance or a challenge. She is a bore, to be avoided henceforth.[41]

A variant of the young girl is described by Frater Taciturnus in "Guilty?"/"Not Guilty?" and by William Afham in "In Vino Veritas" as the clever society woman, who trivializes all things, even the most sacred, into personal adornment. Her thoughtless talk is amusing and charming at best. She is enticing, seductive, fundamentally deceitful because unconscious of herself.[42] Similarly, in his *Journals* Kierkegaard describes women as "virtuosos in lying." They cannot help it, and indeed he finds it attractive.[43]

The second category is woman as she appears in the ethical stage—as wife. Both man and wife are to enter into marriage whole-heartedly. In the ethical stage the universal is emphasized: the ethical person regards the universal in marrying rather than differences between persons. The relationship is the absolute. However, in the case of women the ethical is limited to accepted norms and conventions: her sense of shame or modesty, and her reputation.

Judge William in *Either/Or*, vol. II presents an extended appreciation of his wife.[44] Overall, she "bestows finitude" on man. She is self-sacrificing, hopeful, beautiful, intuitive. A girl (the Judge uses the term inchangeably with woman) has "no conception such as a man has of severe and persistent labor, but she is never idle, is always occupied, time is never long for her." A woman has a "secret rapport with time," which a man cannot understand. Her labor is best compared to the graceful and effortless labor of a bird. When her scholar-husband forgets to come to lunch because of his fascination with a tiny scholarly detail, she dismisses it lightly, "blows it away," and "joyfully the scholar hastens to the dinner table." (Yeh, sure, the reader mutters to herself.) A woman is childlike in her desire to comfort her husband. She is happy and in harmony with existence, because she is at home in finitude. She does not know doubt or despair; she is "man's deepest life," and as such should remain concealed and hidden. The Judge's remarks seem to fit a passage in the *Journals* in which Kierkegaard

---

41. Søren Kierkegaard, *Diary of a Seducer,* trans. Gerd Gillhoff (New York: Frederick Ungar Publishing Co., 1966), esp. pp. 115, 156, 181.

42. *Stages on Life's Way: Studies by Various Persons*, ed. and trans. Howard V. Hong and Edna H. Hong (Princeton: Princeton University Press, 1988), pp. 50–52; 75–78; 290–1.

43. *Søren Kierkegaard's Journals and Papers*, vol. 4, ed. and trans. Howard V. Hong and Edna H. Hong (Bloomington: Indiana University Press, 1975), 4998, p. 576.

44. *Either/Or*, vol. II, trans. Walter Lowrie (Princeton: Princeton University Press, 1959), pp. 306–14.

points out that women have an advantage in living more quietly, and can thus escape convention.[45] "Domesticity" is the highest quality in a woman: she can create silence and peace in her own domain.[46]

The author of "Reflections on Marriage" agrees with Judge Williams' assessment of a wife's grace and beauty. Her inner beauty increases with the years and shines best in maternity: "mother love is as soft as pure gold and pliant in every decision, and yet whole."[47] A woman is selfless and prays for others, for she knows she cannot have her wishes for herself fulfilled.

In his *Journals* Kierkegaard is more realistic than the Judge: he astutely points out the egotism which often infuses this apparent selflessness: "She loves herself through her own." And yet he adds rather touchingly that if she understood this egoism "she would not be that because she is too good to be an egoist."[48]

For the Judge the emancipation of women is a hateful and painful idea. Emancipation is the serpent's temptation. If she stays in her sphere she is strong and secure; if she thinks she could be better than a man in "man's category" then she can at best be a half-man. A woman's long hair is her beauty, by which she binds men to the earth: a woman with shorn hair is a "crazy woman . . . a criminal . . . a horror to men."[49]

There are some passages in which the Judge exhibits his wife in a different light. He tells us that before their marriage his wife was independent, content with little, wholesome; she owes the Judge nothing. As her husband he has been nothing and yet everything to her. "There is in her a power, not hard but flexible, like the sword which could cut stone and yet was wrapped around the waist." Indeed "woman is just as strong as man, perhaps stronger."[50]

According to Vigilius Haufniensis, the author of *The Concept of Anxiety,* women are more sensuous than men, more dependent on their physical constitution. Hence women are more anxious, their anxiety indicating that women unconsciously apprehend that they have an eternal destiny. But this awareness remains unconscious: aesthetically women are meant to be beautiful; ethically they are meant to procreate. Greek sculpture reveals that the woman's consciousness is inessential: Venus is just as beautiful when she is sleeping, whereas Apollo or

---

45. *Journals,* 4992, p. 574.
46. *For Self-Examination* (Minneapolis: Augsburg, 1940), pp. 57–58.
47. *Stages,* p. 137.
48. *Journals,* 5000, p. 577.
49. *Either/Or,* II, pp. 317–18.
50. *Either/Or,* II, pp. 82–5; 115.

Jupiter would be ugly and ridiculous. In romanticism the woman's face is more significant but still the beautiful expression is one of a silent woman, with no history.[51]

The third category in which Kierkegaard discusses women is in the religious stage of existence. We have seen that for Kierkegaard women, despite their value as wife and mother, never really exist as ethical beings. Women pass swiftly as birds from aesthetic immediacy to the religious. At best, a woman's maidenly modesty can become modesty before God. A woman does not experience the "great either/or" of choosing herself in her "eternal validity." Women do not reflect or reach out to the absolute, and do not attain self-consciousness. Instead women remain in immediacy, either that of sensuous, imaginative, or religious feeling. Indeed if women were more spiritual they would never find their culmination in loving a man, because "spirit is the true independent."[52]

Only in *Sickness unto Death,* written by Anti-Climacus but edited by Søren Kierkegaard, do we find mention of reflective women. In a lengthy footnote, the author states that there are exceptional women who experience "manly despair"—despair at willing to be oneself, which assumes that one has a self to despair of.[53] Generally, however, a woman lacks both the selfish sense of self and the intellectuality of man; she is superior in tenderness and fineness of feeling. Her nature is devotion and submission. She is happy when she gives herself away—as a man never can be, due to his self-consciousness.

It comes then as a surprise to the reader that despite all, "inwardly woman is equal before God." In the relationship to God, the man/woman distinction vanishes; both men and women acquire their true selves by means of devotion. Still, "most frequently in real life woman is related to God only through man."[54] Thus, by and large Christianity is not a religion for women or children, because women cannot endure the "dialectical redoubling" of such heroes as Abraham. It takes a man's toughness and strength. Christianity makes men and women equal, but "does not change their natural qualifications."[55]

> Of course every religious view, like every more profound philosophical view, sees women, despite this difference [woman's greater

---

51. Vigilius Haufniensis, *The Concept of Anxiety,* ed. and trans. Reidar Thomte (Princeton: Princeton Univ. Press, 1980), pp. 64–66.

52. *Journals,* 4989, p. 572.

53. *Fear and Trembling and The Sickness unto Death,* trans. Walter Lowrie (New York: Doubleday, 1954), pp. 184–5.

54. *Ibid.*

55. *Journals,* 5007–8, pp. 582–4.

sensuousness], as essentially identical with man; but it is not foolish enough to forget for that reason the truth of the difference, esthetically and ethically understood.[56]

Thus is a feminist disappointed in her reading of Kierkegaard. Kierkegaard's achievements are many and significant, among them his helping us to see the role of the author in all writing, as well as the elusiveness of the unique individual with respect to the general. Kierkegaard understands as Hegel did not that the individual cannot be *aufgehoben* by the universal, that the dialectical process is not synonymous with the general or universal.[57] In the religious stage of existence, which expresses itself in paradox, the individual is both particular and in a love-relationship with the absolute, who is Subject and not Object. Existential truth can be communicated only indirectly, by means of device, deceit, and distance, in order to open up a space for the other to freely appropriate the communication.[58]

But despite all these innovations, Kierkegaard sees women as severely limited beings, incapable of the full range of human achievement and awareness. His philosophy exhibits a male bias similar to that of Hegel in its misogyny, distortions, and omissions.

Yet Kierkegaard's conception of reason is much less male than Hegel's. Ultimately an individual must offer all of her or himself to the absolute in a relationship which includes the personal and unique. Thus reason is not inherently triumphant over estrangement and particularity, as it is in Hegel, but self-sacrificing in the face of Holy Mystery. The abstraction, universality, and objectivity characteristic of Hegel's idea of reason fail for Kierkegaard to comprehend existence, though they have a place in the ethical stage. Existence is not finally comprehensible. But still, Kierkegaard has not got it right. For him the body, instinct, sexuality, are all obstacles. And perhaps they were, for him. But they are also aspects of experience which have been traditionally left to women to take care of and bear the burden of. Kierkegaard, while he called attention to the category of the individual, ultimately interpreted that category in his own male image.

---

56. *Journals*, 4989, p. 572.

57. Mark C. Taylor, "Natural Selfhood and Ethical Selfhood in Kierkegaard," in *Søren Kierkegaard,* ed. Harold Bloom (New York: Chelsea House, 1989), pp. 224–29.

58. Kierkegaard refers to himself as more a reader than author of his own works. *Point of View*, p. 151.

Contributors

Susan Armstrong is Professor of Philosophy at Humboldt-State University, California. She writes on Whitehead, speculative philosophy, and environmental ethics and has published articles in *Process Studies, Environmental Ethics,* and other journals.

John D. Caputo is the David R. Cook Professor of Philosophy at Villanova University and the author of *Against Ethics: Contributions to a Poetics of Obligation with Constant Reference to Deconstruction; Demythologizing Heidegger; Radical Hermeneutics; The Mystical Element in Heidegger's Thought;* and *Heidegger and Aquinas.*

William Desmond is Professor of Philosophy at the Katholieke Universiteit Leuven, Belgium, and the author of *Perplexity and Ultimacy: Metaphysical Thoughts from the Middle; Being and the Between; Art and the Absolute: A Study of Hegel's Aesthetics; Beyond Hegel and Dialectic: Speculation, Cult, and Comedy; Philosophy and its Other; Ways of Being and Mind;* and *Desire, Dialectic, and Otherness: An Essay on Origins.* He is a former president of the Hegel Society of America.

Robert J. Dostal is the Rufus Jones Professor of Philosophy and Religion and current Provost at Bryn Mawr College. He is the author of numerous articles on continental philosophy and hermeneutics in *Man and World, Philosophy and Phenomenological Research,* and other journals.

Shaun Gallagher is Professor of Philosophy at Canisius College. He was Visiting Scientist at the Medical Research Council, Applied Psychology Unit, University of Cambridge in 1994. He is author of *Hermeneutics and Education* and co-editor of *Merleau-Ponty, Hermeneutics, and Postmodernism* (both published by SUNY Press), and author of a forthcoming book, *The Inordinance of Time* (1988).

Philip T. Grier is Professor of Philosophy at Dickinson College. He is the author of *Marxist Ethical Theory in the Soviet Union*, and publishes on Hegel and political philosophy in *The Owl of Minerva* and other journals.

H. S. Harris is Distinguished Research Professor at York University, Toronto, and the author of *Hegel's Development: Night Thoughts, Hegel's Development: Toward the Sunlight*, and *The Social Philosophy of Giovanni Gentile*. He is also the co-translator of Hegel's *System of Ethical Life*; and *The Encyclopaedia Logic*.

Walter Lammi is Assistant Professor of Philosophy at the American University in Cairo, Egypt. He has taught at Stanford and is former editor of the Hoover Institute Press. He writes on Heidegger, Gadamer, and multiculturalism and has published in the *Journal of the History of Ideas* and other journals.

George R. Lucas, Jr. is Assistant Professor of Ethics at the United States Naval Academy, Annapolis and a former director in the Division of Research Programs, National Endowment for the Humanities. He is the author of *The Rehabilitation of Whitehead; The Genesis of Modern Process Thought; Two Views of Freedom in Process Thought: A Study of Hegel and Whitehead;* and editor of *Hegel and Whitehead: Contemporary Perspectives On Systematic Philosophy*.

Michael Prosch teaches at Villanova University and Rutgers University. He has published on economic philosophy and foreign trade, Eastern philosophy and ethics, and on the philosophy of Hegel in the journals *Poleia* and the *Owl of Minerva*.

Tom Rockmore is Professor of Philosophy at Duquesne University and the author of *Before and After Hegel: A Historical Introduction to Hegel's Thought; Hegel's Circular Epistemology; Habermas on Historical Materialism;* and *Irrationalism: Lukacs and the Marxist View of Reason*. His most recent book is *On Heidegger's Nazism and Philosophy*. He is also co-editor of *The Heidegger Case: On Philosophy and Ethics*.

P. Christopher Smith is Professor of Philosophy at Lowell College, University of Massachusetts. He is the author of *Hermeneutics and Human Finitude: Toward a Theory of Ethical Understanding*. He is also the translator of Gadamer's *Hegel's Dialectic: Five Hermeneutical Studies;* and *Dialogue and Dialectic: Eight Hermeneutical Studies on Plato*.

Index